RED HARVEST

RED HARVEST

THE COMMUNIST PARTY AND AMERICAN FARMERS

LOWELL K. DYSON

UNIVERSITY OF NEBRASKA PRESS
Lincoln and London

Copyright © 1982 by the University of Nebraska Press
Manufactured in the United States of America

Library of Congress Cataloging in Publication Data

Dyson, Lowell K., 1929–
    Red harvest.

    Bibliography: p.
    Includes index.
    1. Communism and agriculture—United States.
2. Communist Party of the United States of America.
I. Title.
HX550.A37D97   324.273'75   81–8200
ISBN 0–8032–1659–9   AACR2

*The paper in this book meets the guidelines for
permanence and durability of the Committee on
Production Guidelines for Book Longevity of the Council
on Library Resources.*

FOR PAT

CONTENTS

PREFACE

MY INTEREST IN THE SUBJECT of this book was attracted almost twenty years ago when I was studying the middle western farm strikes of the early 1930s. Increasingly in research I encountered that mixed band of Communist party orators, agitators, and organizers who preached to militant farmers that tax and mortgage moratoriums—proposed by the Farm Holiday Association of Milo Reno—were mere bandages on the body of a society whose vital organs were diseased, and that the monetary inflation supported by many farmers was a witch doctor's brew. They challenged their grimly attentive listeners to go for the radical cures: cancellation of all farm debts, rents, mortgages, and taxes; the right of possession to belong to those who did the work and not to absentee landlords; massive federal aid to the poverty-stricken, to be drawn from taxes on the wealthy; and close ties forged with the unemployed and urban workers who were the farmers' natural allies against the upper-class oppressors who had brought on the economic cataclysm.

At first I assumed that those agitators must fit the Communist stereotype of the day: thickly accented immigrant urbanites who were completely out of place in country settings. I soon found that this was false. There were Finns such as Henry Puro and Alfred Tiala, but their farm backgrounds offset their imperfect English. Most of the rest could pass a pretty stiff muster. "Mother" Ella Reeve Bloor, the aged heroine of scores of left-wing causes, for example, had colonial ancestry, was a relative of Thaddeus Stevens, and had been as a child a friend of Walt Whitman. Her last husband, Andy Omholt, whom she married about 1930, was a western North Dakota wheat farmer who was well respected in his region. Bloor's son, Hal Ware, had started farming at an early age in New York and had later organized collective farms in the Soviet Union. The colorful Charlie Taylor had homesteaded in northern Min-

nesota before taking over the operation of a farmers' newspaper in Plentywood, Montana. Most of the best organizers in every area—Josie
Hallquist in Nebraska, Homer Ayres and Julius Walstad in South Dakota, Ashbel Ingwerson in North Dakota, Jack Witt in Wisconsin, and
others—were, or had been, farmers. Ned Cobb was perhaps the most
respected black farmer in his Alabama county. The most effective of
them all, Lem Harris, had renounced a background of great wealth to
become a manure-shoveling farm hand after Harvard College. Like Harris, many of the young Ivy Leaguers, such as Leif Dahl, who were
attracted to the movement in the 1930s, could show more than a superficial familiarity with field and barnyard. When tested by suspicious farmers, they could milk cows and pitch hay.

One factor which intrigued me about these people was their dedication. Some, of course, were incipient party bureaucrats and time-servers,
but the vast majority worked very hard for little material reward. Being
a Communist functionary was a twenty-four-hour-a-day job. All their
time and effort went for the cause. And yet they constantly balanced on
the edge of dilemma. Farmers wanted relief from seemingly intolerable
problems. The Communists could offer them those radical proposals
which would firm up their ownership and individual possession of the
land. Party dogma, however, called for the eventual collectivization of
farms, and that was anathema to American farmers. The Communist
farm organizers could show movies on Russian farming and write articles about the happiness of the peasant under the Soviet system, but they
could suggest that eventual aim for the United States only to a tiny
minority who were receptive.

The party's farm workers faced other problems. There existed the
fear of their cause, which led to oppression and violence. They did not
fare too badly in the egalitarian middle west, but even there, Mother
Bloor, Harry Lux, Alfred Tiala, and others went to jail for assaulting the
majesty of the law. In the South and in California, however, some
Communists were killed, and others spent years in penitentiaries.

All the time that Communist organizers tried to win rural support
for a workers' and farmers' government, they were themselves being
maneuvered by a distant force. However well they rationalized their
allegiance to the Marxist-Leninist principle of world revolution, the
Russian Communist party—which from the late 1920s increasingly
meant Joseph Stalin—manipulated the line that they followed so that it

would best serve to protect the Soviet Union. American Communists had to become adept at shifting during abrupt turnarounds such as happened in 1928, 1934, 1939, 1941, and 1945.

The Communist party has always been the most successful in agrarian nations—witness the revolutions in Vietnam, China, and Russia itself—yet the American party leadership often neglected or ignored rural work. Communists sought to change the very nature of the American agricultural system, but the programs which won them the broadest hearing among farmers were aimed at preserving that system. Those programs rested on a long tradition of American farm radicalism, and yet they could be discarded at almost a moment's notice by a directive from the leaders of the Soviet Union. The agrarian organizers themselves came from backgrounds which represented a cross section of American life, but they often were seen as an alien force. In this book I have tried to explore these ironies and contradictions.

My thanks are many. I want to acknowledge the generous financial help of the American Council of Learned Societies, the Cooperative Program in the Humanities at Duke University and the University of North Carolina, and the American Philosophical Society. This work would not have been completed except for Wayne Cole, Robert Cross, Theodore Draper, Paul Glad, Robert Landen, and William Leuchtenburg. Stowe Persons suggested a vital line of research. E. H. Carr clarified several points. I stand in awe of H. L. Mitchell. I owe a variety of debts to Ivan Avakumovic, Erik Bert, Charles Coe, Dairylea, Inc., Don Grubbs, Stuart Jamieson, Mike Karni, Harvey Klehr, Charles Mast, John Monfross, Carl Marx Reeve, Larry Remele, Dale Rosen, Fred Sexauer, John Shover, Louis Starr, Fred Stover, Tom West, and Gus Williamson. None, however, is responsible for my errors, interpretations, or stubbornness. Indeed, at least one considers me a fascist; another has said that I am "so objective" that I "must be a Trotskyite [sic]"; a third has condemned an earlier article and is sure that I am a Communist dupe. Not bad—for one who has tried solely to collect, synthesize, and interpret the relevant data.

My thanks to librarians and archivists at the state historical societies of Minnesota, Montana, Nebraska, North Dakota, and Wisconsin; the university libraries of California at Berkeley, Colorado, Columbia, Cornell, Duke, Iowa, Iowa State, Maryland, Missouri, North Carolina,

North Dakota, North Dakota State, Virginia Tech, Washington, and Wisconsin; the public libraries of Des Moines; New York City; Omaha; Alexandria, Virginia; and Spirit Lake, Iowa; the Franklin Delano Roosevelt Library, the Library of Congress, the National Agricultural Library, the National Archives, the Immigration History Research Center of the University of Minnesota, and the Iowa Department of History and Archives.

I am grateful to Al Knutson and Charlie Taylor for lengthy letters, small manuscript collections, and honest interviews. Alex Kringlock and Leo Ars freely gave me irreplaceable material. Two people rendered immeasurable service. Lem Harris opened home, hearth, and substantial records with no restrictions, in full knowledge that my interpretations might not agree with his. B. P. Dyson did much of the research for Chapter 8 and gave constant editorial help. My prize typist was Marina Talley.

Finally, I give my appreciation to the following journals for permission to reprint here material which first appeared in different form in their pages: "The Red Peasant International in America," *Journal of American History* 58 (March 1972): 958–73; "The Southern Tenant Farmers Union and Depression Politics," *Political Science Quarterly* 88 (June 1973): 230–52; "The Milk Strike of 1939 and the Destruction of the Dairy Farmers Union," *New York History* 51 (October 1970): 523–43.

1
SEEDTIME: 1919–25

IN THE BEGINNING, American Communists had little time for farmers. During their frantic first year, 1919, they were too busy—debating the question of splitting with the Socialists, busy with the hectic Chicago conventions which saw them torn in two from the beginning, and busy searching for that proletarian revolution which would establish a Soviet America. They neglected, then, the thousands of red farmers who had sung the "Internationale" at Socialist camp meetings, given bulk to the votes for Gene Debs, and paid sixteen hard-earned dollars for dues to the Nonpartisan League in hopes of seeing state-owned banks and grain elevators. And so the new Communists overlooked farmers, perhaps because as city boys they instinctively knew that peasants were reactionary. That was strange—because V. I. Lenin himself had written more on American agriculture than on any other aspect of this New World nation.

The Communist movement in the United States was urban. It sprang from the left wing of the older Socialist party which had always criticized the "streetcar Socialists," like Victor Berger, Meyer London, and Morris Hillquit, who favored gradual reforms through the electoral process. The left wing, defeated within the party in 1912, had won great accessions of strength during World War I and especially after the Russian Revolution, particularly among new immigrants from Eastern Europe.

By 1919 the left wing was riding high. It had its own organ, *Revolutionary Age,* in Boston, and it was denouncing those who would compromise on the issue of the immediate overthrow of capitalism. In the spring elections for the national executive council of the Socialist party, the radicals won a sweeping victory. The answer of the right, which controlled the party machinery, was to void the election, suspend seven foreign-language federations which were the bulwark of the left, and call for an emergency convention in Chicago on 30 August.

The exuberant left, firm in the faith of its historic destiny, met on 21 June to plot a course. A majority favored continuing the fight to win control of the Socialist party and voted by a substantial margin against forming a separate Communist party (CP). The dissenters, mostly from the Russian-language federation, bolted and summoned a convention for 1 September to found a new party.

Three groups came to Chicago in late summer. By this time the Socialist right wing had expelled about two-thirds of the party's members and had tighter control than ever. Chicago police aided them in banishing a band of left-wingers from the floor, despite the arm-waving protests of John Reed, the revolutionary author and former Harvard cheerleader. The left moved first to a downstairs billiard room and later into the hall of the Industrial Workers of the World to form the Communist Labor party (CLP) and pledge allegiance to the Third, or Communist, International (Comintern).

In the meantime the foreign-language federations and various dissident English-speaking groups met separately to establish the Communist party. It too paid strict homage to the fountainhead of the world revolution. The aims of the CP and the CLP were identical. Their differences were mainly ones of leadership and personality, but the factions maintained a quarrelsome schism until 1921, when the Third International demanded unification.[1]

American Communists, like their comrades around the globe, believed in the imminence of revolution in 1919. Labor unrest swept the United States. The year witnessed a general strike in Seattle, a Boston police strike, and major walkouts in steel and coal. Communists saw those as a sign that the Bolshevik revolution had been a pattern and not a phenomenon. They believed themselves an uncompromising proletarian vanguard. As a result they disdained united fronts, whether with Socialists ("Social Patriots"), Farmer Laborites, or Nonpartisan Leaguers. However small the movement might become, it must remain pristine.

And the movement did shrink. The strike wave receded without the Communists playing any appreciable role. Even more disastrous were the antisubversive raids staged by Attorney General A. Mitchell Palmer. If, as Theodore Draper has estimated, the CP and the CLP had between twenty-five thousand and forty thousand members at their genesis, they were left with only about eight thousand a few months later.[2]

The Communists were doubly cut off from the mainstream of America. Not only did they refuse to associate with other radical or progressive groups or take part in elections, but the Palmer raids, deportations, and prosecutions drove them into a sort of clandestine self-contemplation. In addition, a good 90 percent of the membership used languages other than English, and few had more than a tenuous relationship with the labor movement.[3]

If the early American Communists had few links with labor, their ties to that 30 percent of the population living on the nation's farms were even fewer. During the early years they almost completely ignored farmers. Max Bedacht tangentially criticized his former comrades, the California Socialists, for admiring the Nonpartisan League, composed of farm owners, while ignoring migratory workers, the true agricultural proletariat. The official organ of the Communist party dismissed six million farm owners and tenants as a "social ancronism [sic]" because of their notions about property. The six and a half million rural laborers fared little better. They were written off as "flloaters [sic], aliens or disfranchised negroes" who would never become "effective class-conscious voting groups." The Communist Labor party displayed even less interest. The most it could come up with was the report of a survey by the Post Office Department citing growing discontent among farmers.[4]

The formative Communist movement did have at least one farmer in its ranks, however: Harold Ware, the son of Ella Reeve, a veteran Socialist and charter member of the Communist Labor party. The shy and retiring Ware was often obscured by his flamboyant parent, known best to two generations of radicals as Mother Bloor. Ware had taken an interest in farming while living at a Single Tax colony at Arden, Delaware, during the early years of the century. After graduating from the two-year course in agriculture at Pennsylvania State College, he bought a grain and dairy farm in Westchester County, New York, where he introduced the first gasoline tractor in the area.[5]

Ware had wanted the American Communist movement to act on rural complaints, but it turned him aside. Lenin, however had a much stronger interest in American agriculture. He had written extensively on the subject a half dozen years earlier, using census reports. With his usual voracious curiosity, Lenin wanted new information on recent developments. He wrote to the American party, "Have you no farmers in Amer-

ica?" Ware's response was to give up his farm to bum around the country
as a migratory worker. He eventually sent the Soviet leader a detailed
analysis with maps and charts.[6]

In the meantime, the Communist party and Communist Labor party
elements had finally merged in May 1921 at the orders of the Comintern.
Seven months later they broke surface legally by establishing the Workers party, despite the grumbling of those who enjoyed the conspiratorial
atmosphere of the underground existence. The leadership was still not
ready to tackle work in rural areas, however, and Ware marked time. He
was horticultural advisor to the big charitable farm of the Moose Lodge
at Mooseheart, Illinois, and then drifted west again to North Dakota.
The party awarded him the honorific but seemingly dutiless title of
National Agrarian Organizer. He reported on an agricultural conference, called by President Harding, in wry columns for the *Worker.*[7] Not
until 1922 did he find real opportunity to serve the cause to which he
was enthusiastically pledged.

Famine had seized large areas of Russia in the wake of war and civil
war. Numerous Americans, including Herbert Hoover, sought to help.
Ware became secretary of one group, the American Federated Russian
Famine Relief Committee, which gave him the opportunity to do more
than simply provide charity. He wanted to put into practice his ideas on
scientific socialist agriculture. Ware convinced his committee that food
relief was merely a stopgap, and he won from it a grant of seventy-five
thousand dollars for a more permanent project. Within months he had
bought implements, tools for a machine shop, and twenty tractors. He
recruited nine tractor drivers from among his midwestern acquaintances,
and soon the whole crew had sailed for Russia, where they won Lenin's
praise for their work on a state owned farm of fifteen thousand acres in
Perm Oblast.[8]

Ware returned periodically to the United States on purchasing and
fund-raising missions, and he did some work to rally support for the
party among farmers during the summers of 1923 and 1924, but he spent
the bulk of the ensuing decade in Russia. He soon transferred his activities from frozen Perm to the more hospitable steppes of the North
Caucasus. He got the financial support of many American radicals for
the establishment of a huge, mechanized model farm, and he participated
in the collectivization of Russian agriculture later in the decade.[9] It was
ironic that the original agricultural spokesman among American Com-

munists faded from the scene, for a time, just as the party was taking a new look at farmers.

By 1922 Communists were reexamining theory and tactics. In the early days, after the Bolshevik Revolution, enthusiastic supporters had believed that the proletariat would soon seize power around the globe. Postwar revolts in Hungary and Bavaria seemed the fruit of that faith. Both Communists and their opponents believed, moreover, that a soviet state could not maintain itself in Russia, alone in a capitalist ocean. Conditions, however, had changed. On the one hand, the central European revolutions had failed. On the other, neither counterrevolution nor intervention had succeeded in toppling Lenin's government. It appeared that the Bolsheviks might survive even though surrounded by enemies.

In the summer of 1920, Lenin advised the British comrades to affiliate with the Labor party, and he counseled a pioneer American Communist, Louis Fraina, to follow the same path. Early in the following year Lenin adopted the New Economic Policy, which some called a retreat, in order to shore up the devastated Soviet homeland. When the Third Congress of the Communist International met in July 1921, it adopted the slogan "To the Masses!" and ordered its followers to seek a united front on the left. This would provide room for maneuver and win a wider audience for Communist propaganda.[10]

American Communists, in the throes of underground bickering, had not immediately picked up Lenin's suggestion to Fraina that they affiliate with a broader, labor-based party. In May 1922 they issued their first thesis on the subject but seemed to view the idea more useful as a slogan than as a policy. Not until John Pepper published his pamphlet, *For a Labor Party,* in November did it begin to assume practical proportions.[11]

Pepper was an enigma to his American comrades. Under the name Joseph Pogony he had been a journalist in Habsburg Hungary. During the revolution of 1919 he had thrown his lot in with Bela Kun, the Communist leader, and served briefly as commissar of war. After the collapse of Kun's regime, Pepper fled to Moscow, where his factionalism made him unpopular with Lenin. Seeking new pastures, he requested assignment to the United States. He arrived in the summer of 1922 and soon dazzled the American Communists by leading them to believe that he was the official Comintern representative. Within a short time he became a powerful figure and the leading proponent of the doctrine that the Communists should break out of their isolation by striving to build a broad Farmer Labor party.[12]

This reversal of tactics was difficult for many American Communists to accept. Pepper, however, through the force of his personality and argument, built a strong following among a group of younger men including Ben Gitlow and Jay Lovestone, and he soon brought the party secretary, Charles Ruthenberg, into his camp. And so, whereas in 1919 and 1920 the Communists had vigorously denounced the Nonpartisan League and the newly formed Farmer Labor party, by 1923 they were seeking an alliance which they hoped would bring them into contact with a broad spectrum of the labor movement.[13]

The American Federation of Labor, under the aegis of old Sam Gompers, had always avoided sponsoring a political party. A significant faction in the AF of L disagreed with him on this. The leading proponent of a labor party was John Fitzpatrick, president of the Chicago Federation of Labor, who had called a national conference in November 1919 to found a party on the British model. At a convention held in July 1920 this group tried to expand its base by rechristening itself the Farmer Labor party and by appealing for an alliance of the dissatisfied—Single Taxers, Irish nationalists, followers of Henry Ford and William Randolph Hearst, the Nonpartisan League, and the Committee of Forty-Eight (self-proclaimed successors of Teddy Roosevelt's Progressive party). Many from the last two organizations hoped to launch a campaign headed by Robert M. La Follette. The Wisconsin senator first showed great interest, but eventually declined the candidacy when the labor radicals behind Fitzpatrick insisted that he accept a platform aimed at nationalization of some basic industries. The Farmer Laborites then turned to an almost unknown Utah lawyer, Perley P. Christensen, who won less than a quarter million votes.[14]

This nascent party was an amorphous grouping, and state units had only the most tenuous ties with the national office set up in Chicago. The dream of winning significant support from organized labor had foundered on the rock of Gompers's opposition and the lack of interest of the railroad unions. Fitzpatrick's candidate for governor of Illinois had mustered less than 3 percent of the vote. On the other hand, something was astir in the West. Farmer Labor candidates won 35 percent of the gubernatorial votes in Minnesota, 30 percent in Washington, 26 percent in South Dakota, and 23 percent in Nebraska.[15]

A new wave of agricultural discontent had swept through the region where the Populists had battled the old parties thirty years earlier. In many ways the spirit of rebellion had never died. After the Populists had withered away, many western farmers proudly proclaimed themselves Socialists, and their emotional radicalism often embarrassed staid eastern party leaders like Morris Hillquit. They spent the long winter nights poring over party tracts or newspapers such as the *National Rip-Saw* or the *Appeal to Reason.* Farm families would drive their wagons for as far as seventy miles and sleep in tents for a week at Socialist camp meetings in order to hear spellbinding orators like Kate Richards O'Hare or Eugene Debs. These western Socialists adored Debs, and in 1912 they gave him a sixth of the presidential vote in Oklahoma and a substantial, if smaller, portion in North Dakota, Montana, Idaho, Washington, and other states.[16]

Within a few years, however, the Socialist party was all but dead in the West. The cause was not so much the schisms caused by World War I or the red scare which followed but, rather, the rise of the Nonpartisan League. The NPL was the brainchild of one man, Arthur C. Townley —former Socialist, failed entrepreneuer, and one of the most brilliant organizers in the modern world. In 1915 Townley evolved his great plan: pull together the farmers of North Dakota in a tightly disciplined, high-dues-paying association with the purpose of electing state officials, in either major party, who were pledged to a program of building a state-owned grain elevator and milling system, establishing state hail insurance, and a few other relatively mild innovations. In 1916 the league elected a phlegmatic farmer, Lynn Frazier of Hoople, as governor in spite of the opposition's taunt, "Who in Hell is Frazier, and where in Hell is Hoople?"[17]

Townley soon envisioned a National Nonpartisan League. His organizers struck next in Minnesota, and within a year or two he had organizations in every state between Wisconsin and the Pacific coast. In many areas the old Socialist locals moved into the league en masse.

The socialism of the NPL had aroused bitter enmity, however, and American entry into World War I gave opponents a club to bludgeon it. League leaders did not see the problem in time. While supporting the war effort, they criticized a number of administration policies. As Robert Morlan has written, the war "seemed a matter of secondary importance and an annoying interruption of the progress of the League program."

But as early as May 1917, they recognized the need for a positive statement of support. Although it proclaimed, "Our country, right or wrong," it also added several thoughtful provisions, similar to Woodrow Wilson's later fourteen points, on war aims. Conservatives became apoplectic at the softly phrased suggestion that wealth as well as men be drafted.[18]

Leaguers became increasingly the fair game for patriots. Newspapers consistently misquoted Townley, and before the war ended, he had been prevented from speaking on numerous platforms and indicted by local prosecutors in several places for sedition and other crimes. Charles A. Lindbergh, Sr., the NPL candidate for governor in the Minnesota Republican primary of 1918, faced angry violence and was barred from entering various counties. League opponents waged similar campaigns, often accompanied by brutal assaults, in every state where it had an organization. A mob dragged one of its earliest leaders, Alfred Knutson, head of the Washington state group, from his bed and drove him from the town with a covering of tar and cotton batting—in lieu of feathers.[19]

If the war issue presented a wonderful facade for the attacks of the League's enemies, the Russian Revolution gave them another. The *Minneapolis Journal* denounced the NPL platform as "but the beginnings of a Socialist program such as has wrecked Russia." Eastern news reporters swarmed around the North Dakota legislative session convinced that they would observe communism in action. A vitriolic, highly professional, and obviously well-financed antileague magazine, the *Red Flame,* declared that the NPL had "degenerated into pure Bolshevism" led by "international socialists." Another propaganda sheet implied that the organization had sponsored a free-love bill allowing a returned soldier to have his way with any maiden of his choice.[20]

The rhetoric of NPL spokesmen admittedly gave enemies a basis to be jumpy. At the 1918 convention of the Minnesota league, Townley had invited workers to join with farmers in the fight for reform. Lindbergh's campaign emphasized "farmers *and* workers," and he was the first to be dubbed the "farmer-labor" candidate. This alliance frightened conservatives, who had always claimed it to be an unnatural one between groups with different and often opposing interests. To the more literate enemies of the league, its rallying cries may well have sounded a shade too close to the Bolshevik slogan of a "workers' and peasants' government." The capper came when the North Dakota NPL called on the 1919 legislature to establish "a thoroughgoing system of state ownership, not merely a corporate or cooperative organization."[21]

Whatever justification enemies of the league may have felt for their attacks, one result was obvious. Many farmers decided that it was perhaps a badge of honor to be characterized as a red. Thousands of western farmers, without ever becoming Communists, began watching the Soviet experiment with interest and some sympathy. Their representatives—respected men such as Senators William Borah, George Norris, Smith Brookhart, and others—called for diplomatic recognition of Russia.

Writers of fantasy or science fiction may legitimately hypothesize on what might have been. Historians may speculate also on the eventual fate of the Nonpartisan League in a world which saw neither World War I nor the Russian Revolution. These events, however, did occur and affected the nature of the league. Frazier's cohort swept the North Dakota elections in 1918, but Lindbergh lost his primary bid in Minnesota, and similar rebuffs greeted NPL candidates throughout the Northwest. Reacting bitterly, the league sponsored independent slates opposed to the major parties in both Minnesota and South Dakota in November.[22]

The NPL was breaking up by 1920. Many followers were disenchanted by Townley's autocratic methods, and a serious schism had developed in North Dakota. Leaguers in several other states argued that the nonpartisan drive to win in the old parties' primaries had failed—that the professional politicians could outsmart the simple farmers. The only alternative, other than despair, seemed to be a new party. Observers from the NPL attended the Chicago convention of the Farmer Laborites and cheered for La Follette, but they refused to endorse the platform or support the nominee. The third-party trend was unmistakable, however. Nebraska and Washington joined Minnesota and South Dakota in the ranks of states where powerful new parties evolved from the fading league. Two years later the Progressive party appeared in Idaho; William Lemke campaigned for governor of North Dakota as the Nonpartisan League candidate in the general rather than the primary election; and Farmer Labor sentiment grew in Montana, Oregon, and elsewhere.[23]

By 1922, when the Communists took a new look at the Farmer Labor movement, its real strength was among the farmers of the Northwest rather than with the national headquarters in Chicago. Although John Fitzpatrick gained stature as the party's spokesman, the various state groups paid him only the lightest fealty, and the Minnesota Farmer

Laborites, who sent Henrik Shipstead to the Senate in 1922, ignored all invitations to affiliate with the national organization. Fitzpatrick's magazine, the *New Majority,* provided a clearing house for news and ideas, however, especially after the death of the league's *National Leader* in early 1923.

A few Communists had already begun cultivating friendly relations with the new state third parties even before John Pepper signaled his support. They found willing listeners among farmers who were bitter over wartime witch hunts and the postwar collapse of prices. As early as 1919, Alfred Knutson had quietly joined the Communist party while continuing to work for the Nonpartisan League.

Knutson, born in Norway in 1880, had emigrated to the United States at the age of nineteen. He drifted around the country doing various jobs and graduated from the University of South Dakota in 1912. He deplored the intellectual sterility of his college days and went to work as a carpenter in Williams County, North Dakota. The western Dakotas were a radical hotbed, and he soon abandoned his Lutheran faith and embraced Marxism.

The Socialist party was only a way station for Knutson, who joined the Nonpartisan League as soon as it appeared. His innovative use of skis to continue organizing farmers during the winter when roads were blocked by snow caught the eye of Townley, who advanced him rapidly. Knutson spearheaded the drive into Minnesota, started the first branch in Colorado, and served as state manager first in Idaho and later in Washington. His rough treatment there at the hands of vigilantes may well have converted him to the belief in the necessity of revolution. By 1922 he had returned to North Dakota to spread the new gospel.[24]

Another convert was Charles E. Taylor, editor of *Producers News,* the most important league paper in Montana. Taylor, a tough three-hundred-pound mountain of a man, had won notoriety with his columns defending the right to fly the banner of revolution, and for the rest of his life he was known as Red Flag Charlie. His accession to the party came in 1920, although he concealed his membership for a half dozen years and won election to the state senate as a Republican in 1922. As orator, agitator, and publisher he wielded great influence throughout the Northwest.[25]

There were others who, without joining the party, were not afraid of it—perhaps because their conservative opponents had already painted them red. In South Dakota, acerbic former Senator R. F. Pettigrew—the "ancient Pettigrew" in the *New York Times* lexicon—urged formation of a class-based party. He offered his extensive library to Tom Ayres and Alice Lorraine Daly of the South Dakota Farmer Laborites if they would establish a state branch of the Workers party. Ayres—rancher, editor, friend of William Jennings Bryan—and the beautiful Miss Alice, a speech professor fired for pacifism, were not averse to cooperating with the Communists, but refused Pettigrew's offer. On the West Coast, William Bouck, a hard-bitten old farmer who had risen to be master of the Washington Grange, played a similar role. He had opposed the war, praised the Russian Revolution, and cooperated with the labor unions. The exasperated leaders of the national Grange finally expelled him in 1921, but about a third of the membership followed his lead in founding a new group, the Western Progressive Farmers. Elsewhere, Nonpartisan Leaguers like William Lemke in North Dakota and Ray McKaig in Idaho kept a greater distance from the Communists but, at the same time, carefully weighed the value of an alliance.[26]

John Fitzpatrick, in his Chicago office, probably had no idea how radicalized the western Farmer Laborites had become when in March 1923 he issued the call for a national convention to meet in July to build a broader alliance of workers and farmers. He sent out over thirty thousand invitations and assured those who had received none that they still would be welcomed. John Pepper saw this as a splendid opportunity for the Communists to play for high stakes. He had such amazing success in rounding up sympathetic delegations that Fitzpatrick soon was having second thoughts. By early June the latter was trying to amend the nature of the meeting—to hold off forming a new party for the time being and instead simply discuss what its nature and program would be. Several Communists, such as Earl Browder and William Z. Foster, who were active in the Chicago labor movement and friendly with Fitzpatrick, favored a conciliatory approach, but the enthusiastic Pepper carried the day for his viewpoint.[27]

Fitzpatrick's dream of a party to unite the majority of workers and farmers had gone badly awry. There never had been much hope of bringing in the conservative, business-oriented Farm Bureau. The AF of L largely ignored his plans, and the Socialists snippily declined to affiliate with a weaker party. Fitzpatrick's last hopes for a broad convention faded when the United Mine Workers and Locomotive Engineers failed to appear. Even the sympathetic representatives of the Amalgamated Clothing Workers set sail for other ports after a brief attendance.[28]

When the conclave met, 3 July, 1923, the Communists had representation far beyond the positions allotted to the Workers party. Carefully disciplined and captained platoons claimed seats as delegates of such things as the Rosedale Improvement Benefit Club, the United Working-men Singers, the Lithuanian Literary Association of Brooklyn, and a host of other organizations. The Communist leaders, according to their own later count, controlled some two hundred votes—about a third of the total.

The others represented Fitzpatrick's Chicago Farmer Laborites, a grab bag of free spirits, and a multitude of farmers. The latter came largely from the trans-Mississippi West still in the throes of postwar depression. They were as angry as had been their fathers who founded the Peoples party in Omaha, 4 July, thirty-one years earlier. Hal Ware, back in the United States for a few months, brought a contingent of Dakotans calling themselves the United Farmers Educational League and having vague ties to the Communist party. The majority, however, had no such allegiance. William Bouck, an old Populist himself, led his Western Progressive Farmers from Washington. The Wisconsin Equity Society sent Francis Shoemaker, a small-time demagogue and former Nonpartisan League organizer. William H. Green, an editor who had crusaded against the International Harvester trust, represented the Nebraska Farmers Union. Most of the national and state farm organizations were noticeable by their absence, however, and the majority of rural delegates came to Chicago simply as concerned individuals, worried about the future and with a vision of better things.[29]

The farmers and the Communists found common ground at the convention almost at once. They cheered the venerable Senator Petti-grew, who praised Soviet Russia in his welcoming address and demanded, "All power to the men who do the work and create the wealth. . . . Don't buy the mines and railroads, take them."[30] Fitzpatrick was obviously concerned that the convention was getting out of hand, but when he tried to assert control by attempting to exclude the Workers party and its allies, he suffered a resounding defeat. Under Pepper's tutelage, the Communists had rapidly learned to transcend the sectarianism of the underground party. Although they first opposed the Populist panaceas drafted by the majority on the convention's agrarian committee, they soon gracefully accepted the farmers' demands.[31]

By the end of the convention on 5 July, the Communists and the radical farmers had formed an alliance which routed the Fitzpatrick forces time after time. When the Chicago Farmer Laborites made a last attempt to expel any group affiliated with the Third International, Shoemaker of Wisconsin passionately defended his new friends, and the convention voted overwhelmingly to table the motion. Despite Fitzpatrick's futile protests, the delegates moved to found what they christened the Federated Farmer Labor party, which they deluded themselves into believing would attract the broad support of the working class, rural and urban, across the nation. The Communists got the key executive position, national secretary, which went to Joseph Manley, the son-in-law of William Z. Foster. The western farmers got the positions of honor: Bouck became president with Shoemaker and Green as vice-presidents. Communists filled about half the seats on the executive committee, including among their number Hal Ware and V. S. Alanne, educational director of the party-dominated Cooperative Central Exchange of Superior, Wisconsin.[32]

Fitzpatrick raged that the Communists had violated his hospitality and disowned the new party. Conveniently he forgot that he had cooperated with them almost until the day of the convention. In his avid desire to build a broad, class-structured party he blinded himself to the fact that practically none of his colleagues in organized labor shared that ambition.

The question remains, did the Communists win anything of value by capturing the convention? A historian of the La Follette movement has argued that the Workers party planned to use the meeting as a backdoor entry into the labor unions. If so, they failed dismally. They had lost their last friends in the mainstream when they alienated the Chicago Federation of Labor. On the other hand, they gained a good deal more in potential strength than most commentators have admitted. Pepper had acted in line with the growing Comi .tern interest in peasant movements throughout the world by cultivating the seeds of dissatisfaction which had sprouted among western farmers. When Pepper analyzed the convention for party readers, he wrote that Communist acceptance of non-Marxist demands in the areas of money and taxation had provided "one of the most illuminating episodes of the Convention, and the best proof that the Workers Party had learned to maneuvre."[33] The executive committee of the Communist International lauded the new Federated Farmer Labor party, and Israel Amter boasted that the party had contact "above all with the militant farmers" who demonstrated "more radicalism than many of the industrial workers."[34]

Critics of the FFLP scoffed at its claims to influence. *Labor,* the journal of the railroad brotherhoods, reported briefly and disdainfully: "COMMUNISTS CAPTURE SELVES." The *New York Times* wrote editorially that the new party would fail because true farmers could not tolerate Bolsheviks. In a sense this was whistling in the dark. The western Farmer Laborites were clamoring for action and showed little inclination to desert the alliance. William H. Green rapped the critics sharply and claimed that not a single farmer had followed Fitzpatrick when he bolted the convention.[35]

Minnesota voters demonstrated the power of the third-party idea a few days after the Chicago convention when they sent the foghorn-voiced Swedish orator, Magnus Johnson, to the Senate as a Farmer Laborite to fill an unexpired term. Granted, the FFLP could take no credit, because the Minnesota group had not affiliated with it, but the victory bolstered the spirits of the western radicals. Tom Ayres wrote Johnson's secretary that the news gave new courage to the faint hearts in his state who had begun seeking fusion with the Democrats.[36]

Ayres, like many of the state leaders, had not aligned himself with the FFLP, but neither had he condemned it. The Communists thus had an opportunity to capitalize on their victory in Chicago to extend their ties with western farmers, if Pepper could continue to guide them in the path of the broad united front—and if the Communist International maintained its line of courting the peasantry. A most necessary link would be with the Minnesota Farmer Laborites. That party's chairman, Frederick A. Pike, had attended the July convention only as an observer, but he wrote soon afterwards in the *New York Times* that a new national party was necessary and that his organization should be part of it.[37]

On 24 August the executive council of the Workers party met and approved by a vote of nine to three Pepper's "August Theses." In these the ebullient Hungarian vigorously defended the FFLP as being the vanguard of the working class. He predicted that the new party would enroll 250,000 workers and 50,000 to 80,000 farmers by the end of the year.[38]

A spate of articles in the *Worker* explained farm problems to the predominantly urban Communist membership and exhorted them to build bridges to the rural brethren. Hal Ware wrote that American farmers, unlike the peasants of Europe, were true radicals. Another writer explained the vital interdependence of workers and farmers. They were echoed by William H. Green, just before he left for Moscow to attend a Soviet agricultural fair.[39]

During the autumn, Joseph Manley toured the West to assess the prospects for the FFLP. He found a third party existing almost everywhere except in Montana and North Dakota. The strength of the Nonpartisan League in those states had forestalled independent action, but the NPL had fallen on hard days. Henry Teigan, who had served as secretary of the NPL throughout its life, was convinced that strong forces at the North Dakota league convention, 10 October, would opt for a Farmer Labor alignment.[40]

Alfred Knutson, under instructions from Communist leaders, led the fight to convert the league into a political party. He failed, however, because, according to Manley's interpretation, not enough real farmers had attended the Bismarck meeting. Knutson had done the spadework among his old friends though, and the *Worker* promised a more favorable result when the league reassembled in February.[41]

Manley had better luck in neighboring Montana. The remnants of the Nonpartisan League, led by Charlie Taylor, allied themselves with the radicals of the Butte Federation of Labor under William F. Dunne to call a Farmer Labor conference on 23 October. They enthusiastically founded a new party under the chairmanship of State Sen. Jaspar Haaland, a close associate of Taylor and owner of several thousand acres of rich eastern Montana wheat fields.[42]

By early November the confident Minnesota Farmer Laborites were ready to assume leadership of a national movement. A surprisingly harmonious conference in September had unified the previously squabbling urban and rural wings of their party. On 1 November they issued invitations to a small group of progressives to meet in Saint Paul two weeks later quietly to discuss calling a national convention in 1924.[43] A Twin Cities union leader, William Mahoney, emerged as the outstanding proponent of a united front party and played a principal role during the next half year.

Charlie Taylor answered at once. Bill Dunne would provide him the money to attend, he wrote, and had already notified Charles Ruthenberg, secretary of the Workers party. The proposed conference brought the

Communists face to face with a difficult problem: their rural allies wanted Robert La Follette as their presidential candidate, first, last, and only. On 13 November, the executive council of the Workers party met to ponder this question. Pepper had already decided that the La Follette movement represented a "third American revolution" of well-to-do farmers and small businessmen, which would split the capitalist class. He believed that the Communists should work with this movement while building their strength among the working class. La Follette could serve as an American Kerensky, and the proletarian, or "fourth American revolution," would soon follow. His argument carried the day, and the council agreed to support La Follette if the Farmer Laborites nominated him.[44]

When the Minnesota conference met, 15 and 16 November, the Communists tacitly admitted that the FFLP had failed in its bid for leadership of the entire third-party movement. They continued using it, however, as a device for claiming that they represented more than the few thousand members of the Workers party. The titular head of the FFLP, William Bouck, presented no problem, because he told the meeting that Joseph Manley would speak for him.[45]

The delegates agreed that La Follette was the only possible nominee and that a Farmer Labor convention should meet 30 May to get a jump on the two established major parties. This rallying around the La Follette banner was not without its ironies. Fitzpatrick and Jay Brown of the Chicago Federation of Labor now represented the right wing of the movement although their insistence on a radical platform in 1920 had prevented the Wisconsin senator from accepting their nomination at that time. On the other hand, Henry Teigan of the Nonpartisan League, which had refused to cooperate with Fitzpatrick's leftists in 1920, now agreed that La Follette was a great battler but not a true radical.[46]

When the third convention of the Workers party met six weeks later, it endorsed Pepper's policy of using the FFLP as a device to work into the political mainstream. Pepper had aroused opposition, however. A faction led by William Z. Foster and James P. Cannon criticized him for having alienated Fitzpatrick and the Chicago unionists who in the past had been the Communists' only friends in the American Federation of Labor, and the Foster-Cannon group won a majority on the new central executive committee. The Workers party temporized on the question of supporting a La Follette nomination and agreed to submit it for decision to Moscow.[47] During the next five months, while the Comintern considered strategy, the American Communists operated under the assumption that they would be supporting La Follette in 1924.

La Follette, now approaching seventy, left little doubt that he intended to make his run in the coming presidential election. There was only the slimmest chance that the Republicans would nominate him, in spite of the scandals accumulating around the Harding administration. The opportunity to nominate Fighting Bob buoyed the Farmer Laborites with the hope that they could build a major party behind him. Moreover, their chief competitor for liberal, farm, and labor votes—the Conference for Progressive Political Action—appeared closely tied to the Democratic aspirations of William G. McAdoo, Woodrow Wilson's secretary of the treasury and son-in-law.

The Conference for Progressive Political Action was the creation of the fifteen rail brotherhoods. During World War I the rail unions had grown tremendously in size under the benevolent eye of McAdoo, who had served as director general of the federalized railroad system. They had failed after the war to have the rails nationalized permanently, and they were facing the buffets of the postwar antiunion campaign launched by business. As a result they had sent out a call for a meeting of progressives in February 1922. Representatives of many unions, several farm groups, the Committee of Forty-Eight, the Socialists, and the Farmer Laborites attended. This founding meeting of the CPPA resisted demands from the left to form a third party, but followed the well-trodden path of the American labor movement—to reward one's friends and punish one's enemies within the established parties.[48]

The rail brotherhoods convened a second conference of the Conference for Progressive Political Action on 11 December 1922 in a mood of jubilation. The recent mid-term elections had sent a host of new friends, such as Smith Brookhart, Lynn Frazier, and Burton Wheeler, to Washington and retired many enemies. There seemed little need to modify the organization's policy, and when the Socialists and the Chicago Farmer Laborites again demanded formation of a third party, the unionists voted them down, sixty-four to fifty-two.[49] It was this rebuff to the hopes of Fitzpatrick which had led him to call the ill-fated convention in Chicago the following July.

Throughout 1923, the CPPA established branches in many states and worked to strengthen the organization in anticipation of the presidential election. There was little doubt that the dominant railroad men intended to support their hero, McAdoo, although La Follette got occasional nods of approbation. Then, on the eve of the third conference of the CPPA, in February 1924, McAdoo's aspirations were severely jolted. The pe- troleum millionaire, Edward L. Doheny, deeply involved in the Teapot Dome scandal, revealed that he had been retaining the former cabinet member at twenty-five thousand dollars a year for legal services. All of McAdoo's explanations failed to remove the oil slick from the path of his campaign. The candidacy of La Follette suddenly looked much more attractive to the leaders of the CPPA—especially if the radical connota- tions of Farmer Labor support could be erased. The delegates left the final decision to a national convention to be held 4 July, after the meet- ings of the two major parties.[50]

La Follette was in a delicate position and acted cautiously. The Farmer Laborites had long boosted his candidacy but had little money. The rail brotherhoods, in contrast, had overflowing coffers. Talking privately in mid-winter with Henry Teigan and William Mahoney of the Minnesota FLP, however, the old senator gave the impression that he would accept the party's nomination.[51]

Early in 1924 the FLP was picking up steam. When Fitzpatrick and Robert Buck of the Chicago Farmer Laborites called a conference of western third parties in an obvious attempt to steer them in a moderate course and exclude Communists, the meeting ran away from them.[52] Early in February the North Dakota Nonpartisans convened in Bis- marck. Tom Ayres spoke briefly, damning capitalism, lauding the Soviet system, and asking for the formation of a third party in the state. Al- though a majority of the delegates decided to try once more to nominate their chosen candidates in the primaries of the old parties, a sizable number of them met shortly thereafter to set up the framework of a North Dakota Farmer Labor party under the leadership of R. H. "Dad" Walker, the most widely respected nonpolitician in the NPL.[53] The indefatigable Ayres continued to reiterate his support in the *South Da- kota Leader,* and a meeting of the Nebraska Progressive party endorsed the coming convention of the FLP in Saint Paul.[54] In every instance there was the demand that the convention date of 30 May be adhered to. The westerners left no doubt that they wanted La Follette pledged to their party and their program well before the meetings of the Republi- cans, the Democrats, or the CPPA.

Mahoney and Teigan, however, after conferring with La Follette in February, agreed that the Farmer Labor convention should be set back to a mid-June date. By then, they were sure, the Republican convention would have turned its back on La Follette, and he would be free to secede. At that time, the Farmer Laborites, with thousands of delegates flocking to their Saint Paul meeting, could nominate the old senator and present a fait accompli to their CPPA rivals.[55]

John Pepper feared that this temporizing threatened his scheme for a Farmer Labor party in which the Communists would play an important role. In his struggle with Foster for control of the Workers party Pepper was more and more emphasizing the revolutionary role of American farmers. He pointed to their radical past and their current discontent. The world crisis of capitalism, he wrote, might have begun in British and German industry, but it had manifested itself agriculturally in America. He warned that the industrial working class had no chance of seizing power without strong rural support—and here he spoke, of course, without mentioning the fact, on the basis of his own disastrous experience in Hungary.[56]

Pepper remained adamant on the earlier date for the FLP convention, but his own executive committee, now in the hands of the Foster-Cannon faction, voted him down. Foster had little interest in farmers and hoped to rewin a position of influence in the mainstream of unionism which he had lost as a result of the break with Fitzpatrick. Although he was lukewarm toward the FLP, he hoped to gain sympathy among the rank and file by supporting La Follette, whom he thought the conservative AF of L leaders would reject.[57]

Foster and Ruthenberg persuaded William Mahoney to call a conference of national leaders on 10 and 11 March, while the Minnesota Farmer Labor Federation was meeting, in order to make a final decision on the convention date. Charlie Taylor led Pepper's fight to stick with 30 May, but after Teigan insisted that La Follette would not announce his candidacy until after the Republicans met, Mahoney got his way. The convention would assemble in Saint Paul on 17 June.[58]

From March through June innumerable factions wove intricate patterns of rivalry. Within the CPPA the Socialists demanded formation of a permanent third party; the unionists opposed them. Both united in jealous opposition to the Farmer Laborites. The FLP itself was a commingling of disparate groups united only in the hope of winning political leverage. The American Communists fought among themselves. The Fosterites had long argued with the Pepperites about the united front. The former saw it as useful only in giving the Communists an entry into the labor movement; the latter maintained that a La Follette–led FLP would be an essential step toward a Bolshevik revolution. And, finally, when the factions submitted their differences to the Third International, they found that Sanhedrin of Communism torn by the bitter contest between Leon Trotsky and his enemies.

La Follette's candidacy was the focus of these struggles—even to a degree, the one in Moscow. The old man had suffered serious illness in March and April while the pressure on him mounted. Early in April, *Labor* launched a biting attack on the June convention of the FLP and made obvious that the powerful rail unions would not support any candidate selected by it. Covington Hall, an editor of *Farm-Labor Union News* in Texas, warned Lemke that he feared a split between the farmers, who were all for La Follette, and the brotherhoods, who still secretly aimed at nominating McAdoo.[59]

On 28 April, Sam Gompers met with a group of unionists and progressives to warn them against supporting any third party. The aged grand panjandrum of the AF of L raised the red scare, insisting that the Communists controlled the FLP. The message from organized labor was clear. Within a week, Bob La Follette, Jr., traveled from Washington to his father's haven in Atlantic City to warn that the Communists were using the Farmer Laborites to capture the progressive movement. John Fitzpatrick added his weight to the balance on 24 May by announcing that the Chicago Federation of Labor was abandoning third-party politics in favor of the Gompers approach. Although La Follette still tried to temporize, his son insisted that he disavow the FLP on the grounds that is was Communist-infested.[60]

On 28 May, La Follette finally released a four-page letter, largely written by his son, addressed to the attorney general of Wisconsin. He acknowledged that there were friends of his among the intended delegates to the FLP convention and, indeed, that many of them were true progressives. But having made this gesture, La Follette went on to repudiate the Saint Paul convention completely. He cited two recent items from the *Daily Worker*. On 31 March, Ruthenberg, on behalf of the central executive committee, had exhorted members of the Workers party to use the FLP as an instrument to win a Soviet America. Twelve days before the release of La Follette's letter, the Communist newspaper printed a cable from the Third International which called the 17 June convention a "momentous event." The senator affirmed his belief that the Communists had every right to present their ideas to the electorate, but he referred to them as a divisive and chaotic element within the progressive movement.[61]

La Follette's letter barred the door against a Farmer Labor party nomination. The senator had equivocated until the last minute, but there can be no doubt that the union leaders had forced a decision. The Farmer Laborites were demanding a third party which would include all elements from lightly liberal to red revolutionary. *Labor* had made plain that the CPPA would not accept this, and La Follette's chances for winning endorsement from the AF of L rested on his denunciation of the Saint Paul convention.

The release of the letter caused more scurrying than a fox in a chicken yard. The Minnesota senators, Shipstead and Johnson, quietly found that they had business elsewhere on 17 June. Henry Teigan, until now one of the prime movers in the third-party drive, also withdrew. J. A. H. Hopkins, the frenetic chairman of the Committee of Forty-Eight, who had earlier predicted that the attendance of five or ten thousand delegates in Saint Paul would prevent Communist domination, now discovered suddenly that only the 4 July meeting of the CPPA would be truly representative of progressives.[62]

The beleaguered Mahoney saw cancellations pour in on him. After some soul-searching he determined to carry on with the convention, and be predicted that it would probably nominate La Follette despite his stance. Others were less sanguine. Dad Walker began a boomlet in North Dakota for Lemke now that La Follette "had layed down."[63] An infuriated Charles Taylor wrote Teigan that the Wisconsin senator

> destroys the work which some of us have given our blood money for— denounces the very element who have made him, men who stood like a wall for him during the days of the attack on him. . . . My God, man, has not the history of the past ten years any lesson for you. . . . Teigan, you will find out, you will find out! Just you wait.[64]

Less impassioned Communists showed greater equanimity. Alfred Knutson used La Follette's letter to warn against the cult of the great man, while Foster and Ruthenberg rebuked the senator for demonstrating once more that he was the spokesman of the small-business class rather than the working man.[65] Foster, at least, was probably not much disturbed by La Follette's letter, because he had always doubted the correctness of the policy of the broad political united front. In addition, he had just brought secret instructions back from Moscow to his American comrades.

Earlier in the year, during the constant bickering in the Workers party, the major factions had agreed to submit their differences to the Comintern. A three-man delegation, Foster, Pepper, and Moissaye Olgin, had gone to the Soviet capital to attend an enlarged meeting of the executive committee of the Third International held in April and May. They found themselves already pawns in the greater struggle for the mantle of Lenin, who had died in January. On the one side stood Trotsky; on the other was the Old Bolshevik troika of Zinoviev, Kamenev, and Stalin. No one, the Americans discovered at once, had a good word for the policy of supporting La Follette. Trotsky denounced it as deviant opportunism of the worst sort. The bombastic Zinoviev, head of the Comintern, reversed an earlier stand and seized higher ground than his antagonist by denouncing all collaboration with socialists or progressives.[66] On 20 May, the Third International instructed Foster to insist that La Follette give the Farmer Labor party complete control over the financing and operation of his campaign. Since La Follette would assuredly reject this demand, the Communists could then self-righteously renounce him and put forth their own candidates as the only true representatives of the working class. Foster reported these confidential orders to the top leaders of the Workers party on 1 June. He had also won an even more satisfying personal victory in the Soviet capital—the Comintern ordered his nemesis, Pepper, to remain in Russia.[67]

Poor Mahoney! He had plugged away for almost a year to win support for the great mass convention which was to launch the first true workers' and farmers' party under the reformist banner of the old Wisconsin progressive. Now, however, La Follette had refused his support in advance; the liberal and labor cohorts were deserting in droves; and his Communist allies—whom he had never much liked anyway—were secretly preparing to subvert the corporal's guard remaining.

Enthusiastic predictions in the spring had been that as many as ten thousand delegates would flock to Saint Paul. The minutes of the convention claimed that over five hundred did attend, but Elmer Davis and Boyden Sparks, reporting for two leading New York newspapers, each counted fewer than four hundred.[68] Some dogged Farmer Laborites— Daly and Ayres of South Dakota, Green of Nebraska, Meitzen of Texas, and many of Mahoney's Minnesota friends—defied La Follette's injunction and attended, but the Communists obviously controlled the rump session. Once more, as in Chicago a year earlier, representatives appeared from such groups as the Women's Shelley Club of California and the Galesburg Musical Society. Jaded newsmen formed the ad hoc Upton Sinclair Brass Check Local #1 and selected the Communist cartoonist, Bob Minor, as their delegate.[69] The control of Foster and Ruthenberg was so complete and their wrecking plan so firm that they made little effort to instruct or conciliate the western farmers who had once seemed so important in John Pepper's grand scheme.[70]

Mahoney discovered, as had Fitzpatrick before, that he was no longer master in his house. He tried to stall, hoping to evade the issue of making a presidential nomination until after the CPPA convention had selected La Follette, but he had little support. The Communists brushed him aside. The delegates refused him the permanent chairmanship by a humiliating seven-to-one margin and chose the secret Communist, Charlie Taylor. The cooperative Alice Lorraine Daly became secretary.[71]

Although many non-Communists may have voted for the forceful Taylor out of disgust over the way Mahoney seemed to have botched the convention, still the one-sided margin suggested the hold the Communists had. The crucial issue, however, was La Follette. Since the majority of delegates had no knowledge of the secret Comintern instructions to Foster, most of them probably expected to support the senator in one fashion or another. La Follette sent an emissary to insist that his name not go before the convention, but Foster and Ruthenberg were already on public record as saying they would support him if nominated. Mahoney, caught in the middle, tried to win a simple endorsement for the Wisconsin progressive, with a Farmer Labor nomination to follow the Cleveland convention of the CPPA.[72]

By this point, Foster was obviously masterminding the convention. He seemed willing to play the conciliatory role and left Mahoney with his illusions until time came to decide on nominations. With great relish, Benjamin Gitlow rose to castigate La Follette and mock his supporters. Foster casually announced that the FLP might still select La Follette—

provided he gave the party complete control of the campaign.[73] For a few stunned Farmer Laborites it had finally become too much. W. J. Taylor of Nebraska led a walkout by about twenty-five western farmers after bitterly telling the convention:

> If I were La Follette, I wouldn't want your endorsement. . . . This is no farmer-labor convention. It is a meeting of Communists, and when you call it anything else you disguise its real character. Foster and Ruthenberg are the real bosses here, and you know it.
>
> If you Communists are not afraid to sail under your own colors, why don't you hold your own convention. . . . I'm going back and tell the farmers of Nebraska that when La Follette said this would be a Communist Convention, he told the truth.[74]

Foster had still not played out the final intricacies of his strategy. The delegates nominated the Illinois labor leader, Duncan MacDonald, for president and chose William Bouck of the Western Progressive Farmers as his running mate. The pair deluded themselves into believing that they were interim candidates who would withdraw when La Follette accepted the Farmer Labor endorsement after first having been nominated by the CPPA meeting two weeks later.[75]

The CPPA had symbolically chosen 4 July for its gathering in Cleveland. The excited throng which assembled there stood in direct contrast to the aborted convention in Saint Paul. Aged Populists consorted with Jewish garment workers, and "General" Jacob Coxey exchanged ideas with W. T. Raleigh, the patent medicine magnate. Only one dissident group was missing. A hundred sturdy railroad engineers and other guards turned away any suspected Communists, and a chastened William Mahoney found himself under the ban. As expected, the convention nominated La Follette, but as an independent candidate—having refused Socialist demands to establish a permanent third party.[76]

Foster now played the final act of his charade. Communist leaders met on 8 July and withdrew their support from MacDonald and Bouck. Two days later, five of the seven-member FLP executive committee, established at the Saint Paul convention—including the Communists Clarence Hathaway, Alfred Knutson, and Joseph Manley—pulled the Farmer Laborites out of the race. At the same time, fifty delegates nominated Foster and Gitlow as Workers party candidates.[77]

The Farmer Labor movement, which only a few months earlier had looked so promising, was in shambles. The western farmers were in particular disarray. W. H. Green of Nebraska, so recently a happy guest in Moscow, resigned in disgust. William Lemke, who had praised the Saint Paul convention, remained mum, and Dad Walker's North Dakota Farmer Laborites failed to enter a ticket in the November election. The thoroughgoing political confusion in the Flickertail State was demonstrated in November when A. C. Miller, an acknowledged Communist from Williams County, won election to the legislature—on the Republican ticket.[78] Tom Ayres quietly withdrew his party's electors from the field in favor of a slate of La Follette independents, but the latter vindictively put up their own gubernatorial candidate, dividing the South Dakota progressive vote. A bitter fissure opened in Washington State between the third-party people and the CPPA faction.[79]

The adamant refusal of La Follette to head any FLP list had varying effects in other states. The most serious problem was Minnesota. The split ticket meant duplicated activity and fund-raising problems. In the end, La Follette trailed Floyd B. Olson, the Farmer Labor candidate for governor, by forty thousand votes.[80] The Montana Farmer Laborites convened on 10 July, the very day that their national candidates were bowed out of the race. The volatile Charlie Taylor apparently tried to win an endorsement for Foster and Gitlow, but the party put up a slate pledged to La Follette. Taylor then tried to seize control of the Montana Wheat Growers Association to help finance Foster's campaign, but failed once again. It appeared for a time that the Wisconsin senator would accept the Farmer Labor electors in Montana, but eventually he demanded an independent slate. Taylor, who was a candidate for Congress, insisted on keeping the FLP team on the ballot, allowing the La Follette vote to be split in the state.[81] Taylor's erratic behavior displayed that independence and inability to toe the line which led to his expulsion by the Communists a decade later.

If 1924 had proved a disastrous year for the Farmer Laborites, it had not been a joyous time for the Communists. Party leaders undoubtedly noted Charlie Taylor's unreliability and marked it down for future reference. They might better have studied their own performance. John Pepper had dragged them out of the basements of the underground and had showed them the possibilities inherent in bold maneuvering among discontented groups, but many of them scorned the lesson.

The enthusiastic, scheming Hungarian had rapidly adapted to American ways, and however imperfect was his analysis of political forces in the United States, still it was probably better than most of his comrades. He soon recognized the rampant discontent among western farmers and sought an alliance. He knew, moreover, from bitter experience in his homeland that a revolution which ignored the countryside was doomed. Without carrying the analogy too far, it might be said that Pepper was a Maoist before Mao.

Undoubtedly Pepper and his comrades had outsmarted themselves at the Farmer Labor convention in 1923. The loosely structured Farmer Labor movement presented them with an almost perfect device for winning an audience among angry farmers who had heard themselves called reds and revolutionaries so often that labels held little fear for them, but the Communists drove potential allies away through their inexperienced eagerness. Above all else, they roused the suspicions of conservatives in organized labor. The radical farmers remained allies, however.

In the end, it was outside forces which disrupted the alliance. La Follette, who had remained silent until the eleventh hour, finally condemned the Communists under the pressure of his labor supporters. At the same time, the contestants for power in Moscow tumbled over one another to take the strongest stance in opposition to a united front with the non-Communist left. Many American party members were no doubt happy to be relieved of the necessity of placating those who had imperfect faith.

The Communist party appeared on the ballot in a dozen states in 1924 and won about thirty thousand votes. Half the states and about a third of the votes were in the farming west. The party's best showing came in Minnesota and Wisconsin, where the isolated and often scorned Finns in the poverty-stricken northern counties ran up about one-half of one percent of the total popular vote in those states.

This electoral result was miniscule. If the party was to win a popular following in farming areas, something further needed doing. While party leaders wrangled over their factional disputes, the handful of rural Communists turned toward winning the masses of old Populists, Nonpartisan Leaguers, and Farmer Laborites through a campaign of education.

THE UNITED FARMERS
EDUCATIONAL LEAGUE

THE COMMUNIST PARTY emerged from the election of 1924 torn by dissension over its future political role. One faction, led by William Z. Foster, argued that the Farmer Labor party idea was useless and should be discarded. The group around Charles E. Ruthenberg countered that FLP sentiment would revive as disillusionment grew among supporters of La Follette. Emerging as the leader of the Ruthenberg forces was Jay Lovestone, who earlier had opposed ditching the FLP during the presidential election. As the dispute continued between the Foster majority and the Ruthenberg minority, John Pepper, associated with the latter, pulled strings among his friends in the Soviet Union to have a delegation summoned to Moscow, where the Fifth Plenum of the Communist International was scheduled to meet in March 1925.[1]

The Americans found themselves amidst a power struggle which had profound effects on world communism. During much of 1924, Stalin had let Kamenev and Zinoviev lead the battle against Trotsky. In December, however, Stalin moved to the fore with his principle of "socialism in one country"—the doctrine that the victorious Russian proletariat could build a socialist society in a single nation. Trotsky denied the feasibility of this idea and saw it as a betrayal of world revolution, but Stalin forged ahead. By the time of the March plenum, Stalin had hypothesized a period of stabilization for capitalist nations and had laid down tasks for Communist parties, which implied that there was no imminence of world revolution.[2]

Stalin's tactics not only continued the process of weakening Trotsky, who was removed as war commissar in January 1925, but also undermined the position of his supposed allies, Kamenev and Zinoviev. As recently as the Fifth Congress of the Comintern, during the summer of 1924, Zinoviev had ridiculed the possibility of stabilization of world capitalist society. Now, less than a year later, he presided over a plenum which stressed the reverse.[3]

The implications of these larger events may well have escaped most of the American delegation, the members of which were primarily attuned to their own internecine struggles. Jay Lovestone, however, apparently sensed Moscow trends better at this point than his colleagues. While Zinoviev's power was declining, that of Nikolai Bukharin was rising, and Lovestone attached himself to this Bolshevik intellectual whom he had first met in 1922.

Bukharin devoted a great deal of attention during the session to the peasant question. He had already become convinced that world capitalism was not collapsing, and thus he had allied himself with Stalin in support of building socialism in the Soviet Union. Within Russia itself he encouraged the individual peasants to seek profit, which in turn, he reasoned, would create a demand for industrial production, bringing on the socialist state, however slowly.[4]

Just as Bukharin saw the building of socialism at home as a process which should operate at a snail's pace, with firm support from the peasantry, he foresaw a long nonrevolutionary period abroad during which Communists would carefully proselytize in rural areas to win allies for the industrial workers. In lengthy theses and in his address to the plenum, Bukharin argued the importance of the peasantry in the long-term revolutionary agenda. Lovestone echoed Bukharin's analysis in his own speech, which dealt with American farming.[5]

Ruthenberg, Lovestone, and Pepper rode the crests and negotiated the crosscurrents flowing through Moscow in March and April 1925 much more opportunely than did their opponents led by Foster. After a month of debate, the American commission of the Comintern gave a decision which overwhelmingly favored the Ruthenberg group. Without hinting that its own policy, less than a year earlier, undermining the La Follette candidacy, might have been in error, the Comintern now viewed the Progressive vote as a proletarian victory. Moreover, the commission instructed the American delegation actively to build a broad left-wing political party. Finally, in a tortuously constructed compromise, the Comintern ordered the Foster majority on the central executive committee of the party to share power with the Ruthenberg minority—under the chairmanship of a neutral comrade—until a new convention could resolve future control.[6]

In the waning days of the conference another Communist group, the Krestintern (Red Peasant International) held its second plenum in Moscow. In contrast to the sometimes lively session of the Comintern, the agrarian meeting was brief and drab. Its only significance for Americans was the attendance of Alfred Knutson, representing the nation's farmers.

The Krestintern was less than two years old. It had been born with high aspirations but was already beginning a long slide to oblivion. When 158 delegates from over forty nationalities had assembled in the grand throne room of the czar from 10 to 15 October 1923, Zinoviev had been riding high. In his ambition to succeed the ailing Lenin, he had sponsored the Krestintern in the hopes that a new revolutionary surge in Eastern Europe, following the Russian pattern—an alliance of Bolsheviks and peasants—would sweep him to leadership.

The peasant group—usually called the Farmers International in the United States, for obvious reasons—looked impressive on paper, with its congresses, plenums, council, presidium, and secretariat. In reality, however, the Krestintern was little more than a haven for East European émigrés who made up much of its staff. They focused on their homelands, failing to make any detailed analyses of other regional problems, despite the obvious differences among Russian kulaks, Chinese peasants, Masai herdsmen, and Dakota wheat farmers, to name but a few. Rather than examining the practical issues facing farmers and peasants around the globe, the Krestintern secretariat expended its energies talking of ways to win them to the cause of communism, even if only long enough to stage a successful revolution. Since the Krestintern bureaucracy believed that all revolutions must follow the Russian pattern, innovation was stifled.[7]

Alfred Knutson seems not to have been much impressed by his association with the Krestintern, but the new Soviet homeland enthralled him. He traveled some two thousand miles through rural areas in Russia during the spring of 1925, observing the changes which had occurred since czarist days. Whether or not he met Bukharin, the ideas of that cautious theoretician impressed him. Russia needed time to build its economic system, and Bukharin's encouragement of the peasantry seemed to provide a sound base. As for the United States, Bukharin's policies of slow-and-easy meant no frenetic pretense of belief in imminent revolution but rather—and greatly to Knutson's taste—an emphasis on propaganda, education, and proselytizing.[8]

Knutson fell naturally into the camp of Lovestone and Ruthenberg. After the delegation to the Comintern plenum returned to the United States, they and their allies spent a hectic summer lining up supporters for the Fourth Convention of the Workers party to be held in late August. On the face of things Foster had a two-to-one majority. Quietly watching a week of wrangling was the Comintern-dispatched neutral comrade, Sergei Gusev, an old Bolshevik associate of Stalin, who had slipped across the border from Mexico disguised as a businessman. On the eighth day Gusev dramatically pulled from his pocket a telegram from the Comintern, which, its effect, handed control of the party to Lovestone and Ruthenberg. Foster raged at the decision, but his own cofactionalists submitted to the directive, and for the next three and a half years, Lovestone dominated the American party. Knutson, as a Lovestone supporter, became an alternate member of the central executive committee.[9]

The printed report of the convention devoted six pages to agrarian programs and policies. It was a bland document which generalized about the necessity of winning the "rural proletariat" as well as tenant, poor, and "middle" farmers. The program suggested a united front with the Industrial Workers of the World on behalf of agricultural laborers, but, surprisingly, there is little evidence to suggest that the party did any organizing among this economically depressed group during the 1920s. Knutson's interest and influence showed, however, in regard to farm operators—the average-to-poor tenant and owner. The Communist party should, according to the program, work within such organizations as the Western Progressive Farmers, Farmers Union, farm cooperatives, and Farmer Labor groups, to gain "united action with the workers thru an alliance with the Labor Party."[10]

The convention established an agricultural commission which was assigned the tasks of preparing a clearly defined program and the building of an agrarian department and press. The commission had six members, but only Knutson had demonstrated any interest in farmers. With his appointment as salaried agricultural organizer, Knutson became the party's guiding force in rural areas for much of the rest of the decade. Lovestone seemed neither to know nor to care anything about farmers.[11]

Bukharin's policy of caution not only fitted Knutson's preferences, but it also jibed with realities in rural America. The states of the Great Plains and western corn belt had gone through a decade of ferment and change. The Nonpartisan League, the war, and booming land and commodity prices had given away in the early 1920s to collapsing prices, mortgage foreclosures, bankruptcies, and tax sales—as well as to the spread of the conservative American Farm Bureau Federation. When farm income began to rise slowly again prior to the election of 1924, farmers may have joked slyly about the political coincidence, but they gladly accepted the cash. Those who had survived the worst times now faced a level of taxes and debts much higher than before the war. They recognized the necessity of new investment in tractors, hybrid seeds, and improved strains of cattle. From 1925 through 1929 the real value of farm income approached the prewar level—but never quite reached it. Farmers hoped that they were climbing the path toward prosperity, but they recognized that it was narrow and constantly edged the precipice of disaster. A spirit of surly caution seemed to replace the wartime exuberance and the postwar anger.[12]

Knutson hoped to exploit this rural mood by turning it initially toward building a resentment of capitalist exploitation, next to a consciousness of class conflict, and finally, to forging an alliance with urban workers for the revolution. He chose North Dakota as his base of operations not only for his familiarity with the territory but also because it continued to be the center of more left-wing awareness than any other agrarian area in the country. In neighboring Minnesota, Michigan, and Wisconsin, moreover, the party could depend upon a clannish brotherhood of rural Finns (described in the next chapter). In Montana and the Dakotas a thoughtful and articulate minority of farmers had moved successively from the prewar Socialist party, to the Nonpartisan League, into the Communist party in the early 1920s.

Party units existed in Minot, Williston, Max, Bismarck, Garrison, Bowbells, Beldon, and Fargo, North Dakota; Frederick, South Dakota; and probably elsewhere. They had articulate spokesmen such as Arvo Husa, Pat Barrett, State Rep. A. C. Miller, and Andrew Omholt, a Williams County farmer who had barely missed election as sheriff. The Communists enjoyed the active support of former senator Richard Pettigrew of South Dakota and at least the tacit friendship of a number of other public figures.[13]

Sheridan County, Montana, had the most successful party organization throughout this period. Left-wing socialists had abounded in the Plentywood area even before the arrival of Charlie Taylor to take over the fledgling weekly, *Producer News,* in 1918. Most of the leaders of this group had quietly joined the Communist party within a few years after its birth. Between 1920 and 1924 they gained control of the county government and extended their influence into adjoining counties. Much of their strength derived from the colorful Taylor, a three-hundred-pound giant of prodigious energy, who could use his fists in a political brawl but who preferred his acid pen. From week to week the *Producers Week* enraged enemies and rallied friends. Sheridan County surely became one of the most class-conscious areas in the nation, under Taylor's tutelege. The radicals proudly built a Farmer Labor Temple as the center of their activities, and every pool hall and barbershop carried the *Daily Worker* cheek by jowl with the *Police Gazette.* Sheriff Rodney Salisbury peddled the *Worker* to farmers throughout the countryside.[14] Knutson, in other words, did not begin his work in a vacuum.

He sought first to revive the flagging spirit of the Farmer Labor parties in the West. The refusal of La Follette to accept their nomination in 1924 had demoralized many western Farmer Laborites. There remained, however, a corps of veterans, scarred but fervent, ready to assault the ramparts of privilege once more. Ironically—since the Nonpartisan League had sired third parties in other states—North Dakota had never fielded a ticket. The earnest efforts of Dad Walker, Knutson, and others to form a Farmer Labor party early in 1924 had foundered on the confusion of the Saint Paul convention and the La Follette repudiation.

By late 1925, however, serious talk of a new party began circulating around the state. Lending more than normal credibility to the move was the central presence of William Lemke, the gray eminence of the Nonpartisan League in its heyday. Lemke—corporation lawyer, former attorney general, future congressman and presidential candidate—had publicly steered clear of partisanship in 1924 in the remarkably farfetched hope of becoming Calvin Coolidge's ambassador to Mexico.

Although he had failed to win the near crucial support of Sen. Lynn Frazier for a new party, Lemke sent out the call for a mass meeting to found the North Dakota Farmer Labor party, late in November 1925.[15] The conclave on 14 December attracted about seventy participants and stirred a flurry of attacks from those with a vested interest in maintaining the still-existing shell of the old Nonpartisan League. The editor of the

State Record began with references to the "peculiar" convention, hosted by "Lemke and his twelve apostles." By the end of the month, both the *State Record* and the *Nonpartisan* had focused on communism as the issue. The latter paper charged that Communist agents from outside the state had set up the Farmer Labor party in order to split the progressive vote and undermine the American Federation of Labor. The *State Record* printed a long letter from A. G. Gilbert, once editor of the NPL *National Leader,* now a staunch conservative. He hammered at Knutson, Taylor, William Bouck, and Tom Ayres—that political "soldier of fortune" who was now in the Communist camp because he was "too bad for any other."[16]

Lemke was determined to go ahead with the third party even at the cost of temporary victory for reactionaries in the state. He deplored the voters' blindness to existing class distinctions and seemed resigned to being red-baited. At the same time, however, he objected that

> already some ass in this state is sending out literature . . . openly boasting that the Farmer-Labor party is communistic. Of course this fool thinks he is doing some good for the cause, but he is just giving the ammunition to the opposition that they want.

It seems unlikely that Knutson was the culprit. Lemke had defended him earlier against charges of advocating violence, and the two remained in close cooperation.[17]

Knutson and Lemke conferred continually on tactics during the Nonpartisan League's annual convention early in February 1925, but their attempt to win endorsement for the new party proved futile. Only 18 of the 105 delegates favored the move. Undismayed, the Farmer Laborites nominated a full ticket for the general election, headed by Ralph Ingerson for governor and Lemke for the United States Senate.[18]

Knutson could now boast that every state in the northern tier between Minnesota and the Pacific had an organized, class-conscious third party. Granted, they had little coordination, and, aside from the Minnesota FLP, had won few electoral victories. Moreover, neither friend nor foe could seriously contend that the Communists had much influence in the Farmer Labor parties. That mattered little to Knutson. What was important to him was the existence of these political organizations which recognized the reality of economic classes in American society. However fuzzy might be the perceptions of the Farmer Laborites to begin with, Knutson believed that he and other Communists could guide them, in time, to an understanding of the dialectics of Marx and Lenin.[19]

In March 1926 Knutson launched a second attack on the capitalist system among the farmers of the West. He announced formation of the United Farmers Educational League and its monthly newspaper, the *United Farmer.* The UFEL was the revitalization of Hal Ware's conception of three years earlier, which party leaders had rejected. It was the rural counterpart of William Z. Foster's Trade Union Educational League. Both UFEL and TUEL expressed the cautious policies of the Bukharin era in the Communist International.

The program of the UFEL could hardly have frightened any but the most conservative of North Dakota bankers. Far from being strictly Marxist-Leninist, it was little more radical than the utopian moonings of the Bellamyites of the early 1890s. It called for the strengthening of producer cooperatives and for building close ties with consumer coops; for nationalization of railroads, grain elevators, and meat packers; for tax relief through soaking the rich; for land tenure only to those who operated the farms; and for friendly relations with urban workers. In the same spirit, Knutson appointed a national committee which included several non-Communists. He reserved for himself the key position of executive secretary.[20]

Neither Foster's TUEL nor Knutson's UFEL was to be "dual"—that is, competitive with existing groups such as the AF of L in labor or the various organizations among farmers. The UFEL, like the TUEL, would not have chapters or locals. In this period of seeming capitalist recovery, members of the two leagues had the duty of influencing existing organizations—to educate, to proselytize, and eventually to lead. Knutson proposed, therefore, that the adherents of the UFEL should work within the Grange, the Farmers Union, or even the conservative Farm Bureau.[21]

Two other organizations, the Farm-Labor Union and the Western Progressive Farmers, attracted Knutson more than the old-line groups. Each had a vaguely antibourgeois philosophy, and each seemed to have a broad base of regional strength. The F-LU had begun in Texas in 1920 with the collapse of cotton prices. It proposed a sort of price-setting program in which farmers would refuse to sell below a certain level. Membership boomed to 150,000 in December 1922 and peaked at

165,000 in 1924, with locals spreading as far afield as Florida. The leadership consistently attacked middlemen and sought alliances with labor.[22]

The Farm-Labor Union rapidly disappointed Knutson's hopes, however. It had formed political alliances with labor in Texas but failed to win the gubernatorial nomination for its candidates in either 1922 or 1924. In neighboring Oklahoma, a political victory had damaged the organization perhaps more than had the losses in Texas. A farmer-labor coalition had elected the crackbrained Jack Walton in 1922, but his power-mad governorship brought both his impeachment and the disillusionment of many F-LU members. Finally, the abysmal failure of a cotton marketing scheme produced the near collapse of the Farm-Labor Union just about the time that Knutson so eagerly endorsed it.[23]

The Western Progressive Farmers promised greater success for a time. Late in 1925, small town businessmen began hearing disturbing reports of a class-conscious secret order forming in rural Montana and adjacent states. Soon a more public presence emerged.

The organizing force behind the WPF was William Bouck, cherry-orchardist, onetime Populist, and lifelong political rainbow chaser. Bouck had been active in the Washington Grange since the turn of the century and became its head in 1917. The national Grange, since its fling at politics in the 1870s, had grown fusty and standpat. The Washington branch, on the other hand, was like an eager young pup bedeviling its ancient parent. Bouck's predecessor had aligned himself with organized labor, had pursued progressive politics, and had welcomed the Nonpartisan League. Bouck followed the same path but with less finesse. He gave ammunition to his detractors through his criticisms of governmental policies in World War I—bringing him a federal indictment, dropped only when the war ended—and by his alliance with the Seattle labor movement, which had frightened conservatives with its brief general strike in 1919.[24]

The national Grange finally bestirred itself enough to suspend Bouck from office in 1921. Almost undaunted, he took a third of the state members, about six thousand, into his new group, the Western Progressive Farmers. Bouck and his followers plunged into Farmer Labor politics, and their party challenged the Democrats for second place at the polls in the early 1920s. Bouck played prominent roles in the national conventions of 1923 and 1924. He never questioned Communist leadership in the national FLP, and his reward in 1924 was the brief nomination for vice-president. He apparently had taken the assignment more seriously than anyone else in the country and was happily campaigning when the Communists jerked the rug and ended his race.[25]

Bouck angrily charged that his allies had betrayed him, but his wrath was relatively short-lived. A little over a year after his betrayal, Bouck was ready to work with the Communists again. In October 1925, *Producers News* began to tell its Montana and Dakota readers that they needed a new organization to fight the farmer's battle for survival both on the political and the economic fronts. After several weeks of careful orchestration, the editor announced that William Bouck would speak in the county early in December.[26]

Plentywood was the kickoff point in Bouck's plan to transform the Western Progressive Farmers into a major organization which would challenge the Farm Bureau, the Grange, and the Farmers Union for primacy. For the next year and a half the old battler spent a major portion of his time crisscrossing the northern tier, from Washington to Wisconsin and back, tirelessly—if sometimes fecklessly—speaking, propagandizing, organizing.[27]

The WPF in 1926 appeared to have a nearly open field and good prospects for success. By the midtwenties, the Nonpartisan League's wave had receded everywhere except in North Dakota, and even there its substance had ebbed, with many farmers suspecting that it was in the hands of corrupt "pie counter artists"—professional organizers who haunted the lobbies looking for lucrative contracts. A. C. Townley's announced national successor group, the Producers Alliance, had never amounted to much. Farmers Equity, an economic group of some power earlier in the century, was on the rocks. The American Farm Bureau Federation's probusiness orientation appealed mostly to conservative large operators and small-town merchants, while the Grange and the Farmers Union had little more than token organization in most of the Northwest. Bouck's Progressive Farmers, then, bid to fill a near vacuum. It combined drawing cards of family-oriented sociability—ceremonials, dances, and picnics—with the political and economic programs which large numbers of farmers had come to believe were necessary for their survival.

Bouck's proposals differed little from those of Knutson in this era when Communists emphasized a workers' and farmers' government rather than proletarian revolution. They stemmed from the same basic concerns which had persisted since the region's first settlements: prices, taxes, credit, mortgages, and rents; railroads, elevators, packers, and other middlemen; and the responsiveness of politicians as well. Knutson rapidly found great virtue in the Progressive Farmers. Not only did he appoint Bouck to the national committee of the United Farmers Educational League, but he also advised his readers to join the WPF.[28]

By the summer of 1926 Knutson was fully engaged in a multitude of activities. As agricultural organizer for twenty-five dollars a week—when he got it—he was bureaucrat in charge of party affairs in most of the northern plains. As executive secretary of the UFEL and editor of the *United Farmer,* he played the dual role of educating sympathetic non-Communists and guiding them toward the doctrines of Marxism-Leninism on the one hand, and on the other instructing and directing party members in the correct tasks as evolved by the Comintern and the Red Peasant International. Moreover, Knutson took an active part in both the Farmer Labor party and the Western Progressive Farmers.

Bouck had begun organizing locals of the Progressive Farmers in North Dakota several months prior to Knutson's endorsement. He held meetings across the Flickertail State in December 1925 and again the following March. Bad weather and poor advance work hurt his campaign, but on the whole he was pleased. Lt. Gov. Walter Maddock enthusiastically joined, and Ralph Ingerson, FLP candidate for governor, took the chairmanship of the state executive committee of the Progressive Farmers.[29]

A foray into Wisconsin brought surprising gains after Bouck signed on Francis Shoemaker as organizer. The colorful Shooey was an all-around gadfly who, in the early 1930s, would serve successive terms in the federal penitentiary and the United States Congress. In 1926 Shoemaker was between jobs. Bouck let him keep three out of the five dollars taken in for each new member he enrolled. By early April he had signed up 450 in one county alone, and in less than a year Wisconsin had over 6,000 members.[30]

Shoemaker was the most assiduous of several organizers. P. J. "Paddy" Wallace—a crony of Charlie Taylor who claimed to have been a colonel in the Irish Republican Army—and R. B. French operated in Minnesota. Wallace and John Gabriel Soltis stumped the Dakotas. Many of the organizers had worked for the Nonpartisan League in its glory days. Some now undoubtedly saw the Progressive Farmers as the means to carry forward the torch of agrarian reform which the NPL had dropped; others looked upon the group as a meal ticket. Henry Teigan, last national secretary of the league, watched the spread of the WPF with satisfaction. He sent one organizer to Shoemaker with glowing praise and assurances that the man had given up booze after taking the cure.[31]

By autumn 1926 the Progressive Farmers seemed on the verge of becoming a fourth major farm organization, prepared to throw down a politically and economically radical challenge to the Grange, Farm Bureau, and Farmers Union. Membership already stood at around twenty thousand. The founders could hope, not unreasonably, for ten to twenty times that number almost as rapidly as their organizers could work. Large areas in the original states remained uncanvassed, and other states looked inviting. Bouck, moreover, must have speculated that a rousing campaign in the Southwest could pick up many members of the disintegrating Farm-Labor Union.

When Bouck sent out the call for the first convention of the Progressive Farmers, it may have worn the cloak of doomsday rhetoric which farmers had come to expect, but it also barely concealed the spirit of optimistic excitement for the future. The invitation carried the usual litany of complaints about mortgages, taxes, and dispossession. It predicted, however, that the convention would "forge a powerful weapon for the emancipation of millions who make their living out of the soil. . . ." About eight of forty-two signers of the call were Communists.[32]

The founding convention, which met in Minneapolis early in December 1926, went smoothly. The ebullient Charlie Taylor reported the attendance of over a hundred delegates. The actual number was probably closer to fifty, but given vast distances and discouraging economics, the response was encouraging. The portents augured well in other ways. Popular ex-senator Magnus Johnson spent a day of handshaking in the corridors. Bill Mahoney of the AF of L addressed the group, as did cooperative and political leaders. The scent of success also attracted the pie counter artists.[33]

Montana sent the largest delegation, the majority of whom were Communists. Party members from other states attended, but in contrast with the Farmer Labor conventions of 1923 and 1924, they made no attempt to seize control and dominate the proceedings. Knutson played an active part. He spoke about his trip to the Soviet Union and made no bones about his Communist connection, but his conciliatory attitude

gave him a fair measure of influence. He headed the resolutions committee and seems to have had almost free rein.

The delegates approved a statement on the class nature of society that
called for a firm alliance between oppressed farmers and workers. They
had no reservations about the demand to nationalize railroads and banks.
The convention insisted on the end of imperialism in China and the
maintenance of a hands-off policy toward Mexico. A carefully worded
resolution expressed sympathy for the work of the Red Peasant International, without actually endorsing it or asking for affiliation. Knutson
failed to win approval for only one measure—a call to do away with land
ownership through warranty deeds and to replace that system with one
which would redistribute all land to those who actually tilled it. Property
consciousness ran high even among these radical farmers, who sidetracked the resolution for further discussion.[34]

The convention chose Bouck as president, R. B. French as secretary,
and Helmuth Ihlenfeldt as treasurer. In an unwieldly system, dues went
to Ihlenfeldt in Wisconsin; bills were paid by French in Minnesota; and
expenditures had to be approved by Bouck in Washington. The delegates
also elected a six-man national directory. One member, Andrew Omholt
of North Dakota, was an ardent Communist. The chairman of the directory was Paddy Wallace of Montana. He probably held party membership for a time at least. Knutson tried to get the now rechristened
Progressive Farmers of America to take over the *United Farmer* as a
national journal, but the delegates declined after proclaiming it a "grand
paper." They elected him one of the three members of the national
educational committee, however, along with Shoemaker and Myrtle
Bowles of Washington, whom Andy Omholt rather floridly proclaimed
the Mother Jones of the farmers' movement.[35]

The delegates left Minneapolis pleased with their accomplishments
and sanguine about the future of the Progressive Farmers of America.
The directors announced that organizational drives would begin as far
away as Ohio and New Mexico.[36] For a time many radicals thought the
convention had brought the red dawn for American agriculture.

The harmonious meeting boosted morale for radical farmers at an
opportune moment. Only a month earlier they had suffered a series of
disastrous defeats at the polls. In Washington, where Farmer Laborites
had once cast almost eighty thousand votes, their Senate candidate gar-
nered only a few hundred. William Lemke, running for the Senate from
North Dakota got only 4,977 votes to 107,921 for Gerald Nye and

underwent the most embarrassing defeat of his long political career. A. C. Miller, the Communist legislator from Williams County, lost reelection by a seven-to-one margin after the small-town press pilloried him as a stupid fanatic.[37] Similar results in other states laid a wreath on the once significant third-party movement in the Northwest. Only Charlie Taylor's Montana enclave and the Minnesota FLP survived—barely. The popular Magnus Johnson could get only 38 percent of the vote in his race for governor against a reactionary Republican. The more conservative element of Minnesota Farmer Laborites took the defeat as a signal to purge known Communists.[38]

Knutson accepted these political setbacks philosophically. He admitted that the third-party efforts had been poorly organized. He recognized that partisan politics, after all, was not an end in itself but rather a means of reaching the masses. Since the time had not been right for the FLP, then he could pursue other methods. He suggested that the readers of his paper should form United Farmers Educational League clubs not only to discuss issues and educate themselves but also to decide how best to work within other farm organizations most effectively.[39] The newly minted Progressive Farmers of America could not have been far from his thoughts.

Throughout the winter, following the convention of the PFA, Bouck continued his organizing travels. The Wisconsin and Montana units developed rapidly, and in late January 1927, Alex Kringlock, a former Socialist and Nonpartisan Leaguer, began forming locals in Iowa.[40] Behind this rapid growth, however, fundamental weaknesses burgeoned.

National Secretary French accused Shoemaker, the Wisconsin organizer, of misuse of funds and got the state board to expel him. Bouck leaped into the fray with a list of charges against French. Wallace, as chairman of the national directory, suggested that both Shoemaker and French resign. In what should have been a minor crisis, Bouck displayed his ineptitude for calming leadership. He descended into fits of crankiness, while meaningful activity nearly halted. State organizations suspended their dues to the national.[41]

P. J. Wallace again tried to restore harmony by convening the national directors early in September 1927. They voted to remove French and requested Bouck's resignation. They appointed the capable and well-liked Henry Teigan as new executive secretary. Wallace, Omholt, and Dvorak of Wisconsin steered through an endorsement for the *United*

Farmer. These decisions boldly aimed at restoring harmony and giving the PFA a better journalistic voice than Bouck's dull little sheet, the *Western Progressive Farmer.* [42]

Bouck's stubbornness blocked the directory's efforts, however, and on 1 November Teigan withdrew. He saw no hope for the PFA until Bouck was eliminated. The organization floundered on for a few more months. With one last effort the directory appointed a new secretary and called for a convention to meet on 1 January 1928. The now acid-penned Teigan commented only briefly to Wallace: "Really I hadn't thought it possible that even such a half-witted outfit as those presided over by William Bouck would appoint a fellow of such small calibre as O. E. Green as National Secretary." No convention met. The Progressive Farmers of America was defunct except for autonomous locals in a few states. It had failed in every way, and yet it cannot be simply dismissed. It had probed close to the tender nerve of the subdued anger of western farmers in the second half of the 1920s and had missed by an ace becoming their spokesman largely because of the feuding and incompetence of a handful of leaders. [43]

There was proof aplenty that the Progressive Farmers had bungled a first-rate opportunity. More than a year after Bouck had begun his recruiting sweeps across the northern tier, the Northwest Organizing Committee of the National Farmers Union started its own drive in March 1927. It was led by A. W. Ricker, editor of the *Farmers Union Herald*; M. W. "Bill" Thatcher, head of the grain-marketing Farmers Union Terminal Association; and Charlie Talbott, a hearty, ambitious North Dakota farmer. The committee chose a corps of well-known farmers as field men, trained them in the hard sell, and assigned a block of counties to each crew. Thatcher allocated $13.50 of FUTA funds to recruit each new member, although traditional cooperators recoiled from this violation of Rochdale Cooperative principles (under which all profits went to the participants). In November, delegates to the first North Dakota convention represented four hundred locals and thirteen thousand members. By 1929, the Northwest Group, as it came to be known, had signed up sixty-one thousand members in Wisconsin, Minnesota, Montana, and North Dakota. [44]

The Farmers Union, originally organized in Texas in 1902, took on new life in the Great Plains states, where the Progressive Farmers had failed, for a number of reasons. Its leaders shrewdly delighted in the use of radical rhetoric in search of federal aid to the beleaguered farmer. John Simpson of Oklahoma and Milo Reno of Iowa in particular captivated thousands of rural followers with colorful denunciations of greedy bankers and mortgage sharks. Ricker lagged only slightly behind these orators. His attacks on the "class enemy" were carefully calculated to win rural audiences. Both Thatcher and Talbott could ring the same charges when the occasion arose while publicizing the advantages of their farmer-owned grain marketing business. The triumvirate formed a smoothly coordinated team. Bouck and the PFA simply proved to be no match.[45]

Anyone less convinced of the immutibility of the laws of Marxism-Leninism than Knutson would have been immensely discouraged by the failure of these movements—the Farm-Labor Union, the Farmer Labor party, and the Progressive Farmers—which he had hoped to use as transmission belts for the Communist party. Yet even during the early months of 1927, when some positive action on his part might have saved the PFA, he made no move. The *United Farmer* simply ceased mentioning the organizations as the year wore on.

Knutson redoubled his educational efforts. In June 1927 he expanded his newspaper from four to eight pages, and early in December, with the apparent encouragment of the Krestintern, he went to weekly publication. In many ways the paper resembled the man—introspective and thoughtful rather than exciting or inflammatory. It commented approvingly on the revolution in China, opposed American intervention in Latin America, and carried a seemingly interminable series on farming in the Soviet Union written by Carl Reeve, Hal Ware's younger brother.[46]

Capitalism, according to good Bukharinist doctrine, was still in the ascendant, and revolution was not imminent. This was a comforting dogma for Jay Lovestone at the head of the American Communist party in New York as well as for Knutson in Bismarck. A surging economy and rising prosperity gave both men rationale aplenty for the paucity of Communist accomplishment in the United States.

Lovestone obviously relished the power struggles which kept him on top in the American party. During 1927 he strengthened his grip. Charles Ruthenberg, a colorless but respected figure, died early in March, and Ben Gitlow immediately nominated Lovestone to replace him as acting secretary, frustrating the angry Fosterites. A plenary session in May of the executive committee of the Communist International gave Lovestone a chance to meet Stalin and to reforge his ties to Bukharin. A report from the American commission of the Comintern supported Lovestone and reiterated the conviction that since capitalism continued on the upswing in the United States, the party could do little but try to hold its own. When the American Communists held their fifth convention in September, the Lovestone faction won twenty-five of the thirty-eight seats on the central executive committee, including one for Knutson.[47]

Just as the American party began settling into a cautious holding pattern, however, a combination of events began moving the Comintern in a new direction. Overtures made to leftists in both China and Britain had proved to be costly and embarrassing failures.[48] The Krestintern had stumbled in its efforts to win allies in Asia and Eastern Europe. In Russia itself the peasantry resisted grain collection in the fall of 1927, grumbling about low price and the scarcity of consumer items.[49]

These events set the stage for Stalin's elimination of his last competitors. He had used Kamenev and Zinoviev against Trotsky and then Bukharin against the former duo. Trotsky, Kamenev, and Zinoviev had lost their last shreds of power at the Fifteenth Congress of the Soviet Communist party in December 1927. Now only Bukharin stood in Stalin's path to ultimate control. There was little contest. Bukharin had no defenses except for his quick wit and personal popularity. He was vulnerable within the party for his advocacy of concessions to the peasants, his go-slow policy of forging the socialist state, and his theories of world capitalist stabilization. All of these could be attacked as antirevolutionary and right-wing. Beginning late in 1927, Stalin signaled the eventual destruction of Bukharin by his own move to the left.[50]

At the Russian party congress, Stalin predicted the end of capitalist stabilization and the imminence of a new revolutionary upsurge. Bukharin dragged his feet, going only part way with Stalin.[51] The congress followed Stalin, approving in outline form what later became the first five-year plan, with emphasis on industrial growth and the collectivization of agriculture.

Knutson reacted to these signals with his customary caution. In spite of earlier disappointment he continued to find hope for the Farmer Labor party. He criticized the burgeoning Farmers Union, but in mild terms, and encouraged farmers to join it in order to politicize and radicalize it.

He began encouraging formation of United Farmers Educational League locals, but still as discussion, not action, groups.[52]

By the spring of 1928, however, the policies of the UFEL were beginning to show signs of strain. Knutson predicted the continued necessity of educational work among the rural masses for a long time to come, but in the same issue of the *United Farmer* he gingerly acknowledged Stalin's premise that world capitalism was entering a new period of crisis which would result in depression and war. He concluded that "it behooves us to study carefully the problems confronting us and organize ourselves for action."[53]

The continued commitment of the UFEL to the Farmer Labor party deepened Knutson's quandary. He sent greetings to the South Dakota convention, but he quietly removed all reference to the third party from the UFEL program and replaced it with a demand for a workers' and farmers' government. Late in March he mused that Sen. George Norris might be a good candidate for president, but two weeks later he condemned the idea. Shortly thereafter he denounced his onetime friend and ally Lemke.[54]

The *United Farmer* suffered from the difficulties of keeping abreast with the proper line. Only three issues appeared during April and May. Then Knutson found temporary relief from having to make rapid decisions on the party line. The paper announced in June a return to monthly publication because the leader of the UFEL had been "suddenly called to an agrarian conference in Europe to represent the agricultural interests of this country."[55] This was not stating the case accurately. In actuality, the Sixth World Congress of the Communist International met in Moscow from 17 July to 1 September 1928.

The moderate Bukharin strove to convince the assembled delegates that world capitalism in general was continuing along a path of stabilization and that in the United States it was still advancing. But only the politically blind could fail to see that his time was past. Without as yet publicly attacking Bukharin, Stalin made clear his own belief that postwar capitalism had entered its Third Period. After weathering the initial revolutionary surge and then stabilizing, it was now slouching to its imminent collapse. He exhorted Communists around the world to assume sole leadership of the masses in the active struggle which had arrived. The era of education and of cooperation with others on the left had passed. The American delegation applauded, and all factions denounced the "right danger." Lovestone, however, recklessly defended Bukharin's position as not inconsistent with that of Stalin.[56]

Knutson had private doubts about the new line, but as a good party member he accepted it and propagated it after his return home. In the past he had seldom mentioned the Communist party; now he gave it banner headlines. He introduced Benjamin Gitlow, the Communist vice-presidential candidate, when he spoke in Bismarck, and he referred to himself as the Communist candidate for United States senator, although his name was on the Farmer Labor ticket.[57]

The nature of the United Farmers Educational League had begun to change. Knutson had originally envisaged it as a dedicated cadre working within larger organizations, preaching the evils of capitalism and educating the mass of farmers to the necessity of class struggle. He had opposed forming local units, competing with others for membership, and becoming just another farm group. Third Period Communism, however, demanded that the party show its face and assume leadership. Thus, in the labor movement, William Z. Foster's Trade Union Educational League—after several months of foot-dragging—announced the formation of new unions in the textile and mining industries, in direct competition with already existing AF of L units. At about the same time—during the summer of 1928—the UFEL began organizing its own locals, and by the end of the year, the *United Farmer* was castigating the Farmers Union for collaborating with class enemies.[58]

The UFEL began its first attempts to spread beyond the plains states early in 1929. Knutson toured the South and was appalled by the condition of blacks. Some organizing efforts began in New England, and the *United Farmer* consciously aimed its coverage at a more national and less regional audience. To bolster the new role, Knutson announced plans for a school to train young organizers.[59]

The transition to Third-Period thinking did not come easily for the UFEL or its parent party. Loveston continued to maintain that American conditions were an exception to the world trend, and Knutson dutifully wrote that although European capitalism was in crisis, the American economy was still on the upswing.[60] A general convention of the American Communists in March overwhelmingly supported Lovestone, but he, perhaps not fully convinced of Knutson's reliability, demoted him from full membership to candidate status on the central executive committee. The reckless Lovestone, however, was caught in a power struggle far beyond his knowledge or resources. He continued to defy the clear indications of Stalin's demands for conformity and ignore the obvious humiliation of his own patron, Bukharin. In April he confidently headed a delegation to Moscow to defend the idea of American exceptionalism. Step by step, Lovestone was stripped of his illusions of influence. Shortly after the Americans arrived, Bukharin was fired as head of the Comintern; and on 20 May the American party paper, *Daily Worker,* published a Comintern cable blasting Lovestone and Pepper. Early in June Lovestone secretly fled the Soviet Union. In rapid order, the Communist party expelled him and his ally Gitlow. The leadership temporarily fell into the hands of a Stalin-approved secretariat, William Z. Foster, Max Bedacht, Bob Minor, and Will Weinstone. None of these factionalists realized his ambition to dominate the party, and within a year Kansas-born Earl Browder—who had missed much of the infighting of the 1920s by serving the International in China—emerged as Moscow's chosen general secretary.[61]

Knutson held on in the UFEL for another year, but only by bowing completely. In September he apparently wrote a letter lauding the new line of the party and praising it for "rooting out the opportunist elements." He went on:

> The Party is much stronger, much healthier than it has ever been before. The expulsion of Lovestone and other right wingers from the Party is not a sign of weakness but indicates strength and shows that the Party is following the correct path. Factionalism in the Party has been destroyed. . . . Every Party member should read and study the Thesis of the last plenum. Study particularly those passages which deal with the right danger, the Third Period, the false slogan of "exceptionalism" as applied to America.[62]

The condemnation of his onetime friends did not prevent Knutson's position from growing tenuous. He retained his office as secretary of the UFEL, but Andy Omholt became president. He continued to write for the *United Farmer,* but others took over as editor and business manager.[63]

Charlie Taylor watched the shake-up in Communist circles with a certain glee. He greatly admired Trotsky and had quietly stopped paying party dues after the former war commissar's expulsion. Now, with Stalin's turn to the left and the disgrace of Lovestone—that "spokesman for the pseudo-intellectuals, dentists, chiropractors, naturopaths, social workers, liberal cloak and suit merchants and small business men," as Taylor dubbed him—he looked for a reconciliation between Trotsky and Stalin. While on one hand toying with A. C. Townley and his latest promotion, the American Temperance League, Taylor began serious efforts, on the other, to revive the Montana Progressive Farmers as an alternative to the UFEL.[64]

In an open letter to Knutson, Taylor sarcastically addressed him as "My Dear Working Farmer," and accused him of using a "menshevik, counter-revolutionary, opportunistic right-wing and petty-bourgeois slogan." Calling the UFEL "merely a caricature of a mass farm organization," he proposed that the correct slogan for the Third Period should be "FIGHT THE RIGHT WING DANGER AND KNUTSONISM!"[65]

Taylor's suggested motto may not have been bannered across Communist headquarters in New York, but the exigencies of the new era did prompt the central committee to produce a draft program for agriculture. It provided little comfort for Knutson. His work was dismissed in a single sentence: "Hitherto, we must admit, the Communist Party has wholly neglected the agrarian masses, and tasks have accumulated, which, together with developing opportunities, makes it necessary that our party act energetically in order that it play a decisive role."[66]

As might be expected, the draft program stated the American agriculture suffered from the basic contradictions of capitalism. Farmers had become the captives of finance capital, mortgages had reduced farmers to peonage, and yet, capitalists were using the myth that high wages for workers had caused economic depression.[67]

The anonymous author of the program noted that agrarian revolt often become violent but warned Communists against becoming fascinated by this aspect and losing sight of its essentially bourgeois nature. The task of Communists, therefore, would be to win rebellious farmers as allies of the proletariat, to guide their revolt, and to guard against reformist elements who would oppose party leadership and demoralize the masses. In no instance, however, should Communists simply dismiss the farmers as hopeless reactionaries.[68]

The draft report condemned the UFEL for trying to win a rural following through opportunism—and the use of such meaningless phrases as "dirt farmer" or "working farmer"—rather than through hard Bolshevik analysis. Beginning at once, the party must now be prepared to seize leadership—through committees of action which would organize tenants' and taxpayers' strikes, repudiate mortgage or interest payments, and lead physical struggles against dispossession. By winning acclaim through these methods and by freeing farmers from their capitalist shackles, the party could later, following the line of the Sixth Congress of the Comintern, push them into collectives. To do all of this, the UFEL must drop "Educational" from its title and adopt concrete rather than abstract programs.[69]

The *Communist*'s devastating dismissal of the policies of the UFEL prompted Taylor to a new attack. "Knutson has already beaten his breast and torn his hair as penance for his opportunistic sins," he wrote, but rather than boldly outlining a Communist program for farmers, Knutson "hovered around ... like a waif at a wedding supper."[70]

Red Flag Charlie had hit hard on one of the major distinctions between himself and Knutson. The latter was obviously waiting for firm directions before making any policy statement. The Montanan, in contrast, favored marching boldy forth, with or without the ultimate approval of New York—or Moscow.

While Knutson waited and Taylor shouted, a third voice was heard. Harrison George, a charter member of the party and an old Wobbly, wrote articles for the *Daily Worker* defending the agricultural draft program against both right-wing opportunists and the loudmouths of the Trotskyite left. The right-wingers, he implied, would do nothing to win farmers as allies for the proletariat because they preferred to cite statistics which proved that mechanization was producing corporate farms which could be taken over after the revolution. The Trotskyites, at the other extreme, criticized the draft program because it sought to mobilize farmers by advocating immediate demands centering on rent, debts, and taxes. Taylor and the *Producers News* crowd could yell revolution all they wanted, he said, but unless they first won a mass following by leading the fight against dispossession, they were also opportunists, as bad as or worse than the Lovestonites.[71]

In the midst of the argument, the *United Farmer* declined rapidly. With the January 1930 issue it became a small, one-page flyer. It indulged in the seemingly safe pastime of attacking former friends such as Bill Lemke and Tom Ayres. Following the lead of the draft program, it noted that it was now the official organ of the United Farmers League (eliminating "Educational" from the title). Seemingly for lack of anything better, it printed a barely literate letter from one Alex Noral in Moscow ponderously assailing Charlie Taylor and *Producers News.* [72]

Finally, the July issue of the *United Farmer* addressed itself to the "Toiling Farmers of the United States," with an emblazoned, "Strike! Strike!" Denouncing the president, his Farm Board, farm cooperatives, Congress, the courts, and state legislatures, the manifesto called for direct remedies through committees of action in the immediate fight against rent, interest, taxes, and dispossession, as well as, of course, for an alliance with workers in the struggle against capitalism and imperialism. [73]

Knutson had become the exemplar of the good Communist. Unlike his onetime associates, Lovestone and Gitlow, he did not claim insights superior to Moscow, and he did not follow them into their schismatic, tiny, but optimistically titled Communist Party (Majority Group). He bottled up his inner doubts about the line of the Third Period and followed it loyally. The path, however, was not always easy for him. In the midst of criticism and reassessment, he apparently requested release from work with the *United Farmer* and the United Farmers League. [74]

The Seventh Convention of the Communist party of the United States met in June 1930. It confirmed Earl Browder as administrative secretary and eliminated any vestiges of Lovestonism, but it failed to adopt an agrarian program because of disagreements with the apparatchiks of the Krestintern. [75] For a party seeking to rally the forces of discontent on behalf of revolution, it was not the time for indecision. Commodity prices, which still had been above parity in late 1929, were already beginning the precipitous slide which would culminate in disaster or near disaster for millions of farmers in 1931 and 1932.

Knutson spent the summer making a brief organizing trip to Iowa and studying intensively the works of Marx and Lenin. [76] His time was almost expired, however, as the party moved more aggressively into Third Period activities. A meeting of the political committee of District 11 (including the Dakotas) on 1 September severely criticized both the political and financial operation of the *United Farmer* and the UFL. [77] The ax finally fell in late September when the organization department of the party central committee appointed Rudolph Harju, a Finnish-American activist, as secretary of the UFL and instructed Knutson to turn over all records and documents to the new headquarters at New York Mills, Minnesota. [78]

Knutson frantically scrambled to stay in party work. He repudiated his earlier proffer of withdrawal from UFL activities as a weakness on his part and offered to accept any future assignment. Within weeks, leaving his family behind, he departed for the South to do unpaid organizing work under the assumed name Frank Brown. Never again, in a life which lasted until the late 1960s, did he hold high position in the party.[79]

Later Communists sometimes criticized Knutson, but mostly they ignored him. Many of the older comrades wanted to forget their own part in the factional fights of the 1920s; few could claim much glory from their roles. Younger Communists—the generation of the 1930s—looked to the present and to the future. They had little interest in a decade during which American capitalism had reached its supposed apex.

And yet Knutson had faithfully served his cause as best he saw it. He had sought, in his careful fashion, to reach out, especially to those tens of thousands of farmers who had once marched under the Nonpartisan League standard and to enlist them in the newer army of international communism. Granted that his vision was somewhat narrow. He operated in the sphere to which he was most accustomed, and only late did he begin to look beyond the plains states and recognize the problems of southern black or eastern truck and dairy farmers. But still, given the narrowness of his resources and the unsettled nature of party leadership at the time, he recruited and held together a cadre of rural Communists and supporters which would be the foundation upon which an expanded movement would build in the next decade.

Paralleling the United Farmers Educational League in the 1920s was another Communist rural movement. In the inhospitable area of the northern Great Lakes, poverty-stricken Finnish immigrants were building one of the most successful consumers cooperatives in American history.

3
THE COOPERATIVE CENTRAL EXCHANGE

THE COOPERATIVE CENTRAL EXCHANGE was far and away the largest consumers' federation in the United States by 1929. Its sales to some eighty member stores in that year surpassed $1,750,000, and those stores together grossed more than $6,000,000. By almost any measure applied, the CCE had achieved a striking level of success in only twelve years of existence. The results were even more startling on closer examination. The overwhelming majority of the members of the individual cooperative stores were immigrant Finnish farmers—most of whom spoke English poorly or not at all and who lived in one of the poorest agricultural regions in the nation. Few of the managers of this thriving organization had had more than a grammar school education. And, as the climax, in this most capitalist of all nations, every leader of importance in the CCE was a member of the Communist party.[1]

The Cooperative Central Exchange operated its warehouse and bakery in Superior, Wisconsin, a port city on the southwestern shores of Lake Superior. From this headquarters, lines of supply radiated into a broad area of northeastern Minnesota, northern Wisconsin, and the upper peninsula of Michigan. The region serviced was roughly five hundred miles east and west, and one hundred miles north and south, with a population approaching 1,200,000.[2]

The area had a certain geographic and geologic unity. Eons before, the glaciers had scraped the surface almost down to bedrock. Forests later struggled up in the thin soil remaining. But below this unpromising exterior there were rich pockets of copper and iron ore.[3]

The lumber industry had boomed here in the 1870s, and although the greater forests of the West had surpassed it in output by 1900, lumbering remained an important economic factor well into the twentieth century. Copper mining had begun as early as the 1840s in Michigan and had provided great fortunes to a few entrepreneurs. The last great boom came with the beginning of extensive operations in the great Mesabi iron range late in the nineteenth century.[4]

Agriculture ranked as a distant third behind the lumber and mining industries in the Lake Superior region, and as long as richer areas remained open to settlement, few farmers had any incentive to tackle this hard-scrabble land of short growing seasons.[5]

This was the region into which large numbers of Finns began immigrating after 1900. They came, through one of those accidents of history, to a land very similar to their own in climate and topography. The mine owners of the upper peninsula had recruited Finnish miners resident in Norway during the Civil War. Over the next few decades several hundred miners followed, and their letters home probably familiarized the region to thousands in the old country who were growing desperate and restless over changing conditions in the Grand Duchy. The agricultural revolution, when it reached Finland, had rendered a large portion of the peasant population superfluous, and the nation's cities could absorb only a part of the surplus. Moreover, beginning in 1899, stringent edicts from the czar, pointing toward tighter imperial control and eventual Russification, drove throngs of independent-minded Finns to seek a freer society.[6]

Nearly 90 percent of the newcomers were from rural provinces. They were peasants and agricultural workers, driven from their land. They hungered for new farms, but they had no money to purchase them. As a result, they quickly found work in the forests and mines with the vow to scrimp and save until the dream came true.[7]

Employers agreed that the Finns were hard-working and efficient. But they were also clannish and difficult. They argued about working conditions and wages, and when the Mesabi iron miners struck in 1907 and 1916 and Michigan copper miners in 1913, Finnish workers were in the forefront.[8]

The strikes were only one symptom of a growing working-class sentiment among the immigrants, many of whom transferred their hatred for the aristocracy at home to the plutocracy in America. The vast majority of them were literate, and they began founding workers' clubs to discuss their problems. Originally they met in their church or temperance society halls. When these organizations barred them, large numbers broke with the old ways and built workers' halls. These local clubs joined together in 1906 to form the Finnish Socialist Federation, which soon affiliated with the Socialist party and became its largest foreign-language branch.[9]

The cooperative societies grew out of the Finnish workers movement in the United States. During the strikes, the Finns found that the onetime friendly grocer would no longer extend credit. The first cooperative buying clubs, such as the ones at Mass or Hancock, Michigan, were formed to cope with this situation.[10]

In addition, as more and more of the new citizens were realizing their ambition to become landowners, they faced other problems. Their hard-earned savings went into the purchase of forty or eighty acres of cut-over timberland in Saint Louis County, Minnesota; Iron County, Michigan; or similar areas. For many of the more militant among them, the shift from mine to farm came sooner than they had planned because, following each strike, the mine owners circulated a blacklist of those workers who would never again be hired.[11]

The farming Finns thus faced a difficult future. Their land was the poorest in the region. Their farms were probably less than half the size of those in richer areas of the same states, and as a result, incomes were pitifully low. In such a situation, many of the farmers tried to work off-season in the lumber or mining industries, but every penny still counted. When it came to buying necessities, however, the new settlers found prices high. Isolated hamlets like Embarrass, Minnesota, or Eben Junction, Michigan, could barely support a general store, and then only if the markup on goods was huge.[12] The cooperative buying clubs and stores were the solution for many of these new Americans.

During the second decade of the twentieth century, the cooperative store system had spread beyond the mining towns into many of the rural communities. Some of the experiments failed, but a surprisingly large number succeeded in spite of low capitalization and the poverty of the members. In part the success stemmed from adherence to the classic Rochdale principles, and in part it came from an almost evangelistic fervor which the movement engendered. Many of the Finns who went into the labor and socialist organizations found themselves ostracized by their church leaders. Their social lives revolved more and more around the workers' clubs of the Finnish Socialist Federation. Generally the cooperative store occupied the same building as the meeting hall. When employers underpaid and blacklisted the immigrants, when their union leaders proved fainthearted and strikes collapsed, when their little farms barely gave sustenance, and when their American neighbors sneered at their language and customs, then their hopes and dreams centered on the little building which they proclaimed to be the first step toward construction of the cooperative commonwealth which would eliminate those inequities.

The dream was fine, but the practicalities were harsh. Some wholesalers refused to deal with cooperatives. Others decided that the small quantities handled were not worth their time. Still others were frightened off by the threatened boycotts of privately owned grocery stores. The Finnish societies could seldom make cash purchases and were forced to pay premium prices for credit.[13]

American entry into World War I intensified cooperative problems. Many patrons felt that wholesalers discriminated against their stores when distributing goods in short supply. Letters of complaint got a sympathetic response in *Työmies* [Worker], the organ of the Finnish Socialist Federation, published in Superior. On 30 July 1917, delegates from nineteen cooperative stores met for a two-day conference to form their own wholesale society. They called it the Cooperative Central Exchange.[14] The organization of the CCE followed a pattern similar to its individual constituents. Whereas each member of a store society owned one or more shares of stock in it (but had only one vote following the Rochdale plan), and each patron received a dividend at the end of the year from profits in proportion to his purchases, so also each store society owned one or more shares of exchange stock and shared in the annual profits.

The prospects for the CCE were not overly cheery. The part-time manager borrowed desk space in one corner of *Työmies*'s office and by 31 December had accumulated a grand total of $480 in capital. The exchange also faced, on a larger scale, the same problems of hostility that had confronted the store societies. Most manufacturers, with the exception of flour and coffee suppliers, refused to sell directly to it. One rolled oats supplier maintained its defiance even in face of a Federal Trade Commission ruling.[15]

Within a few years, however, the CCE had established itself solidly. It was no doubt aided by the financial boom of the war and immediate postwar period, but so were many of its competitors which failed with the recession following 1920. The big difference perhaps was that the managers of the CCE plowed all profits into strengthening operations for the first few years. They bought a three-story warehouse in 1919 and soon established a bakery to furnish the Finns' favorite food, hardtack. Sales in 1919 were $313,000 and brought a profit of $7,000. By the end of 1921, the exchange membership had grown to fifty-six stores, and its position was firm enough so that it could help constituent stores hurt by the recession.[16]

The founders of the CCE believed that the organization had greater responsibilities than simply acting as a distributor. They recognized that many of the failures of cooperative stores had resulted from poor management. In the past this group had been either untrained but eager young men willing to learn on the job, or small businessmen who had failed in their own stores. The leaders of the exchange set about remedying this by establishing a training school in 1919. They soon followed with a full-time auditing service which taught a uniform system of accounting and allowed many stores to tell for the first time whether they were making money or losing it.[17]

The leaders of the CCE were interested in much more than simply establishing proper business procedures or showing an annual profit, however. They bitterly remembered the shameful blacklists of the mine owners, and every day they could see the backbreaking struggles to win a bare living from the little farms. For a decade and a half they discussed and debated the ideas of Marx and Engels, of De Leon and Debs, and they firmly believed that their cooperative was part of a greater movement which would bring on a more equitable society. And so, from the very beginning, an education department stressed the teaching of history, politics, economics, and the like through night schools and summer camps.[18]

At the same time that the Cooperative Central Exchange was beginning to flourish, greater events were shaking the world. Late in 1917 the Bolsheviks seized control in Russia. Repercussions followed rapidly among Americans left-wingers as we have seen, and in September 1919 the American Communists broke away from the Socialist party.

The Finns watched these developments, as well as the war between reds and whites in their homeland, carefully. As early as 5 October 1919, representatives of the Finnish Socialist Federation in the Midwest attended a Communist session in Minneapolis and promised to join the movement. *Tyomies* marched in the vanguard of the leftward drive, having called for withdrawal from the Socialist party since shortly after the Russian Revolution.[19] After a long period of soul searching, the federation voted by two-thirds majority in December 1920 to leave its old home. A year later the organization participated in the founding of the aboveground Workers party. The importance of the move—at least in dues paid to the party—can be gauged by the fact that the rechristened Finnish Workers Federation made up between 40 and 50 percent of the membership between 1922 and 1925.[20]

The Cooperative Central Exchange had been, in a sense, the protégé of the federation and had looked upon *Tyomies* as its semiofficial voice. When these two went over to the Communists, the CCE followed. There was no formal affiliation, but, it was understood, the party maintained "ideological control."[21] The short biographies compiled by the *American Labor Who's Who* in 1925 disclosed that the chairman, general manager, director of education, and director of auditing were all members of the Workers party. Most of the board of directors were probably Communists, and party affiliation may have been a condition for the hiring of employees.[22]

Control of the Cooperative Central Exchange brought an unexpected bonus to the struggling American Communist movement, but it also meant headaches. The Finns paid their party dues, dutifully purchased literature, and provided a large chunk of the money which got the *Daily Worker* off the ground. On the other hand, Theodore Draper has written, much of the party leadership "contemptuously regarded [them] as hopelessly Right-Wing country bumpkins."[23] William Z. Foster used their votes to maintain control of the central executive committee of the party from December 1923 until August 1925, but the Comintern representative at the Fourth Convention of the Workers party scorned the Superior, Wisconsin, branch as "opportunists," and the executive committee of the party feared that the Finns were going to "the swamp of Loreism" in opposing the "Bolshevization of the party." (Ludwig Lore was a party founder later expelled for right-wing tendencies).[24]

The question of the relationship between the cooperative movement and the Communists was not confined to the United States alone. It nagged at both sides through the 1920s in many countries. In the exciting days following the success of the Bolshevik Revolution, Soviet leaders had paid little heed to cooperativism, because they felt it was hopeless as a revolutionary vehicle. But when the optimistic flush of hope for early worldwide revolution had died down in the early 1920s, officials of the

Communist International took another look at cooperatives and decided that they could provide a forum for the spread of the doctrines of Marxism-Leninism. The Third World Congress of the Comintern, meeting in July 1921, adopted a set of theses aimed at making the already existing cooperatives into "instruments of class struggle."[25]

The relatively low level of esteem in which Communist leaders held the cooperatives as revolutionary institutions was probably what led them to choose to work within an existing framework rather than to form a new organization analogous to the Red International Trade Unions or the Red Peasant International. The Russians applied for membership in the International Cooperative Alliance, and that group, at its Tenth Triennial Conference in Basel, hesitantly admitted them in August 1921. The relationship was an uneasy one. One of the principal foundation stones of the ICA was neutrality in political matters, but a conference of Communist-dominated cooperatives, meeting in Moscow just prior to the Fourth World Congress of the Comintern in 1922, accepted a series of theses which aimed at substituting the doctrine of class consciousness for that of neutrality. Leaders of the British, German, and Swedish cooperatives firmly resisted Communist attempts to politicize the ICA, but the question remained a major point of contention throughout the decade.[26]

The role of the Cooperative Central Exchange in the Cooperative League of the U.S.A. was like the role of the Communist block in the International Cooperative Alliance. The league was the child of its president, Dr. J. P. Warbasse, who had retired from medical practice to nurse its growth after 1915, and Warbasse provided most of its financial support in the early years. The first four national congresses were relatively pallid affairs. The fifth congress, which met in Saint Paul, 4–6 November 1926, was vastly different. The CCE had become far and away the largest consumers coop in the nation, and its representatives turned out in force to claim eighteen spots of the total of sixty-five delegates.[27]

If past congresses had been polite meetings which listened to position papers on the role of the store manager or the evils of granting credit, the Saint Paul affair provided a roaring contrast. The men from Superior may have been "right-wing opportunists" to their Communist comrades, but they seemed like left-wing lunatics to Dr. Warbasse. With adamant persistence they drove through a resolution which abandoned neutralism and declared that the cooperatives were "primarily a working class movement against the present system based on profit." It went on to demand a united front of workers and farmers to overthrow the exploitive system.[28]

The resolution came as a shock to Dr. Warbasse. For the first time in a decade his leadership was seriously challenged, and the mocking manner of his leading assailant, Eskel Ronn, made the situation all the worse. Few Hollywood scenarists could have drawn greater distinctions between two men. On the one hand was Warbasse, the elderly and wealthy graduate of the best American and German universities—respected surgeon and scientist, prolific author, and single-minded humanitarian. On the other was Ronn, the young immigrant, who with only a year of high school had risen to be general manager of the Cooperative Central Exchange. He was every bit as dedicated as Warbasse, but he was also a rollicking, boisterous character who delighted in waving a red flag at the serious physician.[29]

The tactical victory scored at the convention by the leaders of the CCE very soon proved elusive. Only the *Cooperative Pyramid Builder,* their house organ, printed the text of the resolution, and the Cooperative League's board of directors quietly canceled it.[30] Perhaps more importantly, Warbasse launched a counteroffensive against Ronn and his allies. He circulated a lengthy attack on the CCE and warned that the exchange's use of "communist tactics and disruptive methods" would split the Cooperative League. He warned that compromise was impossible and pointedly noted that European cooperatives had expelled Communists.[31]

The resolution and Warbasse's reaction to it stirred a small international tempest. A British Communist complained that the American bourgeoisie were trying to hound party members out of the movement. And for what reason? Merely for trying to break the illusion that cooperative growth would lead peacefully to socialism. As a result, he wrote, Communists were met with suspicion and unreasonably charged with disruption.[32]

Ronn and Warbasse soon locked horns in a larger arena. The Saint Paul meeting of the Cooperative League of the U.S.A. had chosen Ronn and Matti Tenhunen, chairman of the CCE, as members of the American representation to the Twelfth Congress of the International Cooperative Alliance, which met in Stockholm, 15–18 August 1927. They were part of the eighty "working class opposition" among the total of five hundred delegates.[33] Tenhunen made a lengthy attack on the doctrine of cooperative neutrality, and Ronn passionately warned of the dangers of imperialism and war, but the moderates were in full control. Warbasse circulated a letter at the congress denying that these "communist" sentiments represented American feelings. A pessimistic resumé in the Comintern newsletter foresaw a future war to the knife against Communists in the movement.[34]

Warbasse returned from Europe even more convinced that Communism threatened the existence of his cherished cause. He poured out his feelings in a letter to a prominent Nebraska cooperator, L. S. Herron:

> It is going from bad to worse, Ronn and Tenhunen show no intention of reforming. Their falsehoods and disruptive methods are only making the situation more difficult. . . .
> Our temporizing and placating policy causes them to laugh at us.[35]

Herron counseled a policy of caution. Ronn was riding high, and the Nebraskan warned that he could probably now command a majority at any cooperative congress.[36]

As the decade of the 1920s drew toward an an end, the prestige of the Cooperative Central Exchange had never been greater. Its sales and profits were amazing, considering that its twenty-five thousand members were predominantly poor farmers.[37] The exchange canned and packaged goods which proudly carried the hammer and sickle of revolution rather than the traditional twin pines of the cooperative movement. During the summer of 1929, the CCE gave heavy financial support to a camp for the Young Communist League in Superior. Among the speakers was Ella Reeve Bloor, who had just returned from Moscow, where Stalin had denounced her by name for supporting Jay Lovestone in the struggle for control of the American party.[38]

Mother Bloor was earnestly trying to return to the good graces of party leaders, and although she soon departed to North Dakota and Montana to raise money for the Gastonia, North Carolina, textile strikers, her momentary presence reminded leaders of the CCE of the upheavals in the Communist world. Jay Lovestone had never been a favorite of the Finnish-Americans, but his abrupt loss of party control in June marked the beginning of a different era. Under new leadership the American Communists fully accepted the program of the Third period—all-out war on bourgeois institutions. Since Stalin had proclaimed that capitalism was on the verge of collapse, it became the immediate duty of all Communists to labor unceasingly for a workers' revolution. There could be no compromises and no alliances with socialists or progressives. For Communists in the cooperatives, this meant specifically that they must relegate any concern over balance sheets to the junkheap and consider the CCE and its member societies valuable only insofar as they contributed to the preeminence of the party. The resolution of 1926 declaring cooperatives to be working class movements, which had so affronted Dr. Warbasse, was no longer acceptable. They must now be declared nothing more than auxiliaries of the Communist party.[39]

The new party leaders wasted no time in asserting stricter authority over the CCE after having disposed of Lovestone. Citing dire financial distress, they demanded a five-thousand-dollar loan late in July 1929. The party fraction controlling the exchange's board of directors found its loyalty on the line. For several days they stalled, although New York has insisted on an immediate answer. An outright refusal would have indicated complete defiance of party discipline, since the CCE had donated generously of its funds to such radical causes as Tom Mooney, Sacco and Vanzetti, and the Gastonia strikers. Finally the directors unanimously rejected the loan. Their spokesman, Yrjo (George) Halonen wired New York the lame excuse that the exchange itself was so short of funds that it was being forced to borrow.[40]

Within two weeks a new test came. William Z. Foster was about to convert his Trade Union Educational League into the Trade Union Unity League in order to pose a militant challenge to the stodgy American Federation of Labor. Henry Puro, head of the party's Finnish Federation, requested a one-thousand-dollar contribution from the CCE to help finance Foster's convention in Cleveland. After the directors gave only a quarter of that amount, party headquarters recognized that something was amiss. The quadrumvirate which had succeeded Lovestone in power considered the matter important enough to dispatch Robert Minor, one of its members, to Superior with a personal warning: submit to discipline or face expulsion. Minor, moreover, now called on the board for a continuing contribution to party coffers in the amount of 1 percent of annual sales—which at that point would have been about seventeen thousand dollars—to be disguised as legal fees to a fictitious New York lawyer. According to *Cooperative Pyramid Builder,* he told them, "You yourselves know best how to make the entries in the books."[41]

The controversy over funds precipitated a dispute which had been a long time brewing. In the early days of the CCE, the immigrant leaders had felt almost every hand against them, and they welcomed an alliance with the revolutionary party which promised a new world for workers everywhere. The future of their own organization was always foremost in their minds, however, and as it became increasingly successful, their revolutionary sentiments became more and more compromised. As early as 1923, Vieno Severi Alanne, Lenin's one time roommate, the educational director who had participated in the takeover of the Chicago Farmer Labor convention, had angered a training class of radical students by telling them that the consumers' movement was more important than working class action. Alanne was the Communist candidate for governor of Wisconsin of 1924, but by January of the following year he could no longer conceal his disagreement with the party. He resigned to take a new job, where he could promote political neutrality in cooperative ranks.[42]

Eskel Ronn looked upon Alanne as a traitor after his defection and delighted in baiting the pudgy little man.[43] Ronn himself was changing, however, as the exchange became more successful and he met new acquaintances through the Cooperative League. He struck up an unlikely friendship with the crusty Nebraskan, L. S. Herron.[44] The two men attended conventions together and exchanged long letters chiding one another over their respective doctrinal errors. Herron probably raised some hackles at Cooperative League headquarters when he wrote Warbasse, "I must confess that I have come to like the rascal immensely."[45]

Ronn's correspondence with Herron indicated that he may have been taking his Communist affiliation less than seriously by 1929. One man, however, could not have hoped to block the sentiments of the majority, and almost everyone of importance—employees, department heads, and a preponderance of the board of directors—was a member of the party.[46] But the truth was, the Comintern representative had been correct in 1924 —most of the Communists in the CCE *were* right-wing opportunists. They liked to gather at their workers' halls for lectures or dances and to gossip of the inequities of capitalism. They enjoyed seeing Ronn twist the Cooperative League's tail with his resolutions about the working class. They anticipated a workers' and farmers' government—someday —but they had not foreseen the iron demands of discipline, work, and money required by strict adherence to the Third Period philosophy.

The rejection of Minor's ultimatum brought new controversy as party headquarters sought to reimpose authority. Early in September, the political committee summoned Halonen to New York to liquidate the problem. Halonen refused, sending Matti Tenhunen to speak for him. The angry political committee granted Tenhunen ten minutes to speak, and then expelled Halonen from the party.[47]

The party leaders now rushed in the new district organizer to cope with the growing chaos. He was Carl Reeve, the twenty-nine-year-old son of Mother Bloor, who had recently returned from the Soviet Union. He tried to shore up party discipline by demanding that the party fraction secure Halonen's resignation as education director and his replacement by Walter Harju, a more trustworthy party man. The targeting of Halonen had its own ironies. He had been one of the chief baiters of that earlier heretic, V. S. Alanne, and he had served as an alternate member of the central executive committee of the Communist party from September 1927 until March 1929 as an ally of the now dominant Browder-Foster group and an enemy of Lovestone. On 30 October, after a stormy session, the CCE's board of directors unanimously refused to fire Halonen.[48]

Up until this point the controversy had remained behind closed doors, but when the directors asked *Tyomies* to publish its side of the story, the editors refused. On the following day the newspaper trained its big guns on the leaders of the exchange. The issue was plain, it stated: during the Third Period, cooperatives could no longer be simply a *part* of the working class movement—implying a status of equality with the Communist party—they must now unreservedly accept the role of obedient subordinates.[49] The fight was now out in the open, at least for the Finnish-speaking members of the CCE. Reeve reportedly predicted victory within two weeks as a result of rank-and-file indignation at the board of directors. But attempts in November to use party fractions to control regional store meetings failed.[50]

Ronn, Halonen, and a majority of the board firmed up their defenses with a statement to the membership in the November issue of *Cooperative Pyramid Builder.* They reiterated their belief in the principle of class struggle and rejected the bourgeois theory of neutrality, insisting that the cooperative movement should be firmly in the working-class camp. At the same time, however, the directors denied that any outside organization had the right to interfere with management or control of the exchange.[51]

The same issue of the magazine continued the past practice of extravagant praise for Soviet Russia, but the leaders of the CCE found that compromise measures were unacceptable in the new era. When Reeve found the *Tyomies* corporation "fouling its own nest" by printing "filth" in the *Cooperative Pyramid Builder,* he destroyed fifteen hundred copies —either by burning them or by dumping them in a hole chopped in the ice of the river (the sources vary). To cap an already busy evening, Reeve had a physical confrontation with the pro-CCE janitor of the *Tyomies* building which became legendary in Finnish circles. Reeve either dumped a full spittoon on his adversary's head or was chased howling down the street while being beaten on the backside with an axe handle —or perhaps both and more.[52] *Tyomies* and other Communist organs kept up a steady barrage of attacks until Eskel Ronn complained to his friend Herron: "It certainly is a tough lot, this fighting for the working-class. No matter what you do, you get hell on both sides."[53].

With the struggle now in public among Finnish and English-speaking members alike, the two sides concentrated on winning the support of the eighty-odd store societies.

The CCE board, under the leadership of Ronn and Halonen, skillfully played the theme of injured innocents. They responded with sorrow, not anger, when *Tyomies* refused to publish their version of events, and they proceeded to establish their own Finnish-language weekly. On 2 December, they fired Walter Harju, who they felt was a spy in their midst and refused, in turn, to publish his reasoned but impassioned defense of Third Period philosophy.[54] The Ronn-Halonen forces portrayed themselves as under attack from outsiders and New Yorkers. It worked well. Throughout December, pledges of support from youth and women's auxiliaries and chapters of the Finnish Federation poured in. At the same time, enough harsh words were exchanged that Carl Reeve armed himself and a group from the Young Communist League in anticipation of an attack on *Tyomies.*[55]

The Communist party, for its part, brought heavy weapons to bear. It maintained control of the daily *Tyomies,* which most of the Finnish-Americans in the area read. Reeve and others wrote harsh criticisms of Ronn and Halonen, accusing them of abandoning working class principles and of aspiring to convert the CCE stores into just another capitalist chain-store operation. Party units held trials and made explusions in an attempt to maintain discipline.[56]

A number of dedicated Communists were caught in the middle of this accelerating battle. The well-liked and charismatic Matti Tenhunen disagreed with Third Period dogma. He voted with the unanimous majority of the exchange's board in resisting the party's financial demands, but he clung to his Communist affiliation and tried to remain a neutral in the battle. It was impossible. In December Tenhunen accompanied Henry Puro to Moscow to explain the American cooperative situation. In the Soviet homeland he now had a change of mind, repudiating Halonen and calling for all-out support of the party.[57]

Puro and Tenhunen now made an obscure midwestern battle into an international issue. On 26 December, the Finnish Communist party-in-exile cabled an attack on Halonen, and in February 1930, the executive committee of the Comintern linked Halonen to those other rascals, the IWW, Jay Lovestone, and Samuel Gompers. The final battle lines were drawn. On 27 March, the Communist loyalists formed the Left Wing Committee headed by Tenhunen, Oscar Corgan, and Big Jack Vainionpaa.[58]

The battle was over when the annual convention of the CCE met early in April 1930, except for the shouting—but of that there was plenty. The left wing received approximately equal floor time, but they lost every substantive vote by huge margins. The delegates elected four new members of the governing board and removed the three rebellious directors, Corgan, Tenhunen and Vainionpaa, after they had asserted that their only loyalty was to the Left Wing Committee. While the right-wing candidates received an average of 220 votes each, their opponents could muster only from 34 to 68. In a fighting mood, the convention cabled the Communist International that Halonen had been retained and that the three leftists had been booted out.[59]

The embittered Communists began a boycott of the exchange. They retained control of about eighteen stores, with 3,095 members, which refused to purchase any goods from the Superior warehouse. Individual party members took their business away from stores they did not control. Finally, one day before the biennial convention of the Cooperative League of the U.S.A. was to meet in October, the Communist stores formed a competing wholesale society, the Workers and Farmers Cooperative Unity Alliance.[60]

The new organization sent a delegation to the league meeting in order to announce early its adherence to the principles of the Third Period.

Reeve delivered a scathing denunciation of business cooperativism. Ronn answered with nostalgia for his old association, "I have only one regret, comrades, and that is that the good cause of Communism was here so poorly sponsored." Reeve and his followers stalked out, singing the "Internationale," to the accompaniment of catcalls and considerable personal abuse. It was the final triumph for Ronn. He died during the following year, exhausted by the struggle, at the early age of thirty-seven.[61]

The Cooperative Unity Alliance adhered strictly to the precepts of the Third Period. At one time or another it had thirty-seven stores. It refused to do any business with the CCE, but since it was not large enough to can or package its own goods, it turned to capitalistic sources for supplies. A period of great bitterness ensued, and in more than a dozen towns in the Lake Superior region, two angrily competing cooperative stores struggled for patronage, oftentimes in towns too small for one. A few of the stores failed, but the rate of closings was far less than for comparable private business.[62]

The Communist stores refused to cut their ties completely from the CCE, or Central Cooperative Wholesale, as it was renamed in 1931. Under cooperative laws they still owned shares in the old organization, and at each annual convention, delegations appeared from Mass, Ironwood, Eben Junction, and other Communist stores to present their own slates of officers and to demand passage of a united front resolution calling for their own brand of working class unity.[63]

The Central Cooperative Wholesale grew increasingly impatient with the wayward stores. After Ronn's death no leader spoke any longer about the "good cause of Communism," and the organization moved steadily toward political neutrality, although occasionally aroused to sympathy for causes such as Loyalist Spain in the late 1930s. In 1931, the CCW convention dropped its hammer-and-sickle trademark and adopted the twin pines of the Cooperative League.[64]

The Cooperative Unity Alliance found itself more and more isolated. In 1933 the impatient delegates to the Central Cooperative Wholesale convention laid down new ground rules, refusing to entertain any future motions from the Communist stores until they ceased criticism, terminated the boycott, and ended all competing organizations—meaning the Workers and Farmers Cooperative Unity Alliance. On the other hand, until its dissolution in the late 1930s, the CUA provided valuable support for the Unemployed Councils (the party's organization for the jobless), the United Farmers League, and the Farmers National Committee for Action.[65]

After the shift in the line of world communism signaled at the Seventh Congress of the Communist International in 1935, the Cooperative Unity Alliance tried to resume friendly relations with the CCW. The leaders of the older group would have no part of it, however. They refused any negotiations with the Communist organization as an entity and demanded strict adherence to the conditions laid down in 1933. Finally, on 19 June 1938, the alliance announced its dissolution, and most of its member stores quietly sought new ties with the CCW.[66]

Quite probably the Cooperative Central Exchange would have gradually shed its close association with the Communist party even without the advent of Third Period communism. Party members were always a relative minority in the whole movement, at least according to Eskel Ronn.[67] Beginning with V. S. Allane, the leaders of the CCE were moving away from the close relation to the party. Moreover, as the society prospered and new stores opened, many non-Finns, without any affection for Communism, were diluting the ardor for a strictly class-conscious organization.

The hard-line philosophy of the Third Period hastened the crisis, however. The leaders of the exchange played up the monetary demands of the party during the conflict, but in reality this was a minor issue. The vital struggle was over whether the Communists would have complete control over the organization from above. The party's refusal to compromise the point—something it could not do and remain true to the line of the Comintern—led to the loss of its most prestigious ally in rural America just as the onset of the Great Depression was bringing a new wave of resentment and protest among American farmers.

4
THIRD PERIOD COMMUNISM

THE GREAT WALL STREET COLLAPSE came a few months after the disgrace of Jay Lovestone and slightly more than a year after the Sixth Congress of The Communist International had predicted the final crisis of capitalism. Within two years the world economy was in turmoil. Industrial production declined, and unemployment climbed. Agricultural output, however, remained high, and the glut drove commodity prices to nearly unbelievable lows. American farmers reacted slowly at first; then, like some long dormant volcano, they erupted violently, to the surprise of the government, the public, and very likely to themselves.

The Communists, too, were caught by surprise. A central committee plenum, meeting the same month as the crash, created an agrarian department to analyze the farm problem.[1] The group hurriedly wrote a draft proposal for the upcoming convention of the party which was to meet late in June 1930.

The resulting program was not an unreasonable document compared to many others of the Third Period. While it applied Marxist-Leninist logic, it came forth with an analysis which had strong elements of reality.[2] The authors recognized that although "agrarian revolution is a petty bourgeois revolution inherently, . . . it is none the less of extreme importance to the revolutionary proletariat." They used Lenin's writings to bolster the importance of farmers, and they concluded with a series of hard-headed proposals for uniting what they foresaw as an increasingly angry countryside. They accurately forecast a rapid decline of farm conditions as a result of the general crisis. The Communists, they wrote, must rally local "committees of action" to fight against dispossession and to call strikes against rents, taxes, and mortgages. If the Communists did not play a leading role in forging an alliance with the farmers, then their enemies surely would. Without mentioning Alfred Knutson, the drafters of the agrarian program were pitiless in detailing his lack of spadework. In similar fashion they struck out at Charlie Taylor for plunging ahead, without guidance, into possible serious deviation.[3]

At the party's convention, late in June, a high functionary, Harrison George, offered a further practical analysis of the farm situation. He was comtemptuous of the Lovestonite underestimation of the importance of farmers. George foresaw excellent Communist prospects in the near future as the crisis of capitalism brought underconsumption, rising surpluses, and a tightening vise on rural life by finance capital. George, an ex-Wobbly, was particularly attuned to action which would directly involve farmers in the struggle against the oppressor. He worried much less than the dogmatists in the party bogged down in ideology. Let the farmers grasp the idea of strikes against high rent and taxes, and then "there will be one hell of a fight."[4]

Both the draft program and George's report made the strongest case for immediate, pragmatic work in rural areas throughout the country. The effect, however, was dulled by several months of delay. The difficulty was a typical one for the American Communists. They temporized for several months, unsure of themselves, while commodity prices plummeted. Their analyses conflicted with the ruminations of the ideologists of the Krestintern. Those East European emigrés had stated that finance capital played a progressive role by consolidating small landholdings into large efficent units, ripe for plucking as collective farms.[5]

Harrison George had already demolished this argument by noting that capitalists were indeed increasingly involved in the countryside, but their role was reactionary. They continued to tighten the debt screws on small and medium farmers. No "capitalist collectivization" was taking place; a foreclosed owner was merely replaced by an oppressed renter. In spite of George's fervent plea for action, even at the danger of being opportunist, it was not until late 1930 that Earl Browder announced that Moscow upheld the American stand.[6]

This caution and delay boded ill for the Communist dream of mobilizing farm discontent. Fifteen states east of the Rockies had less than half the normal summer rain. Wheat in North Dakota and Montana was especially hard hit. Slackened demand resulting from the economic slump meant a drop in wheat prices from $1.08 a bushel in January 1930, to $0.70 in July. For the country as a whole there was a 25 percent decline in gross farm income. Wholesale farm prices had fallen by 21 percent, while food prices dropped 16 percent and nonagricultural goods fell by only 10 percent.[7] While commodities took this terrible tumble, Communists bureaucrats argued almost as though their real aim was immaterial.

The usually irrepressible Charlie Taylor spent this time minding his newspaper shop. After having spent eight years in the Montana state senate he had tired of what he increasingly believed to be a charade. Moreover, he gave less than deference to his Communist affiliation, at one point kidding his readers about the "Latest Bolshvik Atrocity"—a mechanical chiropractor. On the more serious side he praised Mother Bloor's speech at the Farmer Labor temple on behalf of the Gastonia strikers, but he blustered angrily at her attack on Trotsky. In September he accepted the futile role of Farmer Labor candidate for senator against the popular Tom Walsh.[8] Although Taylor often witnessed his sympathy for Trotsky, he plainly drifted through most of 1930 and early 1931.

The Finns to whom the party had handed control of the United Farmers League were obviously incapable of breathing much life into it. Henry Puro, the newly appointed head of the party's agrarian department, wrote a seven-point memorandum calling on each party district to make contracts in the countryside and learn rural demands, but his heavy accent made him a poor public spokesman. Mother Bloor seemed the only live wire in the whole group. The constant stump speaking of this septuagenarian would have tired most workers half her age. In January 1931, she became North Dakota organizer for the UFL and made constant forays into Montana and South Dakota as well.[9]

By July 1931, when the price of wheat had fallen to barely thirty-six cents a bushel, Taylor could resist the revolutionary call of the party no longer. At a huge farmers' picnic he appeared along with Bloor, Hal Ware, and young Lem Harris, the latter two of whom were making an economic survey of the nation after returning from the Soviet Union. Taylor, always favoring activism, had probably been influenced by that portion of Puro's letter calling for formulating immediate demands.[10]

The UFL began making gains once Taylor's ardor was aroused. After a mass meeting in October, he claimed fifteen hundred league members in Sheridan County, Montana, and began looking further afield. Mother Bloor had already prepared the ground in northeastern South Dakota with calls for a five-year debt moratorium. Taylor now arranged a well-publicized swap of North Dakota coal for South Dakota wheat, which the drought-striken northerners needed.[11]

The party recognized Taylor's great value as an organizer, and he in turn was pleased by the directives coming from Moscow. At a plenum late in August the central committee of the Comintern had decreed that all "toiling peasants" had to be won over as allies of the proletariat by party seizure of leadership in day-to-day struggles.[12] In November 1931, a rising young bureaucrat, Erik Bert, took over the editorship of *Producers News.* Taylor set up his headquarters for a time in Frederick, South Dakota, and he soon had flourishing UFL units in both Dakotas, fanning eastward from Frederick.[13]

The league also began growing in the Upper Peninsula of Michigan under the tightening economic pressures. On 24 November, some two hundred farmers blocked a mortgage foreclosure sale in Ontonagon County. UFL secretary Rudolph Harju claimed locals in Michigan, Minnesota, the Dakotas, and Montana, although he was unhappy that the league had not spread further geographically. Puro was more sanguine. He foresaw the party in a position to lead mass struggles for relief and against dispossession.[14]

Communist leaders recognized that some areas might be unprepared to accept the party apparatus or the radical UFL. In such places Communists should organize committees of action and even accept nonparty leaders, just as long as a strong party fraction provided guidance.[15] This led to some confusion. *Producers News,* for example, called on Nebraska farmers to stay in the Farmers Union—rather than forming UFL locals —but it chided the union's leaders for lack of forcefulness in the agricultural crisis.[16]

The UFL itself admitted that although requests to organize mass actions were pouring in, its own experience was limited. In the meantime, however, the farm protest movement was building everywhere. Charlie Taylor shifted his efforts to the sandy soil of northwestern Minnesota. He labored to build a taxpayers' league to cut levies. Erik Bert sniped at him, complaining that such associations were tools of the rich farmer. He demanded the formation of a class-conscious group which would lower taxes for the small farmer and raise them for the large.[17]

As spokesmen for distressed farmers, the taxpayers' leagues, committees of action, and the UFL itself were soon to be caught up with and surpassed, however. In stolid, Republican Iowa, a roughneck, sixty-six-year-old Farmers Union leader, Milo Reno, was about to launch one of the truly revolutionary movements of the twentieth century—the Farm Holiday Association.

Reno came by his hell raising naturally. His mother had been a Granger and a Greenbacker, and young Reno had stumped for the Peoples party in the 1890s. His emotional brand of reformism, however, had been out of place with middle-class reformers like Woodrow Wilson in the new century, and he returned to farming. But in the first postwar depression of the early 1920s, Reno had risen to the presidency of the Iowa Farmers Union.[18]

As early as 1920 Reno had argued that farmers had the right to place their own prices on commodities and refuse to sell for a lesser. Throughout the 1920s, Reno had damned low prices and had occasionally suggested a farmer strike to raise them to the level of cost of production.[19] Most farmers, however, retained too strong a faith in the established system to listen to Reno's advice. He retired as president of the Iowa Farmers Union in 1930, but he stayed at the head of its insurance companies and effectively controlled the organization until his death in 1936.

The National Farmers Union had the reputation of being the most radical of the general farm organizations. In reality it was a conglomerate of bitterly contesting factions. By the 1920s its strength was in the Midwest and plains states. The national president, elected in 1928, was Charles Huff of Kansas.[20]

Huff had eagerly accepted President Herbert Hoover's Federal Farm Board program of 1929 as a panacea. The Farm Board tried to stabilize commodity prices through a floating fund used by cooperatives. The leaders of the Northwest Group of the NFU supported Huff's policy because they saw great advantages accruing to their Farmers Union Terminal Association operating in Minnesota, North Dakota, and Montana.[21]

Milo Reno, after the briefest of flirtations with the Farm Board, had condemned it as a delusion. He was joined by a close ally, John A. Simpson, president of the Oklahoma Farmers Union, largest in the organization. Simpson and Reno believed that cost-of-production prices could be achieved, but not through the Farm Board. They were gradually evolving a cost-of-production plan aimed at restoring economic health to the farmer.

Most chroniclers of the Hoover and Roosevelt years have given short shrift to the theories of Simpson and Reno, but they deserve more attention. The cost-of-production plan, far from being antiintellectual, gave a major role to professional economists. They were to predict the commodity needs of the nation on the one hand and the expense to the farmer of filling these wants on the other. Experts would determine the cost of producing a given commodity by totaling the rates of interest on land and equipment, the depreciation of buildings and machinery, and the price of seed and fertilizer; the government would thereupon forbid the sale of the product for less than the determined cost. In 1932, for example, E. E. Kennedy, an economist for the Farmers Union, estimated the cost of producing a bushel of Iowa corn was ninety-two cents at a time when farmers were receiving twenty-five cents.[22]

The cost-of-production plan implicitly admitted the existence of a domestic surplus. To control this, the theorists would again turn to the trained economist who would estimate, in advance of the planting season, just how large domestic needs would be. They would then apportion this total to the states, counties, and townships, and finally to the individual farm. Each farmer would then receive an allotment in terms of the sale unit, whether bushel, pound, or bale. All buyers of farm commodities would be federally licensed and forbidden to pay less than the established price or buy more than the farmer's allotment. The farmer himself could raise more than his allotment if he wished, but he could not sell it on the American market. He could store it or sell it abroad, but proponents claimed that eventually he would tailor production to fit demand.[23]

In 1930, the cost-of-production forces defeated Huff and elected Simpson president of the National Farmers Union. The victory was narrow and almost hollow. Kansas and the Northwest Group continued their cooperation with the Farm Board. Nebraska, second only to Oklahoma in membership, hewed close to Rochdale cooperativism and cried a plague on cost of production as well as the Farm Board.[24]

In the growing economic crisis of the early 1930s, Simpson and Reno plunged ahead, seeking support for their theories. They worked together closely with but one major disagreement. Simpson had strong faith in the Democratic party. He strenuously lobbied Congress for farm relief as well as for that old panacea, inflation. At one point he cried, "What we need is remonitization of silver, and maybe a good supply of paper money, and a sprinkling of counterfeits." When the 1932 Democratic Convention met, Simpson wrote its farm plank, and he obviously wanted to be secretary of agriculture in a Roosevelt administration. Reno, although agreeing with Simpson on the need for inflation, had no trust in the major parties and wrote, "The policies of both are very largely dictated by Wall Street."[25]

Reno and his Iowa followers soon began stepping ahead of Simpson in action to raise commodity prices. The tinder was struck at the 1931 convention of the Iowa Farmers Union when young John Bosch of Kandiyohi County, Minnesota, called for peaceful withholding of crops from market until prices rose. Encouraged by the response, Bosch and Reno tried to get a resolution from the convention of the National Farmers Union to refuse to buy, sell, or pay taxes until cost-of-production prices were reached. The majority, however, voted to table the resolution and to send another delegation to Washington.[26]

For Reno, the time for pleas to Congress had ended. When the prickly editor of the *Iowa Union Farmer,* H. R. Gross—later a longtime Iowa congressman—denounced bankers for calling a "bank holiday" whenever their assets were threatened, some anonymous wit suggested a "farm holiday." Perhaps simple humor in the midst of tragedy, but the new name spread like crab grass.[27]

On 19 February 1932, a thousand or more Boone County farmers formed the first unit of the Farm Holiday Association. In March A. W. Ricker of the Northwest Group began touting direct action, having finally lost faith in Hoover and the Farm Board. Speakers fanned out across Iowa and adjacent states. More than two thousand men and women massed in Des Moines on 3 May to found the National Farm Holiday Association. They presented an unusually short program of demands—only 360 words. John A. Simpson attended and attacked his favorite targets. The Holiday platform deferred to Simpson by calling for national legislative relief, but the key plank was one of direct action. The Farm Holiday movement pledged to organize farmers throughout the nation to withhold their commodities until cost-of-production prices were reached.[28]

Foundation of the Farm Holiday Association gave the Communists a powerful adversary in the fight to radicalize farmers. The response from *Producers News* was almost immediate. The editor charged that "misleaders" had organized the Farm Holiday to keep farmers out of the

United Farmers League. He condemned the Des Moines resolutions, contrasting them with the league program. A strike for cost-of-production prices, Bert wrote, would be a strike against the farm family itself and its already pitiful living standards. In contrast, the UFL called for a real farm strike—one against taxes and dispossession.[29]

At a time when the Farm Holiday Association was aiming at a broad alliance of all farm groups, veterans, labor, and progressive businessmen to save the farm home, Bert and *Producers News* pursued an opposite course. Bert carefully followed the line of the Third Period and attacked not only the Farm Holiday, Farmers Union, and taxpayers leagues but also the Minnesota Farmer Labor party—all as the fascist agents of Wall Street.[30]

There was little pretense by this point that *Producers News* was not a Communist party paper. Communist candidates, often members of the UFL, were endorsed in Minnesota, Ohio, and North Dakota, where Mother Bloor ran for Congress. In the paper's home precinct, Sheridan County, Montana, the party put up a full ticket against the fearful opposition of fused Democrats and Republicans. William Z. Foster, the Communist candidate for president, spoke to several thousand farmers near Plentywood, calling for free emergency relief, no taxes for poor farmers, and no forced collection of rents or taxes.[31]

In the meantime, as the depression continued to worsen, Hal Ware and Lem Harris finished their year-long investigation of American agriculture and set up shop in the nation's capital. They established the nonprofit Farm Research Incorporated to study farm legislation and give "timely accounts" of the farm struggle in a mimeographed *Farm News Letter*. "It is a time for thinking, of course," the editors wrote, "but especially it is a time for action."[32] Washington, however, was a long way removed from the action, and the *Farm News Letter* showed more signs of scholarly analysis than of charging the barricades.

Milo Reno had talked since spring of a peaceful withholding action, and in early August he claimed that 180,000 Iowa farmers were prepared to fight to gain cost-of-production prices. When the farm strike began, however, its violent nature was a surprise to him and a dilemma for the Communists. The hot summer of 1932 had fairly passed, when, in early August, milk producers demanded higher prices from Sioux City dairies. The Farm Holiday was strong in the area, and Reno may have foreseen a milk strike acting as a trigger when he announced a general farm strike to begin on 8 August.[33]

The strike began slowly, and commodity receipts appeared to be affected not at all.[34] Various leaders around the state began to talk of the necessity of picketing, but it was the Sioux City milk farmers who precipitated action.

The diary industry nationwide had tailspinned badly in the depression. Iowa farmers claimed it cost $2.17 to produce a hundredweight of milk with 3.5 percent of butterfat. In Sioux City they received only $1.00.[35] They were angry, but they recognized the club they held over distributors if they cut off the flow of perishable milk. Even in the worst of time, milk, like bread, was a staff of life, and the strike could have an immediate affect.

On 11 August, dairy farmers threw up ticket camps on every Iowa road leading into Sioux City. In cooperation with the Farm Holiday, they soon were halting all commodities flowing into the city—except moonshine.[36] The strike had a twofold aim: to raise the price paid for milk by Sioux City distributors and, with the hoped-for collaboration of farmers in the rest of the nation, to raise all commodity prices.

The Sioux City strike caught the Communists unprepared. An editorial in *Producers News* had just damned a proposed wheat strike in North Dakota, calling any price strike an evasion of the real issues of mortgages, evictions, and taxes. Harrison George later snappishly condemned unnamed purists in the party who paralyzed it when the need for action came. As the strike entered its second week, *Producers News* shifted to cautious support, noting that the strike was against the dairy trust and not the consumer. Henry Puro called upon the party to support the strike and to raise its level. Poor farmers, working through the UFL, should seize control of the movement, he wrote, and direct it against interest, rent, and taxes.[37]

Events in Iowa did not wait on party decisions. Violence soon erupted at picket camps as determined truckers tried to ram their way through the lines. Bricks and stones smashed windshields, and eventually the simple device of a long plank studded with spikes stopped any vehicle short of a steamroller. By 14 August an estimated fifteen hundred pickets patrolled the access routes to Sioux City from Iowa. Four days later, strikers in Nebraska and South Dakota had completed the ring around the city.[38]

The blockade shut off the flow of milk and brought on a settlement which paid dairy farmers 80 percent more than previously received.[39] It might not have been the theoretical cost of production, but it was an epic gain. A continued drop in hog prices, however, demonstrated the futility of blocking only one major packing center, in the larger strike aimed at raising all commodity prices.

Sporadic picketing closed some smaller market cities, but soon the Holiday men aimed at larger targets. On 21 August, area farmers voted to picket Council Bluffs, Iowa. The Council Bluffs strikers faced a formidable opponent, Sheriff Percy Lainson, a combat veteran of the Rainbow Division. After several clashes, Lainson arrested fifty-five pickets, only to be challenged by a mob of one thousand farmers from all over the state. They threatened a march on the courthouse to free the prisoners even in face of Lainson's machine guns. Fortunately a truce was arranged. The state capital, Des Moines, faced a blockade a few days later, but lacking much local support, it was soon smashed by the sheriff.[40]

National attention refocused on northwest Iowa. Mayor W. D. Hayes of Sioux City suggested a midwestern governors' conference to meet the crisis. The Minnesota Farmer Laborite, Floyd B. Olson, embraced the idea and—true to his self-proclaimed radicalism—demanded that the governors use troops to enforce the commodity embargo until cost of production was reached. Iowa's governor, Dan Turner, ignored Milo Reno's endorsement of the conference, but Warren Green of South Dakota, faced with a full-scale strike in his state, hurriedly issued invitations to fifteen governors to meet in Sioux City, 9 September.[41]

Reno faced two problems: sporadic violence was occurring not only in Iowa but in adjacent states, and a settlement of the Sioux City milk strike had brought renewed enthusiasm to picket lines rather than the reverse. A cowardly nighttime attack with firearms on a Farm Holiday meeting near Cherokee, Iowa, resulting in fourteen wounded, gave Reno a rationale to call a truce until the governors met.[42]

The rapidly unfolding events of August kept the Communists off balance. The small cadre of party members in Sioux City had offered aid in distributing free milk to the poor early in the strike, but they lost their welcome status when they reportedly suggested violent tactics. By late August, *Producers News* was made up with an eye on distribution among the pickets. Rather stupidly, however, the 26 August edition laid emphasis on attacking an obscure Minnesota Farmer Laborite named Garrenstron—a step guaranteed to glaze the eyes of any Iowa readers. From that point onward, *Producers News* kept a steady drumbeat of attack on Milo Reno, John Chalmers, and other Holiday leaders.[43]

Lem Harris distributed a much shrewder message in the *Farm News Letter.* He approvingly quoted an earlier Reno statement that farmers could expect nothing from legislation, while contrasting it with Reno's call for a truce in hopes the governors would somehow achieve results.[44]

Once Reno called the truce, the United Farmers League redoubled its attacks through mimeographed and printed flyers. Taking for granted that Reno was a sellout, the UFL called on locals of the Farmers Union and Farm Holiday to form united front committees with the UFL to prolong picketing, to block negotiations, and to expand the strike against the marketing monopoly in order to include also the monopoly of finance capital. Almost casually they called for support of Communist candidates in the November election. Someone in the party—most probably Hal Ware—had the wise idea of using the governors' conference as a platform for publicizing a slightly disguised UFL program and for sending out a call for a farmers national mass meeting in December.[45]

On a hurried drive from Des Moines, where Bloor had addressed a crowd of five hundred, Ware composed a series of demands to be presented to the governors by a "rank-and-file" delegation. In Sioux City, Bloor found thousands of farmers milling around with no apparent leadership. She finagled an invitation to speak as the wife of a "busted North Dakota farmer." She aroused so much enthusiasm that soon she was precariously perched on the cab of the lead truck of a massive parade down the main street.[46] That evening, W. W. Morphew read the rank-and-file proposals to the governors. Removed of rhetoric, Lem Harris reprinted the demands in *Farm News Letter:*

1. We demand a moratorium on all debts, mortgages, and taxes.
2. Because we made our homes and have fed the people of America for generations, we proclaim our right to remain on our farm homes. We demand that all foreclosures, t x sales or evictions of farmers be stopped.
3. We demand the right to fight, by picketing the roads against the food trusts and middlemen who rob both producer and consumer.
4. We demand protection by our sheriffs and officers against armed thugs and gunmen who are hired to break our picket lines.
5. And we demand the right to continue this strike until we receive more than the accepted local cost of production from the middle-

men. This must come out of their profit and not from the increased
prices to city consumers. . . .

Therefore, be it resolved that we call upon all groups of rank and
file farmers in all sections of the United States, whatever their race
or creed, to form committees of action and join with us in sending
delegates to a Farmers National Emergency Relief Conference in
Washington, D.C. on or about December 1st, to present our demands to Congress and to the Nation.[47]

The proposals seemed so reasonable to the conservative *Sioux City Journal* that they were editorially lauded.[48]

The session of rank-and-file farmers—estimated at anywhere between
fifty and a thousand—wrote Lem Harris, requesting him to act as executive secretary of the national relief conference. Signer of the letter was
Harry Lux, former IWW, Nonpartisan Leaguer, and friend of Ware for
a decade.[49]

In formulating the demands to the governors, Ware had practiced the
art of compromise. Unlike the leaders of the UFL or the agrarian department of the party who were wary of strikes for cost-of-production prices,
Ware had gone further, calling for *more* than the local cost of production. On the other hand, Reno had learned from the left at the conference: among his proposals was one that there be a moratorium on all
foreclosures and dispossessions until cost of production was reached.
John Bosch, now president of the Minnesota Farm Holiday Association
told the governors, "The very foundations of government are trembling
. . . our homes must be saved or there will be a revolution."[50]

The recommendations of the governors were rapidly disposed of.
They revived the tired demand for an upward revision of farm tariffs, for
an expanded currency, for assistance with farm, seed, and feed loans, and
for the restriction of foreclosures by federal agencies. Finally, in rejecting
Olson's state-imposed embargo, they grandly announced that all farmers
could work together for their own embargo.[51]

To cries of "Sellout!" from the left, Reno accepted the advice to halt
picketing. A two-week blockade of Saint Paul and Minneapolis simply
revealed further the futility of spot strikes.[52] As autumn dissolved into
early winter, farmers thoughts turned away from commodity prices and
focused more and more on saving the farm home.

A week after the governors' conference, sixteen hundred Nebraska farmers met in Fremont to form the Nebraska Holiday Association. After an address by Reno they adopted their platform and elected officers. They gave pro forma approval to the standard cry for cost of production prices, but the bulk of the program consisted of what soon came to be known as the Madison County plan:

1. A moratorium on mortgages and interest for poor farmers until they can afford "the good things of life."
2. Cancellation of government feed and seed loans.
3. Exemption of the heavily mortgaged land of poor farmers from taxes —immediately.
4. A moratorium on rents until cost of production prices plus a decent living is reached.
5. No evictions.
6. Increased commodity prices to come not from city workers but from middlemen and money interests.

The conference also supported the call for a Washington relief meeting.[53]

Harry Parmenter, a crony of Reno and well-known old Nonpartisan Leaguer won the presidency, but the vice-presidency went to Tony Rosenberg of Newman Grove, a friend of Ware and Harris. On the whole, the conference was a decided victory for the left-wing forces. The triumph was not principally a Communist one. It belonged to what John Shover has called "a remarkable, tiny group of farmers" from Newman Grove in Madison County. Their leader was Andrew Dahlsten, successively a Populist, Socialist, and Nonpartisan Leaguer.[54]

The upcoming Washington meeting shared attention in many rural homes with the presidential election in November. The organizers scored a united front coup when the Montana Farmers Union unanimously endorsed the conference. Over the opposition of the leadership the Montanans also adopted a Madison County-like plank on evictions. A week later the South Dakota Farmers Union favored the Washington meeting. Letters poured into Washington as UFL sections and committees of action pledged delegates by the car or truckload. Before long, the *Farm News Letter,* originally intended as a staid purveyor of statistics, had become the beacon light leading the caravans to Washington and, by the by, pointing out that the elections had been controlled by big business and so made a "determined and resolute fight" by farmers all the more important.[55]

Soon the old trucks began the drive to Washington. The farm families accepted hospitality along the way from Unemployed Councils, the Salvation Army, church and union groups. They pleaded everywhere for the farmers' cause. In Washington Lem Harris peacefully arranged a reception from the police to prevent another Bonus Army riot.[56]

On 7 December, almost 250 delegates representing twenty-six states, thirty-three farm organizations, and several local mass meetings, convened in the Typographical Union Hall in Washington. Probably no more than 25 percent were Communists, and the party kept carefully to the background. Arriving late were 6 black sharecroppers. The opening session elected Tony Rosenberg of the Nebraska Farm Holiday as president of the conference.[57]

A great deal of time during the three-day session was given to individual farmers' reports on conditions in their regions. The honesty and intensity of feeling moves the reader today as much as the sight of the "huge men in overalls with bright-red faces and yellow hair" impressed a contemporary observer, the literary critic Malcolm Cowley.[58]

The resolutions committee wrote a program which the delegates thoroughly discussed. The preamble stated that farmers had come for the first time to lay their story before Congress without "high-paid leaders" or lobbyists in order to stop creditors threatening "to sweep us from our land and home." It condemned all talk of the abandonment of scientific and technical advances and a return to subsistence farming or peasantry. It called on Congress to suspend rules to hear a reading of the program.

The demands of the conference came in eight resolutions:

1. Immediate allocation by Congress of five hundred million dollars for relief of the distressed farm population.
2. Governmental purchase of food and supplies for the urban unemployed from farmers for cost of production plus enough to provide a decent standard of living; processing and transportation to be regulated to prevent monopolistic profits.
3. Rural relief programs to be administered by locally elected committees.
4. Popular election of a regulating body to raise commodity prices for farmers, lower prices to consumers, and reduce the profits of middlemen.

5. Defeat of any legislation based on the theory of surplus production.
6. A system credit which would allow access by all farmers, not just the rich possessing collateral.
7. A three-point resolution containing the core of the Madison County plan:
    A. A moratorium on mortgages, interest, and rents for farmers who until the crisis had maintained a decent standard of living.
    B. The cancellation of mortgages, interest, feed and seed loans, and debts for supplies for farm families who had always been below a decent standard of living—that is, principally, marginal farmers and sharecroppers.
    C. The cancellation of back taxes and moratorium on current taxes until the crisis ends.
8. No evictions.[59]

After thorough debate and occasional flares of temper, the delegates approved the program. The conference then endorsed twelve other resolutions introduced from the floor—approval of a veterans' bonus, demand for withdrawal of American troops in foreign lands, recognition of the Soviet Union, no recourse to the sales tax, strict government economy, and so on.[60]

Groups of delegates laid the program before their congressmen, and received, as well, pleasant hearings before President Hoover, Vice-President Charles Curtis, and House Speaker John Nance Garner. If the delegates had serious hopes that their radical program would be accepted, they were sorely disappointed. After Curtis and Garner had the proposals placed in the *Congressional Record,* the nation's leaders returned their attention to more prosaic means of alleviating farm distress.[61]

The Communist fraction was prepared for this rejection. The farmers now voted "to make their conference permanent, consolidate their power, and in a friendly alliance with the workers, fight against Wall Street and the middlemen for the safety of their homes and livelihood." They elected Lem Harris executive secretary of the Farmers National Committee for Action, established headquarters in Washington, and voted to publish the *Farmers National Weekly.*[62]

The farm strike had failed to bring the relief of higher prices to producers. The governors' conference had dallied. The winter of Washington inaction was setting in as desperate mortgagors, tax gatherers, and lenders sought money from equally desperate farmers. The United Farmers League, the committees of action, and Communist fractions in older farm groups had the program the farmers wanted. Their shouted slogan, "Women and children have the first mortgage!," could bring alliance with large groups of farmers unless Reno or the politicians of that terrible interregnum winter could counteract them—or unless the cautious functionaires of the party hog-tied the growing strength of those pragmatic ideologues, Hal Ware and Lem Harris.

5
THE MUDSILLS OF AMERICAN SOCIETY

LENIN HAD TAKEN GREAT INTEREST not only in American agriculture but also in its various subclasses, especially those on the very bottom: the sharecroppers and the agricultural wage-workers. Few organizations had ever paid them much heed. The Industrial Workers of the World had had a phenomenal but relatively brief spurt of success with the migratory workers of the Great Plains, and there had been a few small sharecroppers' organizations about the time of World War I, but all had faded rapidly.[1]

At the Second Congress of the Communist International, meeting July and August 1920, the theses of the executive committee had clearly exhorted its members not to believe that a labor union elite could shut itself off from other workers, especially those in the countryside. Revolution had to have support from rural areas, and two classes in particular required leadership to become firm and faithful allies of the urban proletariat: hired laborers and small peasants who depended partially on wages.[2]

During the decade of the 1920s, however, no group had actively interested itself in the sustained work of organizing this bottom rung of American society. For the Communists it was probably a matter of priorities. They were, after all, a tiny minority in what seemed to be a burgeoning and self-satisfied society. The party could maintain an agrarian section in the Northwest because of the allegiance of already experienced radicals such as Alfred Knutson, Andrew Omholt, and Charlie Taylor. They had no such leaders on the great fruit and vegetable ranches of California or the plantations of the South.

The combination of Third Period Communism and the onset of the Great Depression challenged the party in the early 1930s as never before.

As economic conditions worsened and unemployment rose, more and more idealistic young people placed their services in the hands of the party, just as the conditions for sharecroppers and agricultural workers degenerated badly.

Following the lead of the Sixth Congress of the Communist International, William Z. Foster founded and became general secretary of the Trade Union Unity League at a Cleveland convention, 31 August–1 September 1929. The TUUL was intended to form the biting edge of an American revolutionary proletarianism and to compete with the conservative American Federation of Labor for leadership. It began with more or less viable unions in coal mining, the needle trades, and textiles. It aimed especially at organizing the unorganized in steel, automobiles, the maritime trades—and agriculture.[3]

The prospects for organizing field hands were at once the best and the worst in California. The sylvan myth of the family farm was a charade in the Golden State. Since the days of the Spanish land grants, the bulk of the desirable land had been controlled by a small group of corporations such as the Southern Pacific Railroad, Union Pacific Railroad, Bank of America, Calpack, the Crocker National Bank and wealthy growers such as Philip Bancroft.[4]

The Census Bureau defined large-scale farms in 1930 as those with thirty thousand dollars or more annual income. California had more than one-third of these in the nation. California had 30 percent of the large-scale cotton farms, although it produced only 2 percent of the nation's cotton crop. Its national percentage of large-scale farms in other commodities were: 40 percent in dairying; 44 percent in general crops; 53 percent in poultry; and 60 percent in fruit.[5] The concentration can be seen in other ways. In 1935, 3.5 percent of operating units controlled 62.5 percent of farm acreage, and in the fabulously verdant Imperial Valley, 6 percent of the farms had 43 percent of the land.[6] The Irrigation and Reclamation Act of 1902, limiting farms to 160 acres, had obviously had no effect.

The economic and political power of the growers had inhibited any protest against their methods. The seasonal workers had infinitesimal power. They traveled the year-round circuit of the state—grapes to cotton to fruit to cantaloupe to cherries to berries—so that they had no fixed abode, no franchise, and no political clout. In addition, during the 1920s, the growers had created a worker surplus by trebling the importation of Mexican-born laborers—valued for their "industriousness, docility, and tractibility."[7]

Even the quiet Mexicans had made some small protests in the late 1920s, but they were quickly salved over. But by 1930 the feeling of impending disaster, combined with the recent hard line of the Communist party, brought new unrest. The previously subservient Mexican Mutual Aid Association started a strike in the Imperial Valley in January 1930, which the Communist organizers soon took over. They demanded a 25 percent wage increase, union recognition for job committees, and rehiring of fired strikers. Resentment by the strikers of the takeover by these brash outsiders, however, combined with organized violence used by growers to bring a sudden collapse.[8]

The Communists retreated only slightly abashed. They now organized their own union, the Agricultural Workers Industrial League, affiliated with the TUUL, and prepared to strike the cantaloupe harvest in the spring. Their plans disintegrated when state and local authorities raided their headquarters, arrested 103, and sentenced 8 under the criminal syndicalism laws.[9]

Over the next two years conditions in the fields degenerated dramatically. In 1929 and 1930, wages had averaged from thirty-five to fifty cents an hour. By 1933, they had dropped to fifteen or sixteen cents. At hearings in 1933, a seven-year-old testified that he had picked cotton from seven in the morning until dark for sixty cents a hundredweight. By sundown, his sixty-five pounds had brought him about three cents an hour.[10]

The Agricultural Workers Industrial League became the Agricultural Workers Industrial Union and finally, in 1931, the Cannery and Agricultural Workers Industrial Union (CAWIU). Under whatever name, however, the union was a failure in the early 1930s. During the depths of the depression, 1930–32, there were only ten agricultural strikes; most were small and unsuccessful. The Communists were involved to some degree in five—and they lost them all.[11]

Perceptive leadership in the party had seen that the one group with the greatest growth rate was the unemployed. From 1930 to 1933, the party had plowed its slender resources into organizing Unemployed Councils, with their structured rent strikes, hunger marches, relief demonstrations, and so on. By the time the New Deal era approached for California, the Communists had organizational experience, trained cadres, idealistic and self-sacrificing young workers, and a district organizer, Samuel Adams Darcy, who was committed to work the farm valleys rather than the more familiar maritime front.[12]

In the meantime, the Communists had become involved in complicated maneuverings in the Southeast, most notably in rural Alabama. The party newspaper, *Southern Worker,* pursued a confusing line in 1930 and 1931. In the fall of 1930, the paper carried a long dialogue between a Communist and a farmer in which the latter was exposed to the joys of collective farming in the Soviet Union. Later, farmers were advised to write to the United Farmers League in Bismarck, North Dakota, for the solution to their problems. The early months of 1931 saw district organizer "Tom Johnson" attempt to organize Farmers Relief Councils in the poor, mostly white hill counties of Birmingham, with demands centered chiefly on relief and noneviction.[13]

This breakthrough in the rural South might normally have cheered party headquarters, except for the peculiar circumstances of the nationality question. Stalin and the Communist International had decided that blacks in the South formed a separate nation, which must be freed in order to lead other blacks out of colonialism. Black nationalism became intertwined with the agrarian question, and by the summer of 1931, the party had shifted its organizational efforts to rural blacks.[14]

In the late spring of 1931, Mack Coads, a black steelworker from Chatanooga went to Tallapoosa County, Alabama, to organize the Sharecroppers Union. With the growth of heavy industry in Birmingham, Alabama, blacks had gained more self-confidence than normal in the South of that time. Rural workers drifted in and out of the steel mills and coal mines, and those who remained at home heard tales of greater freedom in the city. At the same time, Tallapoosa and neighboring counties had witnessed the small growth of a class of semiindependent, sometimes landowning black farmers. There were tensions from the process of modernization, however. The increase of mechanization on the farm had tended to deprive many other blacks of the contractual relationship of being sharecroppers and had driven them one rung down the ladder to the status of occasional wage-worker—needed only during cotton chopping (weeding) in the spring and picking in the fall. And finally, the coming of the depression had placed every class—banker, merchant, landlord, sharecropper, and wage worker—on the fearful defensive.[15]

The first actions of the Sharecroppers Union had nothing to do with the black nation or even with advancing the cause of equality. They were defensive battles to retain a semblance of what they had had. In July 1931, landlords cut off food allowances for sharecropping families during the slack season in Tallapoosa County until 15 August. Under Coads and two local brothers, Ralph and Thomas Gray, the union countered with demands for food advances, the right to grow small gardens, the right to sell their own crops, getting picking wages in cash, and a decent rest interval at lunch time, as well as a nine-month school for their children with a free school bus.[16]

Not only the program but the existence of the SCU itself was a challenge to the prerogatives of the landlords and their legal servants. On 15 July, the sheriff and his deputies broke up a union meeting. On the following evening the lawmen returned. Ralph Gray and the sheriff wounded each other. Gray's friends carried him home, but the posse returned to kill him and burn down the house. In the end, after great sound and fury, the authorities could sustain no charges against any surviving union members.[17]

Murder and terror had cracked an aboveboard union, but such was the growing black desperation that within a year the union was reorganizing underground. Sub rosa units of ten formed locals and spread the gospel to Macon, Lee, Chambers, and Elmore counties.[18]

Once again violence resulted from what had begun as a defense of property, not so different from that taking place among the white farmers of the Midwest. A union leader, Cliff James, owed more on a purchased farm than he had at the time of the sale in 1924. The mortgagor hoped to discredit the union by seizing James's livestock for the debt. Once again there was a shoot-out. The sheriff and his deputies killed James and others. The courts indicted nineteen blacks; several pled guilty; seven were tried. Of the six convicted, one man, Ned Cobb, served twelve years in prison, and another died under mysterious circumstances.[19] The Sharecroppers Union had won great loyalty from its members, but its most unfortunate crop was martyrs.

The coming of the New Deal in March 1933 brought new conditions for both Communist farm workers unions, the SCU in the Southeast and the CAWIU in the West. With the upswing in employment and prices attributed to the National Recovery Administration during the summer of 1933, Sam Darcy was now ready to unleash his trained—and, idealistically, unpaid—cadres among the California workers.

The growers very unwisely tried to maintain the 1932 rate of fifteen cents an hour for field work. This was so niggardly that even they later recognized their mistake. The CAWIU had prepared for the new crop year by organizing thoroughly—from a headquarters in San Jose, through sections, subsections, and most importantly, locals.[20]

For the next year hardly a day passed without CAWIU involvement in a struggle somewhere in California. The year 1933 saw more agricultural workers on strike than any other. Some 57,000 workers stayed off the job; of these 48,000 were in California; and the CAWIU led 80 percent of them.[21]

The early results were a mixed bag in spite of work and enthusiasm. A pea-picking strike was lost in April despite careful preparation. Much more successful was a Santa Clara cherry pickers' strike in June. Although the wholesale prices had risen by one-third, the growers reduced wages one-third. Within a few days over nine hundred strikers were out, and cherries were rotting. The strikers, moreover, had no compunction about raiding the orchards and driving strikebreakers off the job. Law forces soon rallied and arrested twenty-seven and injured fifty, but the strike held firm. By 24 June, the CAWIU had won wage demands but not the important factor of union recognition.[22]

The CAWIU leaders followed this victory with a confusing loss among El Monte berry pickers. There was a melange of white organizers, Mexican pickers, Japanese growers, and white landowners. The Japanese offered a ridiculous nine cents an hour. The union called for twenty-five cents and began a mutually suspicious collaboration with a local Mexican union, Confederación de Uniones Obreros Mexicanos (CUOM). A grower offer of twelve to fifteen cents per hour was soon rejected, but, although the strike remained solid, friction was growing between white Communists and Mexican rank and file. The frantic growers finally offered twenty cents an hour plus union recognition. The Communist leadership rejected this and demanded more money. Recriminations and violence flared, until the strikers finally went back to work for conditions less favorable than those the Communists had rejected.[23]

After a brief convention to discuss and solidify tactics, the union marched into the fray once more. After quickly winning a pear strike in August, where they first received union recognition, and following up with a peach victory, the workers lost sugar beet and grape strikes in the face of growing vigilantism.[24]

The union leaders, however, had been building up for the confrontation with the climactic target—the cotton growers of the San Joaquin Valley. Here the great corporations held power undreamed of even by the plantation owners of the Black Belt or Delta South. Here the forces of law and middle-class society united with the representatives of great wealth in opposition to the union. Here the newspapers stressed the happiness of the workers if only they were left alone by the atrocious reds.[25]

As early as August and September, Union organizers covered the six cotton counties, establishing nineteen locals and finding many workers with loyalty from previous battles. Fifteen thousand hands were necessary for the harvest; 75 percent of them were Mexicans; most of the rest were Okies. Communication was better than in the past: many subleaders spoke both English and Spanish. The economic issue was real. In 1932 the growers had paid forty cents per hundredweight for cotton, a drastic drop from the late 1920s. The union set its demands on 17 September: a dollar per hundredweight, the hiring of workers through the union rather than through labor contractors, and no discrimination.[26]

The growers met in Fresno, 19 September, to set, as usual, standard wages for the whole valley. They listened to union organizer Pat Chambers read his demands but allowed no discussion. After strong arguments for holding the line, the growers advanced a picking price of sixty cents.[27]

The union rejected the offer and called the strike for 4 October. It covered an area a hundred miles long by thirty to forty miles wide. The union patrolled it with jalopy-borne pickets. Eventually twelve to fifteen thousand workers joined the walkout. The growers decided to crush the strike through support of the local authorities in a threefold plan: (1) evict all strikers from the plantation; (2) drive the strikers completely from the San Joaquin Valley; (3) use armed force against picketing.[28]

All the growers' methods backfired. The evictions meant that the strikers now were concentrated in a relatively small number of camps donated by friendly small farmers, where they entertained and policed themselves and were not intimidated by the growers. For perhaps the first time, government relief supplies went to striking workers. And the crude attempt by King County authorities to throw all strikers out of the valley simply focused national attention on the dispute.[29]

The growers now turned to the chilling stage of step three: vigilantism. At an open air union meeting in Pixley, addressed by organizer Pat Chambers, a mob of growers fired again and again into the workers, killing two and wounding nine. On the same day, Kern County vigilantes murdered another striker. No one was ever convicted of the crimes.[30]

The violence finally appalled state and federal authorities. The growers refused any direct contact with the union, but both sides accepted a fact-finding panel. On 22 October, the board reported, recommending seventy-five cents a hundredweight and making a vague appeal to the growers to observe the civil liberties of the workers.[31]

The two sides muttered angrily and stalled. Pressures built up. The Federal Intermediate Credit Bank told growers to accept the terms, while the State Relief Administration threatened cutoff of food to the strikers. After two days the growers caved in, citing patriotic reasons: "to forestall the spread of communism and radicalism."[32]

Still the CAWIU under its slender twenty-one-year-old secretary, Caroline Decker, held out, demanding eighty cents an hour and union recognition. The National Guard mobilized, and relief ended. After one more show of strength, the workers went back to the fields at the proffered seventy-five cents on 26 October. The CAWIU had won its greatest victory—and its last. When the cotton harvest ended, the workers drifted elsewhere, the locals collapsed, and the structure began to disintegrate.[33]

The year 1934 brought more confidence in the future and, consequently, less militance among agricultural workers. Strikes were smaller, fewer, and less successful. Decker and Chambers tried desparately to hold the CAWIU together, even beginning publication of the mimeographed *Agricultural Worker,* which ran for three numbers. Not only had the enthusiasm of the workers declined as the year advanced, but the forces of finance capital gathered swiftly and mightily to oppose radicalism. The Farm Labor Committee of the California State Chamber of Commerce, meeting 10 November 1933, called for an enlarged citizens' committee to combat Communism in every way possible.[34]

A series of meetings led to the formation of the Associated Farmers of California to fight agricultural unionism. Associated "Farmers" they may have been, but their huge antilabor funds came from American Can Co., Santa Fe Railroad, C. and H. Sugar Co., Canners League of California, Fibreboard Products, Inc., Holly Sugar Co., Pacific Gas and Electric, Southern Pacific Railroad, the San Francisco Industrial Corporation, and other banks and industries to the tune of somewhere around $28,000 during the first year. By 1936, the intake was $162,785.76.[35]

The cost of fighting bolshevism seemed to bring no complaints from the contributors. Receipts to the union ran slightly less. Although the CAWIU at its peak probably had the allegiance of eighteen to twenty thousand workers, and its nominal dues of $0.05 a month might have brought in $1,000.00 every thirty days, a financial report for December 1933 and January 1934 showed actual dues totaling $11.25 for the former and $16.10 for the latter. Total income for December was $107.94 and for January, $44.88. The two paid officers, Caroline Decker (secretary) and Pat Chambers (organizer) received, respectively, $7.50 and $5.00 per week.[36]

The Associated Farmers soon coordinated the counterattack of financiers, investors, industrialists, and railroad and power magnates on behalf of the planters. The beginning of the end for the union could be seen in the Imperial Valley in January 1934. A fruit pickers' strike under the Union of Mexican Field Workers was faltering when the CAWIU moved in on 8 January. The growers, with the forces of law under their thumbs, treated constitutional rights with contempt. Irving Bernstein has written that Imperial Valley was less a labor dispute than a "proto-Fascist" offensive by the grower-shippers and the corrupt local officials they dominated to suppress civil rights in order to destroy unionism.[37]

The physical attacks began at once. On 9 January, some eighty-seven strikers were arrested at Brawley. Three days later, Brawley police teargassed a hundred Mexicans. The strike was broken from that point onward, but the aftereffects lingered to give an ill odor to the valley. The authorities forbade an American Civil Liberties Union lawyer to speak in Brawley. When a court injunction ruled in favor of free speech, vigilantes kidnapped and beat him. Authorities made no prosecutions.[38]

A National Labor Board investigation, submitted 11 February, denounced violations of civil rights, but its call for federal action brought only the appointment of retired General Pelham D. Glassford as conciliator. In the meantime, vigilantes beat attorneys for the union and the International Labor Defense. Glassford, even while trying to butter up the growers in order to get scraps for the workers, saw only continued violence and left with a blast at the growers.

The Associated Farmers cared naught for denunciatory reports. By April 1934, they had ushered antipicketing laws through twenty-three counties, effectively destroying not only picketing but the right of assembly and free speech as well.[40]

The culminating blow for the CAWIU came from elsewhere. On 9 May, longshoremen struck the entire West Coast. On 13 May, the teamsters voted their support. The strike broadened and dragged on into June, involving more and more workers in the port of San Francisco. At a meeting on 23 June, the San Francisco Industrial Association, the chamber of commerce, the police commissioners, the chief of police, and the harbor commissioners decided that they would break the strike.[41]

Increasingly, during the maritime strike, those in established positions had raised the red scare throughout the state. On 24 June, police raided the Sacramento headquarters of the CAWIU. They arrested Caroline Decker, Pat Chambers, and twenty others. After being jailed for six months, fifteen went on trial for criminal syndicalism on 15 January 1935. The jury convicted five men and three women, including Chambers and Decker. The judge sentenced them to immoderately long terms. Not until 1937 did a higher court reverse the decisions and free the prisoners.[42]

By 1935, the Cannery and Agricultural Workers Industrial Union on the West Coast was dead several times over. The organizational core was immobilized for three years, in jail and in prison. The growers, through the Associated Farmers and vigilante methods, had frightened members away. And finally, the Communist party had withdrawn support from the union. As seen elsewhere, the tough policies of the Third Period were changing rapidly in 1934 as Stalin sought allies against the rise of Hitler. In June 1934, Jack Stachel, the party's labor expert, spoke of winning the millions within the American Federation of Labor, and on 17 March 1935, the Trade Union Unity League and all of its units dissolved, for the purpose of working within the AF of L.[43]

Despite its short life, the CAWIU had left a lasting mark. In 1933 it had led more agricultural workers in strikes than any other union in American history. It had fought hard not just for Marxist revolution but for decent conditions for one of the most deprived groups in all of American society. It had stirred the souls of a host of young idealists and a large number of writers who would later contribute stories and novels of the migratory worker. And, in a practical sense, it had raised the wages of California's migrants in a fashion which probably influenced rates for the rest of the decade.

The Cannery and Agricultural Workers Industrial Union had made its greatest mark in California in the early years of the decade, but it had been active elsewhere as well. It organized cotton workers in Arizona, sugar beet workers in Colorado and Montana, and vegetable and fruit workers in various states. In 1934, just as the fortunes of the western district were waning, the eastern district—there called the Agricultural and Cannery Workers Industrial Union (ACWIU)—faced a dramatic confrontation and produced a new leader for party work.

Southern New Jersey was a region of labor-intensive agriculture with crops grown for the nearby urban areas. The majority of units were small farms, but by 1930, Clarence Seabrook had amassed a four-thousand-acre enterprise near Vineland, similar to the factory farms of California. In early April 1934, the ACWIU struck Seabrook for wage hikes and union recognition. The time was critical for replanting seedlings from hothouse to field, and the company surrendered in four days.[44] Both sides recognized, however, that this was merely the preliminary skirmish.

Over the next weeks and months, lines were drawn. Seabrook, an innovative self-made millionaire, appealed to substantial growers, cannery owners, industrialists, and other businessmen, warning of the red menace.[45] The union, for its part, worked assiduously to build a united defense front behind its leader, Donald Henderson.

Henderson, a slender, sharp-faced young man was already something of a cause célèbre. As a student he had traveled to the Soviet Union with Rexford Tugwell in the 1920s. He taught economics at Columbia University in the early 1930s while working his doctoral dissertation. Activism held more charms than scholarship, however, and Columbia sacked him for not finishing the degree. For a time, Henderson's firing was one of the great causes among students in New York City.[46] Henderson now chose the path of becoming a Communist functionary. While organizing Seabrook, he held the title of Acting Section Organizer of the Communist Party.

In the interim between the April contract and late June, Communists rallied the unemployed in nearby towns and cities to gain sympathy and to prevent their recruitment as strikebreakers or vigilantes. This campaign was helped immeasurably by being led by William O'Donnell, an ex-state trooper and a member of the executive board of the local American Legion post. Some middle-class merchants and professionals, especially Jews, expressed sympathy for the workers. And finally, the party sent in one of its more experienced farm cadre men, Leif Dahl, to organize small farmers into locals of the United Farmers League.[47]

Seabrook forced a strike of his 250–300 workers late in June by reducing wages and cutting the laboring force. Each side accused the other of violence and of the importation of thugs. A small vigilante group of fewer than 30 was finally deputized by the sheriff, and law officers began arresting pickets. At one point the Communists claimed that 200 armed "Brown Shirts of America" rallied in Hammonton, only to be frightened off by a hastily organized antifascist league.[48]

After fifteen days, John A. Moffett, conciliator for the United States Department of Labor managed a settlement. Seabrook restored wages and rehired workers. Henderson opposed the settlement because it included a five-man mediatory board which the union did not control. Only a show of force by his supporters prevented a physical attack on him by vigilantes.[49]

The strike had served to polarize the area. The union had won and began a campaign of expansion. Its opponents, however, emphasized the Communist connection and launched a counterdrive which included such things as anti–free speech ordinances. The nature of the attacks on the union won great sympathy from liberal and labor groups, and the Agricultural and Cannery Workers Industrial Union did not suffer the crushing repression of its California counterpart. As a result, when the Trade Union Unity League dissolved early in 1935, the Seabrook union won a charter from the AF of L, and Donald Henderson, despite no particular display of competence, had laid his claim to national leadership in a campaign to organize agricultural workers.[50]

While the onset of the National Recovery Administration had stimulated activity among agricultural workers, particularly in California, and the optimism it had produced had encouraged the drive for higher wages and better conditions, the Sharecroppers Union faced critical problems caused by Roosevelt's reforms. The principal agency established for farm relief was the Agricultural Adjustment Administration. The Triple-A (or AAA), quite simply, operated under the thesis that there was a substantial surplus of agricultural commodities which had driven prices to their unprecedented low. The answer to this problem, bringing renewed prosperity, was to cut production through subsidy payments for taking acreage out of production. Since Congress had passed the law after the 1933 planting season, the administration instituted a one-time plan to cut production. It paid farmers to plow up every third or fourth row of cotton.

The sharecropper stood to gain little from the New Deal. Since payments, whether for crop destruction or acreage restriction, went to the planter, he had little incentive to share the check with the cropper. The planter himself, as often as not, was in economic difficulties, but he at least had political power. The voteless sharecropper had practically none. Moreover, when the planters cut the number of acres cultivated, after 1933, they had no reason to keep as many sharecroppers on the land as before. And if, through one fashion or another, the cropper brought pressure on the planter to share the government check, it encouraged the latter to desert the sharecropping system entirely and farm through the use of day laborers. Richard Hofstadter, writing in the late 1930s, conservatively estimated that almost one hundred thousand farmers in the Southeast, mostly sharecroppers, were displaced between 1933 and 1935, largely as a result of acreage reduction programs.[51]

The Communists, pointing to the hungry and ragged masses of unemployed throughout the country, did not subscribe to the surplus commodity theory of the New Deal. Articles in the *Southern Worker* attacked the AAA as a scheme to enrich planters and speculators while robbing tenants, croppers, and laborers through evictions, foreclosures, and chattel sales. The planters controlled selection of the local committees, and there was little that the union could do. Such was the desperation of the hapless sharecroppers, however, that by November 1933, the Sharecroppers Union claimed 5,500 members, and the *Southern Worker* reported that they were refusing to sign government checks made out jointly to planter and cropper.[52]

In 1933 and 1934 the Sharecroppers Union organized heavily in Alabama in the Black Belt counties of Lowndes, Dallas, and Montgomery. Here the progress of mechanization was much advanced over Tallapoosa and the earlier bases of strength. The plantations were more akin to the factory farms of California, and the use of day labor was heavy.

As a result the union claimed a rise in membership to ten thousand by December 1934.[53]

The recruitment of day laborers meant that the SCU became heavily involved in the problems of relief programs. A limited pickers' strike in the fall of 1934 led to higher wages on at least one plantation in Tallapoosa but also resulted in a new and worrisome confrontation with state and federal programs. The state relief administrator announced that all cotton pickers offered employment were expected to accept it, and he invited citizens to report those who did not.[54]

The SCU had become so effectively involved with the day-to-day problems of the poor rural black in the Southeast that it was much less affected by the shift in the world Communist movement in 1934 and 1935 than other party organizations. Rather than fading from the scene in March 1935 as did the Trade Union Unity League and the Cannery and Agricultural Workers Industrial Union, the SCU flourished, both in territory and membership, as it acquired a new secretary and expanded into Georgia, Mississippi, and especially Louisiana. When Clyde Johnson ("Tom Burke") took over as secretary early in 1935, he found a list of only twenty locals. After three months' travel, he located over two hundred, each with fifteen to twenty-five members.[55]

In May 1935, fifteen hundred union members staged a cotton choppers strike for a dollar a day wages and for the right to organize and picket. The planters intimidated the workers with the usual methods. There were several beatings and at least one murder, but the union claimed wage rises on about thirty-five plantations.[56]

Johnson began preparing for a fall pickers' strike. He moved the union headquarters to Montgomery and issued the mimeographed *Union Leader* along with propaganda flyers. On 19 August, pickers in Lowndes County spurned the proffered forty cents a hundredweight and demanded a dollar. All of the well-tested means of vigilante violence blossomed. The union reported at least six deaths and twenty beatings. Planters tried to hunt down union organizers, and Johnson had to flee Montgomery. He claimed that government trucks carried relief workers to be strikebreakers at fifty cents a hundredweight in addition to their relief wages. By mid-September, the pressures had become too intense for the strikers in Lowndes, and they went to work at the forty-cent rate.[57] In September the strike shifted to Tallapoosa, Chambers, Lee, and Randolph counties. Violence was less, and the union made substantial gains.

In the end, the SCU claimed that it had won total raises of forty thousand dollars for pickers outside Lowndes County.[58]

The strikes of 1935 were to be the last. In 1936 the union established its first open headquarters office in New Orleans, it held its first convention, and it began publishing the well-printed monthly *Southern Farm Leader*. These were only the final flourishes for the organization. The Popular Front line of the party and the dogmas of Donald Henderson soon spelled an end for the Sharecroppers Union.

Early in 1934, the Communists had papered together a National Committee for Unity of Agricultural and Rural Workers (NCUARW). Under this rubric they had submitted an extensive proposed budget, requesting $3,385 from the left-wing American Fund for Public Service (usually called the Garland Fund). In June, the directors of the fund granted $2,200.[59] Henderson used the money well to produce a showcase National Conference of Agricultural, Lumber, and Rural Workers in Washington, 9 January 1935. The majority of organizations represented former affiliates of the Trade Union Unity League—bitter opponents of the American Federation of Labor. Now a mood of sweetness and light prevailed. The convention recognized formal existence of the NCUARW and elected Henderson president. The Popular Front goal now was formation of a national farm workers union which would win a charter from the AF of L. The relatively new and naïve Southern Tenant Farmers Union was the major non-Communist group represented, and party leaders assiduously courted its good will.[60]

The NCUARW spent 1935 seeking AF of L charters for its locals. In August it began publishing the monthly *Rural Worker*. By summer there were twenty-three scattered catch-all locals, which included both agricultural and nonagricultural workers and eight purely agricultural locals in California, Florida, Washington, Arizona, Michigan, Ohio, and New Jersey. Organizers and money from Henderson's group contributed to eighteen strikes involving 13,500 workers outside California in 1935.[61]

As national prosperity seemed on the verge of returning in 1936, the fortunes of the agricultural workers locals flourished. With the aid of the teamsters and the longshoremen, farm unionism was even reviving in California. The National Committee to Aid Agricultural Workers (the rechristened NCUARW) claimed a total of seventy-two locals and confidently looked toward the upcoming convention of the AF of L for an international union charter.[62]

Henderson had now carefully sorted out in his mind the guidelines for organization in the South. In 1936, the word went out to the Sharecroppers Union to dissolve as an independent entity. In its birth state, Alabama, the small farmers, tenants, and sharecroppers were to apply for charters in the Alabama unit of the National Farmers Union, a move which would obviously aid the growing Popular Front forces in that group. Wage workers, on the other hand, were to join the Agricultural Workers Union of Alabama, which received a federal charter from the AF of L early in 1937. In Louisiana, the SCU moved en masse into the National Farmers Union.[63]

The Sharecroppers Union had outlasted the Cannery and Agricultural Workers Industrial Union by almost two years. Each in its own fashion had contributed hope and perhaps some financial advancement for its hard-pressed supporters. But now the Communists had decided that their day was done. Unity of all nonfascist forces was the byword within the party.

Henderson went to the 1936 convention of the AF of L with high hopes for a union charter. He met with frustration and obstruction. The American labor movement was in great turmoil as John L. Lewis moved forward with his drive for industrial unionism in defiance of the craft union barons of the federation. Poverty-stricken agricultural workers and their Communist organizers were of small import among these larger events.[64]

Henderson and the Communists were to persist in their fight, however, and before the end of the decade, they would have their union within the new Congress of Industrial Organizations. But work among society's mudsills would founder in an acrimonious ideological and personalized duel between Henderson and H. L. Mitchell of the Southern Tenant Farmers Union.

THE FARMERS NATIONAL COMMITTEE
FOR ACTION AND
THE UNITED FARMERS LEAGUE

THE WINTER OF 1932–33 was perhaps the worst for the American people since that of Valley Forge during the war for independence. A repudiated president sulked for four months in the White House, almost as powerless as the president-elect, who could only await the day of inauguration. Unemployment grew to staggering proportions. Hoovervilles of cardboard and tin shacks blossomed in city dumps and public parks. Tens of thousands of youths—male and female—rode the rails to none knew where. Businesses failed, money disappeared, and banks closed their doors.

In the Midwest, farmers burned corn in cookstoves and furnaces. The *Des Moines Register* printed recipes for meals made from dried field corn. Thrifty homeowners used cracked corn in place of ashes on icy sidewalks. State agricultural colleges experimented with grain alcohol as a cheap substitute for gasoline.[1]

Into this atmosphere, those who had attended the Farmers National Relief Conference brought home a program of hope in the midst of despair. The solid cornerstone of the program was the demand to save the family farm from tax sale, foreclosure, or dispossession. Planning began almost at once to hold a series of state relief conferences as legislatures assembled early in the new year, but even before these were held, a variety of organizers and speakers carried the program to rural areas.

In Nebraska, the left, as represented by advocates of the Madison County plan, already had strategically placed advocates in the Farm Holiday Association: vice-president Tony Rosenberg, secretary-treasurer Andrew Dahlsten, and state organizer Harry Lux. The latter, a flamboyant, red-wigged orator, stormed around the state handing out memberships like lollipops. By spring, he had distributed some thirty thousand of the Farm Holiday's red cards. Lux was either a party member already or became one within the year. Rosenberg and Dahlsten may have briefly joined the party—the evidence is tenuous.[2]

In eastern South Dakota, delegate Roy Miller organized a meeting late in December 1932, which gained the United Farmers League two of its strongest workers. Knute Walstad, a respected Norwegian farmer who had been candidate for railroad commissioner on old Coin Harvey's Liberty party ticket, became an especially effective proponent of a legal moratorium on all debts. His son, Julius, soon developed into an even more fiery speaker and organizer. Working with the Farm Holiday and the Unemployed Councils, the UFL made dispossession almost impossible through a broad swath of South Dakota.[3]

The Communist-sponsored local committees of action were perfect weapons to use in the farmers' fight to retain their land, and if no stronger organization had entered the field, they might have won great popularity in wide areas during this time of troubles. To the Communists' chagrin, however, Milo Reno and his Minnesota and North Dakota lieutenants, John Bosch and Usher Burdick, had stolen at least half a step on them.

As early as 19 September 1932, the Farm Holiday Association executive committee had ordered units to use all power to stop foreclosures. Glenn Miller, head of the Iowa Farmers Union, wrote in the 19 October issue of his newspaper that even if a new president were elected to replaced Hoover, thousands might be landless before he could act—if farmers did not. By November the Farm Holiday Association had perfected its instrument, the local council of defense, made up of from five to eleven members, almost always all farmers.[4] The idea of the council of defense soon spread throughout Holiday territory—Iowa, Minnesota, the Dakotas, Montana, Wisconsin, and even beyond—as pleas poured into Reno's office for plans of operation.

The councils acted as quasi-judicial bodies in handling three types of disputes: (1) between mortgagor and mortgagee, when the latter could not maintain full payments but wanted to retain possession; (2) between the same two parties but with the latter wishing to surrender possession without incurring further debt—as by a deficiency judgment ruled by a court, which could bring the sale of cattle, equipment, tools, and even certain household effects for the benefit of the mortgagor; (3) disputes between owners and renters.

In the first instance both sides could present their cases, and generally the council called for a scaling down of principal and interest during the emergency. In the second instance, the problem could be solved if the council convinced the mortgagor to bid in the foreclosure at the full price of the debt, eliminating the need for a deficiency judgment. In the third instance, the council often tried to reach an agreement by which past rents owed would be scaled down and those for the near future ameliorated.[5]

By early January 1933, Reno was jubilantly boasting that thousands of sales had been stopped. Not all were the result of the mediation of the councils of defense. Reno wrote to a California dentist, "The truth is, that the farmers are carrying too many ropes under their coats for to continue foreclosures in the state of Iowa."[6]

The conciliatory work of the councils of defense received far less publicity than did the instances where no compromise was reached. Each type of case required special techniques. Farm foreclosures were the most difficult, and the absolute rate of success may not have been high once conciliation was refused. By early 1933 most insurance companies were willing to accept some form of moratorium if their interest were preserved.[7] Joint-stock land banks, individual investors, and the receivers of failed banks often demanded satisfaction in full, however.

To block a sale was difficult, but fear of dispossession led to desperate measures. Local leaders would first try to persuade the sheriff not to call the sale; if this did not succeed, they sometimes held him captive till the hour had passed. All else failing, a gathering crowd tried to disrupt the sale or prevent bidding. The United Farmers League had staged an early action of this type in Ontonagon County, Michigan, 24 November 1931, and John Bosch used a similar technique in Minnesota at about the same time.[8]

Foreclosure sales at less then full value were a particular bane to the poor farmer. They brought on deficiency judgments and, in turn, the auctions of animals, machinery, and goods to make up the deficit. The farmers first tried to persuade the lender or his agent to bid in the foreclosure at full mortgage value, precluding any judgment. When early in January, a Le Mars, Iowa, lawyer attempted to bid thirty thousand dollars for a farm mortgaged for thirty-three thousand dollars, farmers from a mob of 750 grabbed him, kicked him down the courthouse steps, and hauled him to the telegraph office with a noose. The cowed attorney wired New York Life Insurance Company for permission to bid in the full price, stating, "My neck is at stake." Within a few hours the company agreed, but the attorney later had a mental breakdown.[9]

In resisting chattel sales, resulting from deficiency judgments, rental disputes, or failed personal loans, the farmers combined hardheaded realism with humor by inventing the "Sears Roebuck" or "penny," sale. The mechanics were simple. A crowd of farmers gathered at the sale and quietly informed any prospective buyers to remain silent. When the auctioneer began, selected bidders signaled two or three offers, and then the bidding stopped. A team of horses might go for $0.50, a tractor for $0.25, milk cows for $0.10 each. At auction's end, the items went back to the original owner. Theoretically, the debt was settled. Woe unto any unauthorized bidder! He tempted the fate of being dunked in the horse trough or worse. Farmers took pride in the first penny sale in their area but usually had vaguely heard of an earlier one. Apparently the first reported by the newspapers was held near Moville, Iowa, in August 1932. A former landlord seized the cattle of a distressed farmer, but on the day of the auction a host of farmers submitted a strange assortment of bids, amounting in all to $11.80. The debt had been legally settled, however, and the purchasers donated the cattle to the original owner. Six weeks or so later, the Madison County, Nebraska, Farm Holiday group similarly came to the aid of the widow Theresa von Bonn and bought her chattels for $14.00.[10] As the penny sale became more systematized, prices became even lower.

In one further instance farmers organized to protect their property from sale for tax delinquency. As early as December 1931, farmers in at least twelve Iowa counties had peacefully halted all tax sales, according to Sen. Smith W. Brookhart.[11] Tax delinquency sales presented fewest problems. Farmers knew the date in advance; county officials were neighbors and friends who had to face biennial election. The plan followed in Woodbury County, Iowa, late in 1932 reflected that of hundreds of others throughout the Midwest.

The county treasurer prepared to put hundreds of acres on the block to satisfy $450,000 of unpaid taxes. But not a square inch changed hands. An estimated crowd of five hundred pushed into the treasurer's office and jammed the corridors as the sale hour neared. When the first parcel was called, dead silence reigned. Soon the official speeded the process by reading only the description of the first property in a township and asked for bids on any other in that township. Within fifty minutes the procedure was over, and the sale postponed for thirty days, when a similar process would occur. Postponements of tax sales occurred in two-thirds of Iowa counties on that day.[12] For months afterwards the same ritual was followed until conditions ameliorated.

The Farm Holiday Association was not alone in fighting to save the farm home. A loosely organized United Farmers of Iowa, begun in the fall, followed the same tactics of conciliation but with less emphasis on direct action. In various places there were the Modern '76ers, the Farmers Relief League, the Loyal Order of Picketeers, and others.

The United Farmers League, as the originator of the slogans of direct action for preserving the farm home, and the Farmers National Committee for Action, as its united front extension, stood as Reno's most prominent rivals in the battle against dispossession. Once the Communists became aware of the rise of the councils of defense, they denounced them bitterly for being mere pale copies of the committees of action.[13]

There were intrinsic differences between the two. The councils of defense sincerely tried to compromise and conciliate, and sometimes they even found in favor of the landowner or mortgage holder. They disrupted foreclosures or staged penny sales only when negotiations failed. By their very nature they recongnized the condition which created them as being extraordinary but temporary. In a year or, at most, a few years, the old verities would apply and the old system—modified, perhaps—would work. The committees of action, on the other hand, scorned compromise and sought confrontation. They were built on the belief that the old order was breathing its last. A new order—the dictatorship of the proletariat —was in store for the near future. Confrontation sharpened class conflict. Physical clashes and arrests would demonstrate to farmers the classic unfairness of the old order, and they would inevitably be led to see that the last hope for a decent life lay in an alliance with the urban workers, their only friends.

Not that the individual farmer in the midst of debt and poverty was expected to recognize these differences. The immediate aim was to preserve the farm home. And so it was that in Iowa and much of the rest of the Midwest the Farm Holiday Association and its councils of defense went about their task in a fashion not too different from the UFL and the committees of action in the northern sections of Michigan, Wisconsin, and Minnesota, in eastern South Dakota, and much of Nebraska. In North Dakota and Montana, and, indeed, in many of the states already mentioned, the organizations worked together on the local level and oftentimes were indistinguishable.[14]

The Communist leadership, however, always pressed for ideological distinctions from the other organizations. When the angry farmers of Le Mars, Iowa, halted the foreclosure action on 5 January, 1933 and roughed up attorney H. S. Martin, Mother Bloor soon appeared on the scene and encouraged the crowd to march on the state legislature to present demands for a halt to all dispossession. The local council of defense blocked the proposal for the time being, but in neighboring states the Communist-influenced organizations staged a succession of relief marches and conferences.[15]

Nebraska was the state for which the party held great hopes. The erratic governor, Charles W. Bryan (William Jennings's younger brother), had done little to soften the terrible farm problems, and the party seemed to have a strong cadre for seizing control of the state Holiday Association in the Madison County group. The party prepared, moreover, to send its most persuasive functionaries to the Nebraska relief conference, headed by Lem Harris, executive secretary of the Farmers National Committee for Action.

Harris, just beginning his long career as the party's agricultural expert, sometimes had problems convincing skeptical farmers of his bona fides. Tall and slender, with receding hairline and rimless glasses, he looked more like a college professor than a regular dirt farmer. Put to the test, however, he could skillfully milk cows, pitch hay, and tinker ailing tractors into operation. His agricultural competence came not from family background, although a grandfather had been a western land speculator. Harris's father had gone from a career as a grain exporter to form one of the largest stock brokerage firms on Wall Street. Born in 1904, Harris grew up in the luxury—and loneliness—of a wealthy home. Graduated in history from Harvard in 1926, he went to work on the dairy of a Bucks County, Pennsylvania, Quaker farmer, staying there until 1929. Roger Baldwin of the American Civil Liberties Union introduced him to Hal Ware in that year. Two years in the Soviet Union with Ware, working on collective farms and in farm implement factories, determined him that Communism held the answers for the suffering world. He returned to the United States with Ware in 1931, unconvinced that he could aspire to the exalted status of Communist party member.

Earl Browder, general secretary of the party, persuaded him otherwise and personally signed his membership card.[16]

Although cut off by his father, Harris unselfishly poured the slender allowance provided by his mother into party work. His support kept Farm Research Incorporated, the major interest of the scholarly Ware, in business. He proved himself to be a successful fund raiser in the party, always pleading for money. After some false starts he became a first-rate farm speaker, and he charmed groups, large and small, with a warm and engaging personality.

Harris's first major task after the successful conclusion of the Washington relief conference was to organize the Nebraska, South Dakota, and North Dakota conferences. Nebraska was already presenting some problems for the party. Leif Dahl, a Columbia University student-movement dropout, who had helped Andrew Dahlsten formulate the Madison County plan, had become persona non grata to his former friends. In an enthusiastic article, he had referred to "open warfare" on the "agrarian front," backed by the Nebraska Holiday's "Red Army," and had compared the committees of action to the revolutionary soviets of 1905 and 1917.[17]

A horrified Andrew Dahlsten had complained about the bad effect of Dahl's article and demanded that he be kept out of Nebraska in the future. A red scare was building up among the original Madison County group, which would eventually nullify their utility to the party. On the other hand, in mid-January, Dahlsten was confident of routing the Reno faction in Nebraska, if the problems of money could be whipped. He forced the Farmers National Committee for Action to come up with one-hundred dollars for his treasury and another sixty dollars to cover the Nebraskans' expenses at the Washington conference.[18]

Tony Rosenberg officially announced on 23 January a march on the legislature for mid-February to demand that body legalize the farmers' methods for halting evictions of all kinds. Governor Bryan attempted to start a backfire by appointing a seven-man board of conciliation to get debtors and creditors together. He selected a banker, a businessman, the tax commissioner, and the heads of the four state farmers' organizations —the Grange, Farmers Union, Farm Bureau, and Holiday. The Madison County group leveled such attacks on Harry Parmenter of the Holiday, however, that he withdrew. As the time for the march grew closer, the nervous governor proclaimed a mortgage moratorium—a move purely advisory and without legal force—and the legislators rushed a moratorium bill toward completion.[19]

Although Rosenberg had first predicted a rally of fifty thousand, and later of twenty thousand, the actual number of marchers was about four thousand. The figure was impressive, however, in view of the winter cold and the general farm poverty. Parmenter and Rosenberg signified the split in the state Holiday by presenting separate demands to the legislature. Parmenter called for enactment of a two-year moratorium on foreclosures with administration left to district judges. The Rosenberg group presented the essence of the Madison County plan, calling for cessation of all evictions.[20]

Parmenter and his assistant, F. C. Crocker, cried communism and hinted darkly of Moscow gold distributed in Nebraska. Harris privately complained that Nebraska was "a bare victory." The excited farmers at the conference had gone beyond the bounds of the party's careful program by pushing for a huge issue of greenbacks to meet the debt problem —an inflationary solution which the Communists had long scorned.[21]

Harris enjoyed the relief conferences in the Dakotas a good deal more. They were numerically smaller but politically much more sophisticated. The two Dakotas had strong United Farmers Leagues as well as party fractions in the Farmers Union and Farm Holiday. Behind the leadership of men such as Clarence Sharp, Julius Walstad, and Homer Ayres in South Dakota, and Ashbel Ingerson and Pat Barrett in North Dakota, opposition attempts to disrupt the conferences were dismayed and the usual demands laid before the legislatures.[22]

The North Dakota situation proved particularly favorable. Farmers had suffered from low prices and drouth, taxes and evictions, and grasshoppers and bankers to such an extent that many were losing faith even in their supposedly radical politicians. Charlie Taylor, national chairman of the UFL since his appointment by Browder in December, spent part of February organizing the relief conference. He won endorsement from five legislators and claimed he could as easily have had twenty. He was most sanguine about prospects, not just for United Farmers League but for the Communist party as well. Speakers at a counter-conference called by Charlie Talbott of the Farmers Union were simply echoing the United Farmers League program, and Taylor wrote Hal Ware that concentrated work by the Communists might well win political control of the state.[23]

The farmers' winter of trial and confrontation had begun to produce results even as the state relief conferences met. As early as January the Democratic governors of Wisconsin and Iowa had issued proclamations practically demanding an end to foreclosures.[24] Other midwestern executives followed after. Then, early in February, the Iowa legislature began the parade of laws in the individual states which placed foreclosure moratorium proceedings completely in the hands of the court system. The legislation clearly fit the needs of the financial establishment and nowhere approached either the demand for repudiation, coming from the Farmers National Committee for Action, or the long-term, farmer-controlled moratoriums of Reno's Farm Holiday. Indebted owners petitioned for a continuance of any foreclosure action until 1 March 1935. If the court approved, it became the receiver for the land, apportioning all revenues.[25] Neighboring states adopted laws nearly identical to Iowa's.

Communists began attacking the new legislation at once. The laws, they wrote, had a twofold purpose: to rescue financial institutions whose investments were in danger of complete loss and to halt the mass-struggle movement among farmers.[26]

Legal arguments over the new laws began immediately, with local judges sharply disagreeing over the constitutionality of the legislation.[27] The Communists staged a more direct challenge. Harry Lux, state organizer for the Nebraska Holiday Association, tried to stop a foreclosure sale at Wilber on 15 March, after passage of the new law. The authorities rapidly arrested him, tried him, and fined him $250. Although he appealed to the state supreme court, the conviction and fine stuck.[28]

At the same time that farmers began doubting the efficacy of the state moratorium laws, their anger grew over the dawdling of Congress. On the first day of the special session in March, the national legislature had shouted through an emergency bill to save the banks. Relief for farmers dragged on during March and April as rural exasperation mounted. Then a series of violent confrontations shocked the nation.

Plymouth County, Iowa, had probably produced more pickets during the strike of 1932 than any other area. The Farm Holiday and council of defense had been especially active in fighting dispossession over the winter. The situation grew increasingly tense in April when a sullen band of several hundred farmers prevented the dispossession of a poor family, the Durbands, from their land a number of times.

During a near incredible two days late in April, the frustrations of western Iowa farmers boiled to the surface. On the morning of 27 April, some six hundred farmers attempted to stop a foreclosure sale at Primghar in neighboring O'Brien County. The sheriff, who had been tipped off in advance, met the angry crowd with a force of special deputies armed with ax handles. The sale went ahead, but not before combat on the courthouse stairs which left several of the leading protestors bloodied.[29]

The defeat in Primghar rankled, and many of the mob drove to Le Mars, seat of Plymouth County. There they first threatened to lynch a man who had recently foreclosed a neighboring farm, and then about a hundred trooped to the courthouse. District Judge Charles C. Bradley had on his docket for early May several cases in which insurance companies were challenging the mortgage moratorium law. The farmers had determined to demand from Bradley a pledge upholding the constitutionality of the legislation. Their entry into the courtroom was noisy, and Bradley primly ordered them to be quiet. Their accumulated rage burst forth. They seized the judge, dragged him down the stairs, and tried to force the pledge from him. When he resisted, they hauled him to the edge of town, put a rope around his neck, and began tightening it. Sanity prevailed, however late, and they allowed Bradley to trudge alone back to town, minus his trousers.[30]

On the following day, a flying wedge of wrathful farmers in Crawford County broke up a chattel sale at Denison and gave severe beatings to several state agents. Governor Clyde Herring acted swiftly. Activating several companies of national guardsmen, he placed Crawford, O'Brien, and Plymouth counties under martial law. Within hours the militiamen began rounding up suspects and throwing them into barbed wire enclosures.[31]

The extent of the violence came as a surprise, probably even to those involved, but there is no evidence that the Communists were involved. Hal Ware had visited the picket lines several times during the preceding fall, however, and Mother Bloor had established a regional office of the Farmers National Committee for Action in Sioux City and had good relations with several farmers in the Le Mars area. Some farmers may now have seen the imposition of martial law as the first wave of the fascist repression predicted by Ware and Bloor. At any rate, a delegation of them called on Bloor for arms and men to help. One can well imagine the combination of surprise and momentary exhilaration which must have seized the aged radical at the prospect of the revolution actually beginning amidst Iowa's cornfields. The cautious functionary in Bloor took over at once, however, and she offered the angry farmers cups of tea while explaining that the proper moment for revolution had not yet arrived.[32]

Lem Harris for the FNCA issued a special bulletin appealing to all farm groups to support the arrested farmers, who, it seemed at the time, were to be tried by courts martial. Harris called the moratorium law flimsy at best, but he excoriated judges who refused to uphold it for being tools of Wall Street. He connected the Iowa arrests to the arrest of Harry Lux, the seizure of five Michigan UFL members for "criminal syndicalism," and the murder of four Alabama sharecroppers as part of the "organized persecution" of militant farmers by the "money interests." Harris lightly censured the Le Mars farmers for deserting the proven success of united action for the mistaken policy of individual intimidation of the judge.[33]

Closer to home, the Sioux City regional office of the FNCA circulated a mimeographed flyer, *Why National Guard in Le Mars?* With little subtlety, it attacked Governor Herring and the National Guard as collection agents for Wall Street. It closed with a demand for a withdrawal of the militia and a mass demonstration in Des Moines, 4 May.[34]

National Guard officers had been hinting darkly about outside agitators. The flyer gave them evidence enough. Although Sioux City was not under martial law, the lax observance of civil liberties in the 1930s allowed a detail of national guardsmen to raid the regional headquarters of the FNCA, seize literature, place four people—not including the absent Bloor—under arrest, and lodge them in the city jail "pending further instruction." Three days later they were released from "open charges" along with two typewriters and a mimeograph machine, but not their literature.[35]

Lem Harris had not been alone in questioning the assault on Judge Bradley. Milo Reno had even more directly decried the action, as much as he understood its provocation. Both men discerned that a physical attack on the near sanctity of the judiciary depleted the store of good will farmers had accumulated in their relatively peaceful defense of the farm home during the winter.[36]

The intermittent enforcement of the moratorium laws and the failure of Congress to pass relief legislation had brought direct fire from both the Farm Holiday Association and the Farmers National Committee for Action, even though their solutions to the problem differed greatly. Reno had scheduled a national convention of the Holiday to meet in Des Moines 3 May to assess the situation. Attendance rules were lax, and several farm protest groups were represented. Former State Senator Lars Skromme led a group of the United Farmers of Iowa; the charismatic, goateed, pistol-packing Walter Singler brought a delegation of strike-tested Wisconsin dairy farmers; there were Modern '76ers from the Primghar riot area; and a substantial number represented the FNCA and the left wing of the Nebraska Holiday.[37]

The Communists—Charlie Taylor, Mother Bloor, Harry Lux, and Rob Hall, editor of the *Farmers National Weekly*—acted mostly as observers and reporters. The earlier Le Mars poster had called for a march on the governor's office at ten on the morning of 4 May. The caucus decided not to attempt it, fearing the immediate arrest of Bloor. Lux, as national committeeman for the Farm Holiday from Nebraska, tried to gain the floor to propose a march on the capitol, but went unrecognized. The same was true of Taylor's attempt to read greetings from Lem Harris.[38]

A. C. Townley, the original organizer of the Nonpartisan League, tried to use the convention as a means of staging a comeback through selling a national scrip money program, to be administered by councils of farmers and workers, but Reno carefully shunted him aside as the head of a study committee. The real business of the convention, recognized by all, was whether to vote for a new farm strike to pressure Congress to pass the cost-of-production plan, introduced into the Senate by George Norris.[39]

The Roosevelt administration had rather carefully ushered through its own farm relief program based on the voluntary domestic allotment idea of Professor M. L. Wilson and others. Its basic feature was to reduce the commodity surplus and thus raise prices by taking acreage out of production.[40] John Simpson had gotten the respected Norris to attach the cost-of-production scheme as an amendment to the omnibus agriculture bill. Under this, the president could use the cost of production plan at his option. The new secretary of agriculture, Henry A. Wallace, had a deep hatred for Reno, however, and was determined to block passage of the amendment.

Reno wanted his delegates to vote a tentative strike, which he could call off if he were satisfied with the progress of farm relief. But Walter Singler and other hotheads practically forced a mandatory strike, to begin 13 May, with only narrow exceptions.[41]

Reno backed off from the responsibility for running the strike, and it was placed in the hands of an executive committee headed by Townley. The latter picked Lux as his Nebraska representative. This perplexed the Communist caucus. On the one hand, Lux could propagandize for the united front and for direct action, but on the other, he feared that the wily Townley would claim that he had sold out to the Reno forces.[42]

The Communist position was to favor the strike. They opposed the Roosevelt program as a combination of the economics of scarcity and an attempt to rescue creditors at the expense of farmers. They also, more quietly, were against the cost-of-production plan as a futile delusion. The strike itself, however, would bring confrontations, picketing, and the sharpening of important immediate demands concerning dispossession.[43]

During the next week and a half Reno had to prepare for a strike which he was half-hearted about at best, while Congress struggled to put the farm bill in final form. Wallace fought tenaciously to exclude the cost-of-production plan, and in spite of the support of Senators Norris, Frazier, and Wheeler, it lost on 10 May. Now the strike seemed certain, but Reno frantically searched for a way out. Even without his pet plan, the omnibus legislation which passed had programs for inflation, credit relief, and—in the domestic allotment plan—at least the promise of higher incomes.[44] On the day before the strike was to begin, Reno got assurances from Floyd B. Olson, the Farmer Laborite governor of Minnesota, that President Roosevelt would call for a national mortgage moratorium until New Deal measures could bring relief. It was enough, and Reno called off the strike at the eleventh hour.[45]

Reno's action brought bitterness and near revolt from some of his most devoted followers. The Communists, too, were vitriolic in their denunciations.[46] In the practical sense, Reno had played the right game. Farmers were busy with field work in May and had no major commodities, save perishables, to hold off the market. For the time being Reno was content to let the administration experiment—a sentiment which the majority of farmers seemed to share. Foreclosures and evictions, and the consequent reactions, died down partially as the result of the emergency state laws, however imperfect, and partially because both debtors and creditors expected relief from Washington.

Indeed, the summer of 1933 was a time of rising aspirations and lowered voices. Governor Herring quite sensibly ignored the demands of those who would have tried the rioters under martial law in western Iowa and decided to restore civil government in the occupied areas as rapidly as possible. By August the courts had handed down relatively light sentences—mostly suspended jail terms—to fifty-three defendents in Primghar, Le Mars, and Denison.[47]

Roosevelt's appointments encouraged optimism. Henry Wallace, the secretary of agriculture; George Peek, head of the Agricultural Adjustment Administration; and Hugh Johnson, chief of the National Recovery Administration, had all fought for government assistance to farmers throughout the 1920s. Johnson's noisy crusade during the summer for the new NRA codes of fair practice created a mood of hope accompanied by a moderate rise in prices and industrial activity. The market price of corn began to climb in late spring. In February it had stood at twelve cents a bushel. In May it reached thirty-one cents, leveled off in June, and peaked at forty-seven early in July.[48] Since few farmers still had corn on hand to sell, the boost was mainly psychological, but it contributed to the mood of hopeful anticipation among many farmers in the summer of 1933.

Both the Communists and the Farm Holiday Association faced a time of lull after the long period of hectic activity. The perceptive Lem Harris noted that farm organizations were falling apart as spirit declined. Reno was particularly bogged down. The Holiday Association, despite a following of several hundred thousand, had little in the way of structured organization, and practically no dues flowed to headquarters. Reno operated out of the Iowa Farmers Union offices and charged his telegrams to their account. His nine-thousand-dollar salary as president of the Farmers Union Mutual Insurance Company covered most of the rest of the Farm Holiday Association expenses. A lawsuit, early in June, by two former members sought to place the company in receivership. Reno devoted much of his energy until early fall in fighting the suit and reorganizing his company.[49]

As for the Communists, late spring and summer became a time of self-criticism and analysis, with a modicum of organizational activity.

Farmers with a wait-and-see attitude could no more be forced into action by the United Farmers League than by the Farm Holiday—or, for that matter, by the Farm Bureau. Clarification of positions and consolidation of gains became the order of the day.

The UFL and the committees of action had established themselves firmly, if not in great numerical strength, in upper Michigan, northern Wisconsin, Minnesota, North and South Dakota, and Montana. Charlie Taylor's ambition of opening a full-time office in Minneapolis and transferring *Producers News* to that central location came to naught, however, for lack of money. More distant league units existed among small farmers in the three Pacific Coast states and occasionally assisted the burgeoning Cannery and Agricultural Workers Industrial Union. The closely allied United Farmers Protective Association had over a thousand members in New Jersey and eastern Pennsylvania. Whatever the party line during the Third Period, local leaders often closely collaborated with the Farm Holiday and the Farmers Union in rent, tax, and mortgage struggles.[50]

The great disappointment was the Nebraska Holiday Association. The march on the capital and the militant activities of the rest of the winter had taken away most of the Holiday members from Reno's man Parmenter, leaving him with little more than a paper organization. The Madison County leaders were proving weak reeds, however. Andrew Dahlsten wanted respect as philosopher-king of the movement, and his sons wanted power without work. Tony Rosenberg had turned suspicious and surly, and he had welcomed a Nebraska visit by A. C. Townley, who raised great fears among the Communists because of his charismatic demagoguery. The Communists could depend 100 percent only on Harry Lux, but he was not, strictly speaking, a farmer. Clouding the situation further was the growing resentment and anger of the wives and daughters of the local leaders, who found themselves socially stigmatized because of their husbands' and fathers' radicalism.[51]

By early summer the party had decided to cut its losses with Rosenberg and the Dahlstens. It dispatched Charlie Taylor, Rob Hall, and Otto Anstrom into Nebraska for two months to help Harry Lux revitalize the Holiday Association. Puro referred to them as the party's "best forces." Taylor, of course, was chairman of the UFL; Hall, the editor of *Farmers National Weekly*; Anstrom was a tough war veteran and former North Dakota farmer who had spent the 1920s in the Soviet Union teaching tractor driving to the peasants.[52]

In late June, the Nebraska Farm Holiday Association (Madison County plan) held its state convention in Loup City. Tony Rosenberg, chairman of the Washington conference and leader of the march on Lincoln, failed to make an appearance and disappeared henceforth from the stage of events. A pair of reliable Communist farmers, J. J. Schefcik and Carl Wiklund were elected president and vice-president. Harry Lux continued as organizer. Andrew Dahlsten made his peace well enough to remain secretary-treasurer. If the Reno Holiday Association had practically collapsed in Nebraska, the Communist-oriented Holiday was losing steam. The election of Schefcik and Wiklund signaled a shift of power from Madison County and the rich farmlands bordering the Missouri river to the poorer, drier farms of central Nebraska, centering on Sherman County.[53]

The summer lull brought other developments in the Communist farm movement. During the euphoric days of the Washington conference and the months thereafter, when deepening distress seemed about to push masses of farmers to revolutionary extremes, Lem Harris had attacked dues-collecting organizations and salaried leaders. For him the ad hoc committees of action would arise to meet a special need, radicalize the farmers of the area, and then dissolve. But what, others asked, would maintain the level of radicalism and forge the necessary alliances with the urban proletariat to consummate the revolution?[54]

Hal Ware provided one partial answer. He organized a school on wheels to travel around the country training a revolutionary cadre in Marxist history, philosophy, and tactics as adapted to rural areas. He acquired a Ford van and staffed it with an eager group of young people, led by Jerry Ingersoll, former Amherst student and son of the Bronx borough president.[55] For the next year the school on wheels led a gypsy existence, camping three or four weeks at each locality in Pennsylvania, Michigan, the Dakotas, Nebraska, and elsewhere, teaching both doctrine and method to selected rural leaders.

Although the Communist organizations did not challenge the Farmers Union or Reno's Holiday Association, let alone the Farm Bureau, in strength, their activity and potential influence were amazing, given the thinly spread nature of the leadership. It was a combination of party veterans and the dedicated young. On the one hand were Bloor, Ware, Omholt, Taylor, and Anstrom—none of whom with the exception of Omholt had recent experience in American farming; on the other, there were Harris, Hall, Ingersoll, Dahl, and others, largely drawn from middle to upper-class families and Ivy League education. The party's agrarian secretary, Henry Puro, a largely self-educated Finnish immigrant, had considerable praise for their work in an article published in June. Indeed, he took credit on behalf of Communist leadership for most of the "mass struggles" since the Washington conference and even for the passage of the mortgage moratorium laws.[56]

As much of rural agitation calmed down, however, Puro and others began to find fault. In a speech before an extraordinary conference of the Communist party, 7–10 July, he discovered rampant right-wing opportunism among those associated with the Farmers National Committee for Action. As a party careerist, he carefully avoided mentioning names, especially Harris and Ware, whose close connections to Browder were well known, but the policies he hammered at were patently theirs. Why, he asked, had the party always been kept quietly in the background while it provided the guidance for the Washington conference, for the United Farmers Protective Association in Pennsylvania, and above all, for the Nebraska Holiday Association? Whose fault was it that the latter group adopted the no-dues and no-salaries concept which had led to near collapse? What compromiser had actually editorially welcomed Reno's and Townley's *Farm Holiday News* in the pages of *Farmers National Weekly*—when such scoundrels had always to be attacked? Puro thundered that these mistakes must cease and that American farmers must be familiarized with Stalin's great speech, "To the Collective Farm Shock-Brigade Workers."[57]

On 1 September, Harris announced a second national farmers' relief conference to be held in mid-November in Chicago.[58] In part the strategy may have been to iron out the differences between Puro and his allies on the one hand and the Harris-Ware group on the other, but more importantly, farmer militancy was on the rise again and needed close attention. After the false dawn of commodity price rises in mid-summer, they dropped precipitously almost to the winter levels. Corn, for example, fell seventeen cents between 17 July and 20 July. At the same time the NRA-stimulated prices which farmers paid out rose at a rate higher than any previously recorded by the Bureau of Agricultural Economics. More and more farmers complained that the federal plans for refinancing mortgages were slow, complicated, and—as the Communists had already charged—written for the benefit of lenders, not borrowers.[59]

Emergency programs to reduce surpluses by paying farmers to plow up every third row of cotton and slaughter five million pigs brought cries of outrage from other, unaffected commodity raisers and feelings of guilt among the affected. The Farmers Union, Farm Holiday, and Communists each condemned the program of destruction, while the unemployed went ragged and hungry. A Manson, Iowa, lawyer wrote a grisly story of the poor seining the Missouri River downstream from packing plants to recover the little pig carcasses flushed down the sewers.[30]

Milo Reno, his insurance company problems solved, was about to embark on a new crusade. The annual Iowa Farmers Union convention in late September seated delegates from seventeen other states on the twenty-third and became an emergency session of the National Farm Holiday Association. The resolutions, as usual, laid great stress on inflationary measures, but the greatest attention centered on the scheme for an industrial code for agriculture to be proposed to Hugh Johnson and the NRA that would neatly circumvent Reno's old enemy, Henry Wallace. The code itself was a barely disguised version of the cost-of-production plan.[61] Wallace himself was privately warning Roosevelt that the NRA had overly impressed midwestern farmers. Politically they were very angry and might be able to force price-fixing at cost of production.[62]

A Farm Holiday delegation of Bosch, Parmenter, and Kennedy, which called on Roosevelt, was charmed by his careful generalities. Reno, who stayed home, was not and prepared for a new farm strike.[63] He hoped to win moral support from a new conference of worried farm-belt governors, but Governor Herring of Iowa delayed the convocation. Gov. William Langer then precipitated action in North Dakota by embargoing all wheat, effective 19 October, until prices reached the cost-of-production level. Langer's proclamation aroused Reno's combative spirit. An emergency session of directors of the Holiday Association called a farm strike to begin 21 October.[64]

Reno badly misgauged the mood of the farmers. They were angry at the slowness of recovery, but they had corn prices about three times those of a year earlier. Rightly or wrongly, they had viewed Hoover as their implacable enemy. They saw Roosevelt as a friend who was willing to experiment and eager to help but who had gotten a little too balled up in red tape. Moreover, the majority of them were engaged in the exhausting labor of corn picking, and duty in picket camps on cold October nights held no charms.

Shrewd politicians used the strike as a lever to win gains for farmers. Sen. Louis Murphy of Iowa wired Roosevelt that the situation was very bad, and what was needed was government loans of fifty cents for every bushel of corn which farmers would put in storage. Governor Herring frantically called Henry Morgenthau, Jr. of the Farm Credit Administration to warn that the roads were swarming with pickets. A cabinet meeting advised the president to adopt Murphy's scheme on the corn loans. Roosevelt followed up with a nationwide radio appeal to farmers on 22 October in which he announced selective gold purchases at variable levels for the purpose of raising commodity price levels—which farmers could read as a concession to their inflationary demands. FDR finished with a flourish, promising that if one program failed, then he would try another until he achieved the coveted goal of recovery.[65]

The heralded midwestern governors' conference finally met in Des Moines, 30–31 October. The executives essentially adopted the Farm Holiday program and carried it to Washington for meetings with Roosevelt and Wallace, 2–4 November. One by one, the national leaders shot down the proposals, and the governors returned empty-handed. All were apprehensive of their reception back home. Schmedeman of Wisconsin reportedly fortified himself with strong drink. Langer feared that the hard-working Communists in North Dakota would drive him out of office in a recall election. He concocted a blustery story of having pounded the president's desk and having stormed out.[66]

The strike caught the Communists by surprise. They supported it as a manifestation of desperation and farmer militance, but they severely criticized the lack of goals, planning, or preparation. It was almost, they charged, as if Reno had arranged for it to fail.[67] Violence soon became a measure of the inefficacy of the strike compared to that of 1932. Night riders bombed dairies in Wisconsin and railroad bridges in Iowa.[68] By early November, some of the strongest supporters of the earlier strike had formed organizations to convoy commodities to market.[69]

On 8 November, Wallace announced that the Commodity Credit Corporation would loan forty-five cents per bushel for corn stored under seal—about ten cents above the market price. Wallace made an almost triumphant tour of the Midwest. By 11 November the strike was dead, although Reno did not officially end it until eleven days later. The administration dramatically flew corn loan forms from Washington to Iowa. Before the end of the month, the first farmer had cashed his check, and during the following month, millions of dollars descended like manna to guarantee the first merry Christmas in years. After a spring, summer, and early fall of floundering, the administration had within six weeks won the almost solid support of midwestern farmers.[70]

In the very midst of this drama, the Farmers National Committee for Action staged its second conference in Chicago. The conclave marked the party at the peak of its perceived strength in rural areas. Seven hundred and two delegates drawn from thirty-six states represented fifty-nine organizations and a claimed 114,885 farmers or farm workers. In delegates alone it was almost a threefold increase from a year earlier. Charlie Taylor presided over meetings in which delegate after delegate lashed out at the Roosevelt adminstration, its Agricultural Adjustment Administration which deluded farmers, its National Recovery Administration which betrayed workers, and its loan programs which saved the hides of bankers and insurance companies rather than farmers. The speakers, on the other hand, took great pride in claiming for the FNCA and UFL the credit for saving the family farmer from foreclosure or eviction through their direct action.[71]

The conference declared that salvation lay, not in dependence on corrupt legislators or administrators, but on constant direct action in a united fight against bankers, trusts and middlemen. It warned that as the administration increased its use of force to further its programs, fascism threatened.[72]

As oppression deepened, the conference warned, the farmers must sharpen their demands:

1. Direct cash relief with no collateral.
2. Cancellation of all debts for small and middle farmers.
3. An end to all dispossession and the reinstatement of the previously dispossessed.
4. Higher purchasing power through attacks on profits of the trusts.
5. Reduction or elimination of taxes for busted farmers.
6. Rent reductions.
7. The end of Negro oppression.[73]

To attain these ends, the delegates enthusiastically shouted their approval for united mass action: meetings, demonstrations, and, above all, the strike.[74] It was sadly ironic for the earnest delegates that they were describing and reliving the glory days of the past year. At the very time they met, Reno's strike was failing miserably; government checks were about to fall on the farm belt like a gently nourishing rain; and the vast majority of farmers were sincerely ready to allow the Roosevelt administration to have a fair try.

While the rank and file passed resolutions and applauded every speaker, a devious factional game was being played behind the scenes. Puro had come to resent those whom he felt diminished his stature as the party's agrarian secretary. He had already launched a veiled attack against Ware and Harris, but they were too secure to be assaulted directly. Charlie Taylor had no such protection; moreover, he lacked discipline and had the slight stench of Trotskyism. Erik and Ruth Bert hated the big man because he had ridiculed her for bungling a Young Communist League camp near Plentywood. Hall and Ingersoll tended to trail along behind Puro because they smelled connections to power, and the burly Finn intimidated Bloor.[75]

Puro had rapidly advanced one of his Minnesota Finnish protégés, Alfred Tiala. Shortly before the Chicago convention, Puro made Tiala national secretary of the United Farmers League and obviously tried to present him as its leading spokesman. At the convention, Puro attempted to maneuver Tiala into a position more prominent than Taylor. He failed, but his attacks on Taylor for the next year and a half were unremitting.[76]

Puro used the Chicago convention to win consolidation of three farm papers, the *Workers and Farmers Cooperative Bulletin,* the *Producers News* (National Edition), and the *Farmers National Weekly.* All were amalgamated under the last title, to be published in Chicago under the editorship of Bert and a board of directors controlled by Puro. Tiala set up a Chicago headquarters for the UFL, and Puro moved the agrarian secretariat there from New York. The hard-liners had congregated.[77]

The refurbished *Farmers National Weekly* appeared with the issue of 15 January, 1934. As rural agitation declined, Puro, Bert, and Tiala hewed more closely to the line of the Third Period than had the paper during 1933. Harris had moved the FNCA headquarters to Philadelphia and apparently had less to do with the direction of the paper. Ware remained in Washington with Farm Research. At a time when Taylor felt that Ware's extraordinary abilities were needed to bolster field work and conciliate factional conflicts, he pursued his penchant for statistical analysis.[78]

Despite the program of mass action proclaimed by the Chicago conference, only a handful of eviction fights remained. A Warsaw, Indiana, court sentenced Tiala to six months in prison for obstructing justice in a mortgage foreclosure.[79] What was perhaps the last major case came in a UFL stronghold, Roberts County, South Dakota. An insurance company had evicted Henry Neiland, a foreclosed owner, and replaced him with a tenant. A mob of several hundred drove the tenant off and put Neiland back in possession. The sheriff arrested Julius Walstad and seventeen others almost at once. The courts issued a massive injunction forbidding all gatherings of the UFL or the Unemployed Council. Those groups defied the injunction with several large rallies. At a trial in June, the jury speedily freed all of the accused. It was a splendid last hurrah. The Roberts County UFL declined rapidly thereafter in the face of a mass of federal relief checks and a mounting red scare.[80]

With the waning of mass action, factionalism within the movement rose further. John Barnett, an ideological ally of Puro, attacked the united front tactics of the Farmers National Committee for Action. United front tactics were correctly used, he wrote, only when Communist leadership was openly in the forefront. The FNCA also often skirted the connection for fear of being shunned. In the Dakotas and Wyoming, there had been too much emphasis on influencing the Farm Holiday Association to the detriment of the UFL. And finally, Barnett concluded in another slap at Taylor, the weak leadership of the United Farmers League led it to be dominated by the aggressive FNCA.[81]

Puro and Barnett followed up somewhat later by reproving both the Chicago conference and the FNCA for catering to farm owners—kulaks—rather than tenants and agricultural workers. Attacks on the concept of a national farmer labor party and on Trotskyism may have represented not-so-veiled threats to Taylor.[82]

With Ware busy in Washington and Harris preoccupied for a time in Philadelphia, Puro, the Berts, and their allies targeted Charlie Taylor for ideological isolation. When the Nebraska Holiday Association held its convention in Grand Island, 22–23 March, Puro and Ruth Bert maneuvered to have Taylor excluded. Less than a week later the executive council of the UFL met in Duluth and released Taylor from his duties as chairman.[83] Puro and Tiala increasingly used the UFL as the vehicle of the hard line, and the FNCA took a back seat.

Taylor's humiliation had still another course to run. The Eighth Convention of the Communist party was to meet in Cleveland, 2 April 1934. Lem Harris tactfully made a special trip to Taylor's retreat in Plentywood to take him to the convention. Puro, a member of the party's executive committee, blocked Taylor's seating and delivered a speech blasting him for the serious deviation of favoring a national farmer labor party and for resisting efforts of the party's central committee to correct him.[84]

Earl Browder took Taylor to dinner, listened quietly to his explanations, and ordered him to New York for two weeks. There the executive committee, according to Taylor, exonerated him but refused to embarrass their fellow member, Puro, by publishing their conclusions. Taylor was too valuable a worker to lose, and the party sent him to Nebraska as political advisor to the Holiday Association and its newspaper, the *Loup City Standard.* At about the same time, the party-liners finally expelled Andrew Dahlsten, father of the Madison County plan, from the movement.[85]

With Taylor in exile, the Third Period dogmatists dominated the Communist farm movement. In June 1934, the United Farmers League held its first and only national convention in Minneapolis. Fourteen states, from New York and New Jersey to California, sent 109 regular and 48 fraternal delegates.[86] Puro dominated. He denounced the old political parties and reformist leaders such as Milo Reno, Floyd B. Olson, William Langer, and Rodney Salisbury, the renegade former Communist sheriff of Sheridan County, Montana. On the other hand, he told the delegates, "The Communist Party has again proven to be the only party which is concerned with the lot of the ruined and drouth-stricken farmers." He lauded the farmers emergency relief bill, formulated at the recent Communist convention and introduced into the House by the maverick Terry Carpenter of Nebraska. It called for abolition of evictions and foreclosures, cancellation of debts and taxes for impoverished farmers, and cash relief administered by farmers themselves.[87]

Puro stressed the problems of the terrible drouth in 1934 and called for unity in the relief struggle with members of the Farmers Union, Holiday, and cooperatives—while berating their leaders. Reino Tantilla, later killed in Spain, upbraided those who had not used every struggle to build a strong UFL. From beginning to end the convention speakers stressed the narrowest of lines—with one exception. Lem Harris warned that unless league members sought support from other farmers, they stood in danger of isolating themselves.[88]

New officers reflected the hard line. The delegates ratified Tiala as president, Puro as secretary, and Ruth Bert as one of four vice-presidents —the others being Harry Correll of Oregon, Al Murphy of the Share-croppers Union, and Julius Walstad, the South Dakota firebrand.[89]

At a time when increasing numbers of farmers were turning gratefully to the federal government to receive its proffered help in surplus control, commodity loans to guarantee prices, mortgage assistance, and drouth relief, the United Farmers League launched its bitterest attacks on those programs and their initiators. The spirit of revolt had died down, and Puro was whistling in the wind by trying to pretend that it still existed.

In 1932 and 1933, the Communist farm movement had formed one current flowing freely in the stream of farm protest. By moving generally in the same direction, the UFL and FNCA had gained a certain influence and even prestige. By July 1934, the UFL was bucking the stream. Its influence had been reduced practically to a nullity.

Greater events were stirring throughout the world, however. Just at the point when Puro's Third Period dogma seemed unchallengeable, a mighty shift was about to occur.

COMMUNISTS, FELLOW TRAVELERS AND POPULAR FRONTERS

THROUGHOUT FIVE DECADES, historians have debated the Comintern's reasons for adopting the harsh policies of Third Period Communism in 1928. There are those who contend that the movement's leaders accurately foresaw the economic disaster which struck the capitalist world in the next several years. Others say it was Stalin's spiteful method of attacking Bukharin's desperate prattle about capitalist stabilization. The largest number of western experts, however, argue that Stalin used Third Period dogma to strengthen his case for the necessity of forced agricultural collectivization and heavy industrialization at home.[1]

There are fewer disputes about the sharp move from Third Period Communism to the Popular Front policy of seeking alliances at the leadership level with Socialists and even the liberal bourgeois.[2] The simplest answer is Stalin's fear of the ascendant Hitler and the possibility of a war of conquest directed against an isolated Soviet Union. The Popular Front became Comintern doctrine at the Seventh World Congress in 1935, but 1934 marked the true turning point.

Rioting fascist mobs in Paris, 6 February 1934, had precipitated the fall of the left-center Daladier government on the following day, bringing in a right-center government aimed at mollifying the rioters. French Communists had not collaborated with the rightist forces, but they had demonstrated against the government at the same time. The results may have appalled Communist leadership, because on 12 February their unions cooperated with the Socialist unions for the first time since 1929 in a general strike to oppose fascism. Unity with the Socialists in France was brief, however, in the absence of a clear directive from Moscow. Jacques Duclos and Maurice Thorez, leaders of the French Communists, continued to attack the Socialists as "social fascists" for several more months.[3]

Finally, by spring, Dmitry Manuilsky of the Comintern, with Stalin's tacit approval, had reached a decision. Manuilsky told the French party representative, Albert Vassart, in May that the time had come for a new line. Vassart carried the message to the conference of the French Communist party, 23–24 June, which dumped Third Period dogma and proposed an immediate alliance with the Socialist leaders for workers' unity against fascism—the Popular Front. The two parties signed the pact on 27 July.[4]

The French Communists, as the most powerful party outside the Soviet Union, often served as a doctrinal weather vane to lesser parties around the world. Others cautiously tested the wind until they were sure of its direction. In the same month that the Comintern was pushing a reluctant Maurice Thorez toward rapprochement with Leon Blum and the Socialists, the United Farmers League convention in America enunciated hard-line dogma and elected hard-line leaders.[5]

Through the rest of the summer, the UFL persevered in the policy of attacking liberal or radical but non-Communist farm leaders while trying to win away their followers. During the North Dakota Holiday convention late in July, Ashbel Ingerson, Charlie Taylor's friend, flouted the presence of Milo Reno, Usher Burdick, Governor Langer, and Senator Frazier to win almost unanimous endorsement of the Communists' farmers emergency relief bill, which among other things would have confiscated all farms not directly worked by the owners and would have granted them to the tenant in fee simple. The delegates probably saw Ingerson's proposal simply as one more slap at the hated money power, but Reno was growing increasingly irked at the infiltration of his meetings. He lashed out at "the deluded Communists who would do away with all orderly process." A regular correspondent of the *Farmers National Weekly* answered just as sharply. Reno's speech, according to Roy Dalziel, showed that he was either "a liar or an ignoramus" and that "the National Holiday needs a better man for its president."[6]

The *Weekly* did not neglect to include the New Deal in its list of abominations. Late in August, an editorial, presumably by Erik Bert, blasted Roosevelt's farm programs. It called for complete abolition of the Agricultural Adjustment Administration and claimed that the badly needed drouth relief program had turned out to be nothing less than a bureaucrats' nightmarish attempt to drive thousands of farmers off the land by withholding emergency feed from all except a tiny percentage of the suffering livestock. In the same issue, however, the Philadelphia office of the Farmers National Committee for Action took the moderate line of asking all farm groups to unite in seeking relief.[7]

For a couple of issues the newspaper was uncharacteristically quiet on substantive questions, as it concentrated on a subscription drive and other procedural matters. The number for 14 September, however, could have left the experienced reader with some anticipation. The executive committee of the United Farmers League, with almost full attendance, met for two days in Minneapolis early in September along with representatives of the Nebraska Holiday Association and the Workers and Farmers Cooperative Unity Alliance. The brief and vague report gave no satisfactory explanation for the lengthy session.[8]

The answer came a week later. The national office of the UFL offered the Farm Holiday Association a seven-point program for a united front against governmental policies of crop destruction. The message admitted that the two groups could not agree on all things, but the specific areas of agreement, such as drouth relief, should override previous quarrels. The striking break with the past was in the target at whom the message was aimed. After two years of trying to win the rank-and-file Holiday members away from their "misleaders," the UFL directed its proposals at the national board of the Farm Holiday Association, meeting in Des Moines, 18 September. As a backup measure, Puro ordered the UFL to begin collaboration with Holiday units on the state level wherever possible.[9]

The shift to the Popular Front had begun in American agriculture. It had taken only a short ten weeks from the time the powerful French party had made its initial move. In France, Leon Blum's Socialists had reacted precipitately, out of fear of the powerful rightist leagues. The Communist agricultural organizations in the United States faced a twofold problem: first, few Americans perceived a fascist menace in 1934, and second, two years of attacks had roused a bitter anger in that passionate man, Milo Reno. The Communists had either to win his trust or to neutralize him.

The path to the Popular Front was often strewn with boulders and lined with brambles. The national board of the Farm Holiday Association met in Des Moines concurrently with the convention of the Iowa Farmers Union. President John Chalmers of the Iowa Holiday proposed a new farm strike, but for the first time since 1931, both the Holiday and the Farmers Union refused to endorse the weapon. Reno was in his finest form. He took credit—ruefully—for the federal corn-hog program which he said had passed Congress only to prevent Holiday hell raising. He damned Hugh Johnson as a nascent dictator and attacked Henry Wallace for breaking the Ten Commandments: "And when you violate the principles of Jesus Christ, you're going plumb to hell and nothing in the world can stop you." He brought in his usual first-rate cast of outsiders. Bill Lemke and Ferdinand Pecora, the securities-crime investigator, each gave a stirring expose of the evils of corporate America.[10] But supporters of the new Popular Front line waited in disappointment for any acknowledgment. The Holiday board, meeting without fanfare, unanimously rejected the UFL proposal for an alliance. In answer to a query about the refusal, Reno frankly stated that the "Russian brand" Communists of the UFL had tried to destroy the Holiday and that he had no more desire to work with them than with the fascists.[11]

The Holiday board not only rejected the UFL offer, it did not bother to reply, giving Erik Bert the opportunity to charge the Holiday with a nefarious campaign of silence. The climate for the Popular Front should have been more favorable in Minnesota. Locals of the Holiday and the UFL had cooperated often since the beginning of the movement. John Bosch, president of the Minnesota Farm Holiday and national vice-president, spoke on 12 September to a gathering in the UFL stronghold of New York Mills. He echoed the Popular Front line and warned of the dangers of war and fascism; he called for a government controlled by workers and farmers. It was not enough. Jim Flowers, state secretary of the UFL confronted Bosch with the charge that he and other Holiday leaders were "playing into the hands of the fascists and war makers" by sabotaging efforts at unity. This exchange gave Bert the editorial opportunity to endorse superficially an alliance with the Farm Holiday Association but quickly to revert to the old line of local interaction among the UFL, Holiday, and Farmers Union with implied leadership going to the Communists.[12]

For the next six months one could sense a tension in formulation of policies by the United Farmers League and *Farmers National Weekly*. The Puro-Bert group had great difficulty freeing itself of the hard-line, "united front from below," anti–social fascist attitudes of the previous period. Puro and Bert periodically reverted to their harsh attacks on the leadership of both the Farm Holiday and the Farmers Union. Their ally,

Art Timpson, writing a history of farm unrest, damned the Holiday leaders for having constantly betrayed the farmers. Bert wrote a four-part series arguing that the cost-of-production plan would ruin the small farmer. He followed it up with a blast at Dr. Francis Townsend's old-age pension plan—ironically, soon to be praised—but not endorsed—by the party. As late as March, 1935, Puro denounced Floyd B. Olson, Farmer Laborite governor of Minnesota, who was rapidly becoming the darling of Popular Fronters.[13]

Had the party leadership allowed these policies to continue un-checked, they could have reached no accommodation with Reno, Olson, or other targets for the Popular Front alliance. Perhaps at Hal Ware's urging, however, they soon made two strategic moves. They acted to end Charlie Taylor's exile in Nebraska in order to utilize his undoubted talents on a larger scale, and they dispatched Lem Harris from Philadelphia back to the crucial Midwest.

Harris more than matched expectation, but Taylor had reached the end of his tether. Ordered to attend the Farmers Union convention, he took the scanty travel funds and went to Minnesota, where he wintered on his brother's farm. He wrote Earl Browder, defending his past stands in favor of a broadly based Farmer Labor party. Jack Stachel, standing in for Browder, who was in Moscow, answered encouragingly and in a second letter, according to Taylor, offered him a salaried position at party headquarters if he could wait until Browder made the Popular Front policy official. Taylor's faith was flagging, however, and he equivo-cated. In the summer of 1935, along with his longtime friend, Ashbel Ingerson, he organized an anti–sales tax league in North Dakota. Party functionaries called them on the carpet and were about to give them a party trial when the two walked out. Taylor and Ingerson organized his old following in Plentywood and regained control of *Producers News* in a stormy stockholders' meeting. He ran it on independent radical princi-ples, but the revolutionary times had passed in Sheridan County, and that once proud and literate paper shut down its presses forever early in 1937.[14]

Harris was younger and more resilient than Taylor. He reacted to the new challenge with verve. He dispatched a telegram of greeting to the Minnesota Holiday, gathered in annual convention, 9 and 10 October 1934. He stressed areas of agreement and the desperate need to cooperate in winning adequate drouth relief. The response was favorable, and representatives of the Minnesota Holiday and the Farmers National Committee for Action met in Minneapolis, 29 October, to agree on united action in the fight for better relief programs. The state convention of the Holiday had already taken a strong stand against war and fascism; the Minneapolis pact reiterated that position. In the hope of extending the alliance further, they invited participation by the Minnesota Farmers Union, which soon consented to a joint meeting.[15]

Not everything went smoothly. John Bosch had agreed to present a resolution for united action to the National Farmers Union convention late in November. He reneged, however, claiming that most Farmers Union members opposed working with the radical UFL and Nebraska Holiday. Lem Harris was plainly exasperated. He wrote that the Farmers Union was a great organization but that its programs were childish. Momentarily abandoning his conciliatory approach, he accused Reno of slipping into anti-Semitism by referring to the New Deal as the "Jew Deal."[16]

Bosch was probably correct in his judgment. Not only did he have to handle Reno cautiously, but the Farmers Union was in its usual disarray. John A. Simpson had died recently. His successor, Ed Everson of South Dakota, had little of Simpson's quick intelligence, and he seemed to be dominated by the union's secretary, E. E. Kennedy, originally a protégé of Milo Reno. Kennedy, in turn, was increasingly associating himself with Father Charles Coughlin, the dynamic—many said demagogic—radio priest from Royal Oak, Michigan. Coughlin had recently founded an umbrella organization, the National Union for Social Justice, which he hoped to develop into a third force in America, based on papal encyclicals and some strange economic theories, that was intended to rise above both the reactionary Republicans and the radical New Dealers. Elsewhere in the Farmers Union, the Northwest Group heartily approved of the New Deal and despised Kennedy. Had Bosch trotted the Popular Front through the front door of the convention in 1934, it might well have shaken the faction-ridden structure to pieces.

Harris's setback at the NFU convention was only a detour. Signs of approval for united action recurred. The United Farmers League pushed hard for an alliance with the South Dakota Farmers Union. In North Dakota the UFL and the Holiday worked out a strong Popular Front agreement, not only on drouth relief but also on dispossession and the fight against war and fascism.[17]

Puro and Bert could drag their feet, John Barnett could castigate Lem Harris for mildly praising the cost of production slogan,[18] but Harris was reemerging more and more as the party spokesmen in agricultural strategy. On 25 January 1935, he issued a call for a national drouth conference to be held in Sioux Falls, South Dakota, the heart of the most distressed region. The conveners represented the broad new line: members of the Grange, Farmers Union, Farm Holiday, and even one Farm Bureau director. They also included Frank North, arrested and convicted as a leader of the Denison riot of April 1933; J. P. Russell, onetime Socialist candidate for attorney general of Iowa; and H. L. Mitchell, secretary of the Southern Tenant Farmers Union.[19]

The conference, which met 25 March through 27 March, strove mightily to be a model of the Popular Front in action. It concentrated on the issue which concerned the broadest spectrum of farmers—the devastating drouth of 1934 and what the delegates claimed had been inadequate federal response.

Although 343 regular and 108 fraternal delegates responded to the call, the sponsors had to have been disappointed in the organizational distribution. Of the regular delegates, 93 represented the United Farmers League and another 35 the Nebraska Farm Holiday. Others came from the Sharecroppers Union, party-controlled cooperatives, and unemployed organizations. Slightly fewer than 100 regular delegates claimed to represent the National Farm Holiday and the Farmers Union combined, while Grange and Farm Bureau members were almost completely absent.[20]

Little more encouraging was the dearth of top leaders of other groups. Not even the most optimistic could have been expected Everson, Kennedy, or Reno, but the failure to attract John Bosch of Minnesota or Oscar Brekke and Emil Loriks, rising young Holiday and NFU leaders in the host state, was a blow. Still, the organizers made do with whom they had. The convention report prominently cited the remarks made from the floor by J. W. Batcheller, former president of the South Dakota Farmers Union, and Oliver Rosenberg—brother of the long-departed Tony—vice-president of the North Dakota Farm Holiday. Ole Sundby, a North Dakota legislator, served on the resolutions committee. Another North Dakotan, Jasper Haaland, presided over the convention. Haaland, a wheat farmer, had served in the Montana Senate in the early 1920s with Charlie Taylor, had gone broke, and then had amassed new farm wealth in the Red River Valley. Ostensibly he represented the Farmers Union at the drouth convention; in addition, however, he had been a quiet member of the Communist party since about 1932.[21]

The convention produced the expected results. It attacked New Deal relief programs which seemed to be aimed at driving small farmers off the land or into subsistence agricultural. It demanded increased production and the abolition of the Agricultural Adjustment Administration. It endorsed the Communists own farmers emergency relief bill. And, to fit the climate of the times, it resolved in favor of a labor party and inveighed against fascism and war.[22]

In addition to these public activities, the Popular Front element of the Communist farm movement solidified its position working behind the scenes. The executive council of the United Farmers League met and elected a completely new slate of officers. Julius Walstad, who had just returned from a trip to the Soviet Union, supplanted an increasingly erratic Alfred Tiala as president. Harry Correll, who looked like a Presbyterian minister, according to Henry Puro, replaced the latter as secretary, and Jim Flower of Minnesota became vice-president. The party leaders decided also to consolidate their forces in Minneapolis, the UFL and the *Weekly* going there from Chicago and the Farmers National Committee for Action from Philadelphia.[23]

Departing from Sioux Falls with a strong program and revised leadership, the UFL and FNCA began a bold courtship of those who could be convinced that salvation lay in the Popular Front. In order to show their serious resolve to win federal passage of the emergency relief bill, the convention delegates had selected a group headed by Harris to lobby Washington. When they called on Harry Hopkin's Federal Emergency Relief Administration for minimum wages and locally elected administrative committees, they got a polite brush-off. On the other hand, they found a surprisingly jovial Henry Wallace, who promised to talk further to Hopkins about their suggestions. Wallace's mood turned angry, however, when they criticised the Agricultural Adjustment Administration, and he suddenly showed them the door, saying, "I don't like the spirit in which you come."[24]

The group next testified before a subcommittee of the House Committee on Agriculture. John Walz of North Dakota simply told them his own story. In 1909 he had bought 320 acres of bare prairie for $8,000. He had built his house, the barns, dug wells, strung fences. He had paid

$4,500 in taxes and $14,000 in interest. He had raised about sixty thousand bushels of wheat, five thousand of flax, and $120,000 worth of cattle. And yet, in spite of this productive record over twenty-five years, he owed $14,000 in debt.[25]

Walz and the others were speaking for the record to the committee; congressmen had heard worse and had become hardened to tales of suffering. Perhaps more significant for the future of the Popular Front in agriculture was the confrontation with a Farmers Union delegation. The two groups finally parted after angry words and a near brawl. Although a majority of the membership of the Farm Holiday Association and the Farmers Union would never be aware of it, a two-and-a-half-year struggle had begun between the Coughlinites and the Popular Fronters for the figurative souls of those organizations.[26]

The next step toward united action was a bold move to win approval from the national convention of the Farm Holiday Association for the drouth program. Reno gloried in the showmanship he brought to his Des Moines meetings. In the past he had presented John A. Simpson, A. F. Whitney of the Railroad Trainmen, Senators Smith Brookhart and Louis Murphy, Governors Langer and Herring, Mrs. Gifford Pinchot, and Father Coughlin. In 1935, with a certain devilish humor, he invited the two most prominently mentioned potential third-party candidates for president, Sen. Huey Long and Gov. Floyd Olson. Long jumped at the opportunity to speak outside the South. Olson dithered and then decided not to risk comparison with the Louisiana firebrand.[27]

Harris diligently exchanged messages with Reno in an attempt to get permission to present the drouth conference resolutions. In the end, Reno was still suspicious of Harris and refused to allow him on the platform, although allowing his attendance.[28]

Long typically stole the show before a crowd of ten thousand with an exposition of his "share our wealth" program. Reno enjoyed the proceedings tremendously, but there were others at the meeting who were appalled by the man and his simplistic solutions. More brands were added to the fire of discontent on the following day when Reno gave the platform to a Mrs. Guggen with a monomania for money conspiracies. It was finally all too much for the radical but sensible John Bosch. He pleaded with the convention to adopt a moderate platform calling for a national system of production for use rather than for profit. This set off a strange little anarchist from Manhattan who had somehow made himself the Farm Holiday delegate from New York. He denounced Bosch as a socialist. A bored Reno ended the debate: "It don't mean a thing. It's just a phrase that's being blown around. . . . I don't see any harm in keeping it in." It was.[29]

A few days earlier, Harris and a couple of Iowa Holiday members had met with Reno and thought that they had his permission for Andrew Cunningham, a South Dakota Holiday man, to read a report on the Sioux Falls conference. In an after-dinner session with Bosch presiding, Cunningham read and moved the adoption of the drouth program. In the midst of the debate, Reno flew into the room and began to castigate Harris. When a South Dakota farmer, Fred Hoppe, tried to moderate, Reno turned on him, calling him "Lem Harris's puke," and continued: "You can't talk. You can't argue. Don't try to get the floor, I'm running this meeting. Sit down and shut up. And get out before I really get mad." F. C. Crocker of the nearly defunct Reno branch of the Nebraska Holiday then railed at "Communist Jews" and praised Hitler for persecuting them. Finally the Sioux Falls program was quietly tabled.[30]

John Bosch had been caught in an embarrassing chain of events. Like most democratic radicals of his era, he distrusted Long as a potential fascist. He admired Reno's genuine concern for the underdog but despaired at his lumping together of Long, Coughlin, Olson, Upton Sinclair, John Dewey, and others as equally intelligent critics of the prevailing capitalistic system. Although Bosch had little formal education—an eighth-grade certificate—his broad and deep reading and native intelligence made him the intellectual equal of most college professors. He was no blind admirer of the Soviet Union or of the American Communists. He had too much independence to become a fellow traveler. Bosch was, however, deeply concerned about the rise of fascism. This led him, along with such progressives as Rep. Tom Amlie of Wisconsin, to accept election to the national executive council of the American League against War and Fascism, the leading Communist front organization of the 1930s. While maintaining his independence, Bosch was well on the way to accepting the Popular Front as a necessary defense for democracy. At the Des Moines Farm Holiday convention Bosch privately agreed that a new labor party could include Communists.[31]

Harris saw the utility of building up Bosch as a counterweight to the emotional Reno, but he continued to have problems with the party hard-liners. Bosch had written an article for *Common Sense* calling for a third party, which would have progressive leaders who could give it a powerful voice. This brought an angry rejoinder from Erik Bert, who read fascism into the plea for articulate leadership, although Bert condescended to add, "We don't imply that Mr. Bosch is a conscious fascist."[32]

Despite Bert's grumbling, the forces of unity moved forward. North Dakota, the flagship unit of the UFL, formed a decade before, voted to dissolve and called on its members to play active roles in the Farmers Union and Farm Holiday. *Farmers National Weekly* gave its readers a sympathetic exposition of the Washington lobbying activities of Bill Thatcher, who was building a strong alliance between the Northwest Group and the New Deal. The *Weekly* called on all supporters of the Sioux Falls conference to infuse the Farmers Union with "fighting blood."[33]

An authoritative American Communist leader finally provided strong directional guidance for the rural cadres. Clarence Hathaway— native Minnesotan, skilled machinist, graduate of the Lenin school, and editor of the *Daily Worker*—reported on the farm situation to a meeting of the central committee late in May. He touched on the sins of the Harris-Ware group lightly, suggesting that they had catered too much to the well-to-do class of farmers and had failed to build the party in Nebraska during the heyday of the farm strikes. Hathaway castigated the party's farm leaders, at great length but seemingly half-heartedly, for not analyzing the evils of New Deal agricultural programs more thoroughly. His strongest remarks were aimed at those who, since 1932, had tried to channel the broad movement of the farm revolt into the narrow United Farmers League alone.

Hathaway, unlike the more cautious careerists, did not confine his article to the obvious mistakes of the past. He tried to illumine the path to the future. The party's political bureau, he wrote, had emphasized the necessity of penetrating mass farm organizations in order to influence their policies. The Farm Holiday Association and the Farmers Union should be the primary targets, although even the Grange and the Farm Bureau could be worked with on specific issues. The infiltration of farmer organizations was, however, different from that of worker organizations. In the case of the latter, the goal was proletarian unity. In the case of the former, there was no purpose in a unity of farmers which would include rich capitalists. The Communist aim in the countryside should be to win solidarity of small farmers under proletarian leadership and an alliance with middle farmers against the fascist enemy.

Where did this leave the UFL? Hathaway reported that some Communists wanted to use the analogy of the labor movement, where the party's Trade Union Unity League had dissolved in order to work within the AF of L. For the present, Hathaway advised maintaining the UFL because in certain areas it rallied small farmers who would have no organization otherwise. Perhaps more important, a vital UFL could be used as an instrument to win a united front with the Farmers Union or Farm Holiday.[34]

Hathaway's article must have given pause to those who were still dragging their feet over any alliance with "bourgeois reformers" of the Holiday and Farmers Union. An even more powerful voice very soon left no doubts. The Seventh Congress of the Communist International met in Moscow, 25 July–20 August 1935. Lem Harris was an interested participant. Probably very few people have ever been at once as startled and as gratified as Harris when, listening to a speech by Browder, with Stalin present, he heard his leader exhort American Communists to cooperate with Milo Reno.[35]

Cooperation is a two-way street, and Reno had recently demonstrated considerable dislike for the Communists. For all of his irascibility, however, Reno was both a democrat and a pacifist. Hitler's program of rearmament and Mussolini's bullying of Ethiopia undoubtedly worried him. At the same time that Browder praised him, the old Populist, somewhat grudgingly, began making overtures to the Communists. Early in July he said that if he had to make a choice he would prefer the Communists, who tore everything down and then rebuilt, to the fascists' dictatorship of and for the few.[36]

Later in the month Reno had another chance to speak of and to his recent enemies. The North Dakota Farm Holiday held its annual convention in Bismarck, 22–24 July. The strong hand of the state president, Usher Burdick, was missing. The voters had sent him to Congress in 1934, and he was sweltering out the long summer of Roosevelt's famous Second Hundred Days in Washington. The convention was in the best rowdy tradition of North Dakota politics. The Popular Fronters controlled the daytime session, but the moderates packed the evening meetings with state employees and cooperative gas station attendants. The contradictory votes were often confusing, but the Communists made the most of the opportunity to present their case. Lem Harris's bride, Kay, charmed the delegates with her appeal to resist war and fight fascism. Harry Correll spent an hour damning the Roosevelt farm program, praising the farmers emergency relief bill, and criticizing the nearly sacrosanct Frazier-Lemke proposals for mortgage relief.

Reno gave the main address, and as always, he electrified the crowd. For those whom he had castigated in Des Moines only three months earlier, the climax of his speech came when he shouted: "You Communists fight for me, and I'll fight for you. We can fight together shoulder to shoulder." The Popular Fronters received a bonus when the delegates reelected Oliver Rosenberg as second vice-president. With Burdick much in Washington and the first vice-president generally ineffective, Rosenberg became the key to the well-organized and active Farm Holiday in North Dakota.[37]

The Communist farm movement received a blow on 13 August with the senseless highway death of Hal Ware.[38] Neither an orator nor a glad-hander, Ware had preferred to keep to the background as an economist and strategist. Both Charlie Taylor and Henry Puro respected him, and non-Communists such as Roger Baldwin of the American Civil Liberties Union mourned his loss.[39]

Aside from his outer qualities, Ware had provided a signal service for the Farmers National Committee for Action at a time of dire financial need. In the early 1920s, a young idealist named Charles Garland had inherited nearly a million dollars, with which he established the American Fund for Public Service—a foundation generally known as the Garland Fund. It was independent of his control and was to make loans and grants to radical groups. The Garland Fund supported labor schools and newspapers, and gave needed boosts to the American Civil Liberties Union and the National Association for the Advancement of Colored People. In 1924 it granted Ware about thirty thousand dollars for Russian Reconstruction Farms, his early experiment in socialized agriculture.[40]

A decade later, in 1934, when the Garland Fund was beginning to run out of money, Ware got the Russians to repay $13,000 of the earlier grant. Harris immediately filed for $12,790, to be divided between his own work and that of Donald Henderson.[41] The smoothness of the whole operation caused some consternation among the directors of the fund. Norman Thomas, Ben Gitlow, and James Weldon Johnson rejected the proposal, but a majority agreed to a compromise suggested by Roger Baldwin, to grant $5,000. For the next few years, the Garland Fund provided the major source of support for the Farmers National Committee for Action, together with an anonymous annual donation of $6,000 from the wife of a midwestern public figure.[42]

Even before Hal Ware's death, Lem Harris had largely replaced him as money raiser and strategist and certainly surpassed him in dealing personally with farmers. From the time of Harris's return from the Comintern congress, the grousing against the Popular Front ceased in the *Farmers National Weekly*. Bert stayed on for some months longer as editor, but Henry Puro resigned from his agrarian work to become party secretary in the Upper Peninsula of Michigan.[43]

The newspaper and the Communist farm leaders now went all out for united action with other organizations. In the wake of the Italian invasion of Ethiopia, the North and South Dakota Farmers Unions in separate meetings condemned the aggression. Usher Burdick wrote the *Weekly* about his outrage. Kay and Lem Harris made a circuit of Farmers Union and Farm Holiday meetings during the fall, building bridges and soothing old resentments. Reino Tantilla and Walter Harju met with John Bosch to begin the process of uniting the Minnesota UFL to the Holiday. Harry Correll praised those who placed loyalty to farmers above loyalty to an organizational name.[44]

All this was prologue to a letter of 7 December 1935 to state and local units of the UFL, signed by Correll and Walstad. Lauding the membership for its brave fight during the darkest days of the depression, the two leaders now called on the locals to merge with either the Holiday or the Farmers Union in order to fight the rising tide of fascism and to win the other goals of the UFL.[45]

Within a week, John Bosch wrote an article for the *Weekly* on teaching young people the need to fight fascism. As the Popular Front spirit blossomed, Correll published an article effectively ditching the farmers emergency relief bill and endorsing the Frazier-Lemke farm refinance bill, the cost-of-production scheme, and the Townsend old-age pension plan. Five years of Communist charges that this type of nostrum was inflationary bunkum were erased from the ledger overnight. Finally, even Milo Reno, Harris's most relentless detractor, wrote him to suggest a meeting to discuss issues. The old fighter retreated not an inch from the past, saying, "Your methods were reprehensible," but he called now for a better understanding. He followed this up with a letter to Erik Bert suggesting an amalgamation of progressive groups in order to stave off disaster.[46]

Reno, however, was a declining force. He had slight confidence in partisan politics and was truly, as an associate said years later, a man of the barricades.[47] He had done little to maintain any real organization as the emergency receded. His weekly radio broadcasts by December 1935 were showing a growing sense of despair. He made conciliatory moves toward the Communists, because of his dislike for fascism and probably because he was influenced by the youthful Dale Kramer, left-liberal editor of the *Farm Holiday News*. On the other hand, many of his close associates, such as Kennedy and Everson of the Farmers Union, Chalmers of the Iowa Farm Holiday, and L. M. Peet, who now controlled his insurance company, were pushing him to embrace Father Coughlin. He began to drink more heavily, and on 5 May 1936, Reno died, aged seventy, in Excelsior Springs, Missouri.

John Bosch now became acting president of the National Farm Holiday Association at the age of thirty-seven. Superficially the Holiday had declined dramatically from the heady days of 1932 and 1933 when it could easily claim a half million followers. By 1936, only a few thousand paid dues, but the situation was deceptive. On occasion, when an unfair sale loomed, the old Holiday network could still turn out hundreds of protesters in the Dakotas, Wisconsin, Montana, Iowa, or Minnesota. The organization was like the peacetime cadre of a citizens' army. If the emergency recurred, the Holiday could rally its thousands once more in defense of the farm home.

The strategic position of the Farm Holiday Association and the men who controlled it became increasingly important because of the open factionalism in the Farmers Union. Since the late 1920s, two loose alliances had fought one another. On the one hand were the Kansas Farmers Union and the Northwest Group, which had elected Charles Huff president in 1928. Their leaders, Huff and John Vesecky of Kansas, Charlie Talbott of North Dakota, M. W. Thatcher (head of the Farmers Union Terminal Association), and A. W. Ricker of the *Farmers Union Herald*, believed implicitly in the necessity of powerful regional producers' cooperatives which could battle industry and railroads toe to toe. They had gone along with Herbert Hoover's farm program as long as it poured money into their coffers, and they had turned on him when it failed.

Ricker and Thatcher voted for Norman Thomas in 1932, but they embraced New Deal farm programs at once. Thatcher spend a great deal of time in Washington lobbying, and he forged an important friendship with Eleanor Roosevelt as well as with other New Dealers. When the Farm Bureau began to back away from the New Deal, the Roosevelt administration looked increasingly for support to the cooperative wing of the Farmers Union.

Opposed to Kansas and the Northwest Group was the educational wing, which more precisely could be called ideological. Led by John A. Simpson until his death, this group, which included Reno, Kennedy, and Everson, tolerated the cooperatives as a necessary auxiliary but concentrated its forces on achieving absolute goals: the cost-of-production plan, monetary inflation, mortgage moratoriums, and the Frazier-Lemke proposal to refinance farm mortgages at 3 percent a year. It disdained the half-a-loaf expediencies of Huff, Ricker, and Thatcher. The ideological alliance had defeated Huff in 1930 and elected Simpson president. It made Kennedy secretary-treasurer a year later. As early as the fall of 1933 the leaders had turned angrily against the New Deal. With Simpson's death in 1934, Everson inherited the presidency, but Kennedy became the real leader. He organized new state unions in Ohio, Indiana, Michigan, Illinois, and Alabama, which were strong in numbers and in Kennedy's ideology but almost completely ignored cooperative activities.[48]

As Kennedy and Everson crushed all opposition at the national conventions of 1934 and 1935, the strong Nebraska Farmers Union, which believed in small local cooperatives, opposed all federal farm legislation, and despised both the Northwest Group and the Kennedy clique, withdrew completely. The leaders of the Kansas Union the Northwest Group were in near despair and contemplating secession and the establishment of their own Cooperative Farmers Union.[49] For John Bosch and Dale Kramer, the threatened schism offered the possibility of an alliance with the cooperatives in which the progressive Farm Holiday would replace the increasingly Coughlin-influenced Kennedy followers.

In 1936, conditions in American agriculture, especially in the Midwest, threatened to become explosive. Many farmers believed that the drouth relief and seed and feed loan programs of 1934 were inadequate. The Farm Credit Administration, in the eyes of many, seemed capable of refinancing only those farmers who really did not need it. And finally, in January, a unanimous Supreme Court struck down the Agricultural Adjustment Act of 1933. Kennedy exulted, believing that Congress would now be forced to pass the cost-of-production plan. Other opponents of AAA, such as Bosch and Harris, recognized that even with its shortcomings, the program had brought much money to farmers and would have to be replaced rapidly. The leaders of the Northwest Group were angry and dejected.[50]

A meeting—which never would have occurred a few months earlier —drafted a "Farmers' Program" for congressional consideration. Of the nine participants, at least four represented the cooperative enterprises of the Northwest Group, including A. W. Ricker; at least two were Popular Fronters, John Bosch and George Nelson, national board member of the Farmers Union from Wisconsin and soon to be vice-presidential candidate of the Socialist party; and two, Lem Harris and John Schefcik, were Communists.[51] The proposals tried to rescue as much as possible from AAA by demanding full payment on all contracts and relief supplements to farmers where necessary. They insisted on security for the farm home through passage of the Frazier-Lemke refinance bill, paid lip service to the cost-of-production plan, and demanded curbs on the Surpreme Court.[52]

Congress ignored the "Farmers' Program" and rapidly enacted the Soil Conservation Act of 1936, a weakened form of Triple-A but one accepted by the Northwest Group because it continued subsidy payments. The *Farmers National Weekly* grumbled that it represented a "scarcity program" but wasted little criticism on the new legislation. Kennedy and Everson, however, angrily opposed the SCA.[53]

All elements of the Farmers Union and its allies united behind Lemke's efforts during the spring to bring his farm refinancing proposal before the House for a vote. The administration and congressional leadership quietly threw every obstacle available in its path. Lemke doggedly plodded forward, signature by signature, to get the majority of representatives to release the bill from committee. Kennedy camped in Washington to use his considerable lobbying ability. *Farmers National Weekly* sponsored a letter-writing campaign. Father Coughlin tried to force Roosevelt into an open stand. The Kansas Farmers Union and Northwest Group gave tacit support. All was for naught. The administration shrewdly used adverse testimony from William Green, head of the AF of L, and from the Farm Credit Administration to undermine the bill, and it lost on 13 May by a vote of 235–142.[54]

John Bosch commented that the defeat caused great disappointment among farmers, but his statement concentrated on future struggles. The Northwest Group's chagrin was little more than *pro forma,* because it had achieved passage of the Commodity Exchange Act, which prohibited exchanges from discriminating against cooperatives—a battle of twenty-five years' standing finally won. For Coughlin, Kennedy, and Lemke, however, the effect was harrowing. Kennedy closed down his Washington office and returned home to Illinois. In mid-June he hinted of dramatic political events to come.[55]

Father Coughlin had reached a point of great personal frustration by June 1936. He had achieved national recognition for his powerful weekly broadcasts on political and economic issues in the early 1930s. During the presidential campaign of 1932 he had strongly supported Roosevelt and had obviously hoped to be a close advisor of the new president. Roosevelt, however, had kept the priest at arm's length, and by 1934, Coughlin was attacking Roosevelt's intimates and, by implication, the president himself. He formed his pressure group, the National Union for Social Justice, in whose simplistic program some saw purer economic democracy and others saw fascism. He took the congressional defeat of the Frazier-Lemke bill as a personal affront by Roosevelt and decided to strike back in this electoral year.[56]

Bill Lemke was angry also. He too had supported Roosevelt in 1932 but now felt that that support had gone unrecognized. He was prepared to join Coughlin and others in a bid to torpedo Roosevelt's reelection effort, as long as it did not undermine his hold on his House seat from North Dakota. On 19 June, Coughlin announced that Lemke would be the presidential candidate of the hitherto unheard of Union party. Shortly thereafter, Kennedy and Everson met with Lemke to express their support.[57]

Lemke's candidacy threw the liberal and radical wings of the farmers' movement into a state of consternation. Coughlin, like most Catholics, was strongly anti-Communist, and the Communists in turn called him a fascist. Popular Fronters such as Bosch and Kramer soon subscribed to the same view. Ricker, Thatcher, and Talbott of the Northwest Group recognized the advantages which the New Deal had brought to their cooperatives and to most farmers, and they despised Kennedy and

Coughlin for endangering them, although they maintained a cautious sympathy for Lemke the man.[58]

Coughlin and Lemke hoped to rally an alliance consisting of labor, farmers, the followers of Huey Long, the adherents of Dr. Townsend, and Coughlin's great radio audience. An early test of one portion of that coalition came at the Fifth Convention of the National Farm Holiday Association in Saint Paul, 30 June and 1 July.

The meeting was the first since Milo Reno's death and the first held anywhere other than Des Moines. John Bosch presided. Since early in the year he had been accepting the proffered alliance of his former foes, the Communists. In January he and Harry Correll, erstwhile secretary of the United Farmers League, had made a joint speaking tour. Some time later, he appointed Correll to be a Holiday organizer.[59] Communist support proved crucial to him in staving off the efforts of Lemke supporters at the convention.

Three hundred delegates convened in the auditorium of the state office building in considerable confusion. Nine state organizations claimed representation: Iowa, Minnesota, the Dakotas, Wisconsin, Wyoming, Nebraska, New Mexico, and Maryland. Iowa favored a pro-Lemke resolution; Minnesota and South Dakota were opposed; North Dakota and Wisconsin split. The other four states held the balance. The Nebraska and Wyoming delegations represented not the old National Farm Holiday groups but rather those of the pro-Communist Madison County plan. The Maryland and New Mexico presidents, who had no visible organizations behind them, lined up with the Iowa leadership.

At first no one could find a copy of the bylaws, which spelled out the method of voting. After a bitter debate the delegates tabled a proposal to settle all questions by a majority of those on the floor—an obvious advantage for the host state. Bosch appointed a bylaws' committee made up of four Communists, tw' Popular Fronters, and one Lemke supporter, Chalmers of Iowa. When a copy of the bylaws finally appeared, it gave sole voting power to the president of each state delegation. This would have allowed a majority for Lemke and the Union party. Bosch made an impassioned appeal for democracy, and the bylaws' committee reported a compromise calling for one vote per state plus an additional vote for every hundred paid-up members. The delegates voted to suspend the bylaws and adopt this rule.

Bosch now had his majority. The convention rejected the Lemke endorsement, and five state presidents stalked out. The remaining delegates now unanimously elected Bosch national president, George Nelson vice-president, and Dale Kramer secretary-treasurer. They adopted a strong antifascist, antimilitarist platform, but also paid careful lip service to the hoary cost-of-production plan and the Frazier-Lemke proposals. To balance their rejection of the Union party they also refused endorsement of the Farmer Labor Party, but later, in a civil liberties resolution, praised the FLP.[60]

The seceding presidents established a rump organization with Usher Burdick as president, William Keane of Iowa as vice-president, and Walter Groth of Minnesota as secretary. On paper it seemed a strong challenger, since Burdick and Keane were state presidents and Groth the Minnesota secretary. The schismatics rapidly folded, however. Burdick was running for reelection to Congress and was also Lemke's national campaign chairman. He not only refused the leadership of the rump Holiday but also soon handed over his North Dakota position to Oliver Rosenberg, a Bosch ally. Groth had no following in his own state, and only Keane, along with Reno's old friend, John Chalmers, was left in Iowa to mutter and growl about the "Communists" who had taken over the national organization.[61] There was a superficial validity to their charges. John Bosch had told the state convention of the Wisconsin Holiday: "If I have to choose between a stalwart, rock-ribbed Republican or Democrat and a Communist, I would choose a Communist. In Minnesota, we don't make an issue of Communism." Shortly thereafter, the 14 August issues of the *Farmers National Weekly* and the *Farm Holiday News* announced their merger as the *National Farm Holiday News.* Kay and Lem Harris now joined Harry Correll in working closely with Bosch and Kramer.[62]

The lines were rapidly drawn in the national election campaign. As usual, the Grange and Farm Bureau stayed aloof from the campaign. The Farmers Union and the Farm Holiday, constitutionally economic and educational organizations, were also supposed to remain nonpartisan. Emotions ran so high, however, that neutrality became almost impossible.

Kennedy led the pro-Lemke forces. He campaigned heavily for his candidate, and by October the Ohio, Indiana, and Illinois Farmers Unions had either officially or informally endorsed Lemke. The Illinois president resigned to accept the Union Party's nomination for lieutenant governor. Kennedy used his control of the *National Union Farmer* to insist that there were three major parties in the 1936 election, only one of which stood by the farmer.[63]

The Northwest Group and its allies, with a strong interest in Roosevelt's reelection, emphasized their neutrality. Ricker denied that he would head a pro-Roosevelt committee. Talbott, in a blast obviously aimed at Kennedy, warned against partisan activities at Farmers Union meetings. Chester A. Graham backed the Coughlinite board of directors in Michigan into a reluctant affirmation of neutrality—and lost his own bid for reelection as state secretary-treasurer.[64]

Bosch and Kramer of the Farm Holiday had fewer inhibitions. Kramer used his editorial columns to lambaste both Lemke and Coughlin. When the archbishop of Cincinnati reprimanded the latter for a particularly venomous attack on Roosevelt, Coughlin, strangely enough, compared himself to Mohammed, who, he said, had also been persecuted. Kramer was highly amused. With allusion to Coughlin's mania about monetary questions, he wrote that Mohammed had founded a faith "where when you die you go to a place where forty black-eyed damsels await you; under Father Coughlin, in all probability, you merely sit around in Congress coining money and regulating the value thereof."[65]

Bosch was more somber. He told the convention of the Minnesota Holiday that he had known Lemke long and well, but that the North Dakotan had made a terrible mistake to run for president as the representative of an undemocratic party. Bosch said that he had little time for Roosevelt, whose program had not really helped farmers. He had fought hard at a conference early in 1936 for a national Farmer Labor ticket, he told them, but labor unions had opposed it because of their gratitude to Roosevelt. And so, Bosch said, when it came down to it, he would support Roosevelt over Landon and Lemke. Bosch went on to castigate Coughlin for supporting the Spanish fascists, whereas the Holiday Association had cabled its support for the Republic. By this time the Communist party had reached the same conclusion about Roosevelt, and they too were supporting him by indirection although, technically, they had their own ticket in the field.[66]

Kennedy had overestimated his personal support among Farmers Union members. As opposition to his backing of Lemke grew, Kennedy vigorously fought back. His followers in the Indiana Farmers Union gave rude treatment to George Nelson, vice-presidential candidate of the Socialist party and a high official both of the Farmers Union and Holiday. The state convention of the Illinois Union condemned the "so-called" Farm Holiday Association in Minneapolis. As the campaign drew to a close, Kennedy grew more intransigent. In a speech to the convention of the Indiana Farmers Union, he denounced communism, assailed the principles of the Farm Holiday Association for being contrary to the flag and Constitution, and singled out the daughter of the liberal state secretary as a target for red-baiting. The exasperated secretary wrote Charlie Talbott denouncing Kennedy as a "fascist." Kennedy ended the campaign writing a front page editorial for the *National Union Farmer* commending the election of Lemke.[67]

Although Lemke returned to the House of Representatives from North Dakota, he suffered a total defeat in the presidential election, coming in a distant third not only in the nation but even in his home state.[68] For Kennedy the question now was whether he could maintian his position within the Farmers Union.

The national convention of the NFU met in Des Moines, 17 and 18 November 1936. Lemke gave a bitter and poorly received address. The ineffectual Everson won unanimous reelection. John Vesecky of Kansas replaced the pro-Kennedy C. N. Rogers of Iowa as vice-president. Finally the nominations for secretary came. Illinois nominated Kennedy, and a rebellious Oklahoma delegate defied the majority of Simpsonites to name J. M. Graves. Tension ran high as the ballots were counted, and a young man from Ohio took the occasion to denounce Communists and Socialists while praising Kennedy. When the tellers reported, Graves had outpointed Kennedy, 56½ to 50½. Kansas, North Dakota, Montana, Wisconsin, and a newly readmitted Nebraska supported Graves; Ohio, Indiana, Illinois, Iowa, and Alabama went for Kennedy; other states split their votes. In the end, both sides agreed that the 6 Michigan votes cast by Chester A. Graham swung the victory to Graves, despite the Coughlinite sentiments of the Michigan union.[69]

A coalition of the pro–New Deal cooperatives and the Popular Fronters had engineered Kennedy's defeat. It was that same alliance which had been temporarily forged earlier in the year when the Agricultural Adjustment Administration was invalidated. The one believed that Kennedy damaged the NFU's necessary ties to the Roosevelt administration, and the other looked upon him as a fascist. Young Popular Fronters such as Bosch and Kramer, Loriks and Brekke of South Dakota, and Graham of Michigan created the atmosphere for his defeat. The visceral sympathies of the older leaders of the Northwest Group were probably aroused also. Ricker, after all, had been a Populist, Socialist, and Nonpartisan Leaguer. Thatcher's background was similar. Their distaste for Kennedy and Coughlin was obviously deeper than a disagreement over the Soil Conservation Act. Even cautious old Charlie Talbott concluded that Kennedy was an "avowed fascist . . . dangerous to the future of the Farmers Union" and charged that Kennedy had accepted a "hot check" for dues from Alabama in order to get their three convention votes. Kennedy reciprocated by imputing years of disloyalty to Talbott.[70]

The defeat of Kennedy was a major victory for the Popular Front group and their allies, but the balance within the Farmers Union remained uneasy. The largest state unit, Oklahoma, was split between followers of the new national secretary, Graves, and John Simpson's son, William. Nebraska, next in size, had seceded for two years and could easily do so again, even though that conservative group now had a Communist, John Schefcik, among its vice-presidents. The third largest, Michigan, was firmly in the hands of Kennedyites, furious with Chester Graham. Ohio, Indiana, and Illinois were also angry over Kennedy's defeat. The rapidly growing Alabama Farmers Union was divided between the newly-admitted progressives from the Sharecroppers Union and those like the state president, R. H. Sartain, who pledged "to wipe, yes sweep, communism from the South."[71]

Kennedy had given a graceful farewell speech to the convention after his defeat. He soon began having second thoughts, however. Early in 1937 his supporters began a recall petition drive, aimed at replacing the newly elected officers with the old ones, charging "subterranean methods" and "political bludgeoning." Everson concurred with the charges and recommended the recall. The national board threw out the petition, ruling that it did not have sufficient signatures, but this was only the first of a series of moves by Kennedy and Everson to reassert control.[72]

Throughout the fall of 1936 and early in 1937, as the Farmers Union was an unsure battleground between the Kennedy-Coughlinites (fascists to their opponents) and the cooperator–Popular Front alliance (Communists to *their* enemies), John Bosch and Dale Kramer saw plenty of reason to preserve and indeed to rebuild the Farm Holiday Association. They found close allies and willing workers among the Communists.

Lem Harris got them an organizing grant of two thousand dollars from the Garland Fund. To Bosch, who had been paying the bulk of Holiday expenses from his own pocket, this was munificence. He toured the region, cajoling the Wisconsin Holiday, which had leaned toward Lemke. He traveled South Dakota with Oscar Brekke and North Dakota with Oliver Rosenberg. Frank North, of the 1933 Denison riot, tried to revitalize the movement in Iowa. Kay and Lem Harris worked for the newspaper and spoke for the Holiday when the occasion arose. Otto Anstrom forged a connection between the organization and the Workers Alliance (a jobless and relief group). Julius Walstad and Harry Correll contributed their talents.[73]

Kennedy's loss of his powerful position in the Farmers Union, however, began to undermine the reason for a separate Farm Holiday Association. Early in December 1936, Bosch spoke to a committee of the National Farmer Labor Political Federation about his dream of a powerful coalition of the Holiday, Farmers Union, Sharecroppers Union, and Southern Tenant Farmers Union which could meet organized labor as an equal partner in a new political party. In January a conference of state Holiday officers pursued the same line. A sure sign of declining faith in the future of the organization came, moreover, when Minnesota vice-president Harry Haugland and others began writing nostalgically of the earlier times when the Holiday had been a power in the land.[74]

In February Bosch attended a conference in Washington with Henry Wallace—something Reno would have spurned. He came back praising the administration for being more advanced than farm leaders. It was one indicator among many in the country at the time that the Popular Front was trying to latch on to the New Deal. Bosch's brother, Richard, a former teacher at Commonwealth College and a sort of one-man brain trust for the Holiday since its early days, defended the Roosevelt court-packing plan while Kennedy and Everson attacked it. John Bosch was growing tired of the travels involved in organizational work and had acquired a taste for hobnobbing with the likes of Henry Wallace and Elmer Benson, the new governor of Minnesota, who had appointed him to the sinecure of state miller. He proposed that he devote his time in the future to meeting with other leaders to influence them in the direction of Farm Holiday programs. In June he addressed the League for Industrial Democracy in New York, and in July he greeted the founding delegates of the United Cannery, Agricultural, Packing and Allied

Workers of America (CIO) in Denver. Bosch sent a friendly open letter to John L. Lewis, and Kramer wrote wistfully of the possibility that the Holiday could become the CIO of the farmers.[75]

In the meantime, Kennedy and his allies continued their last-ditch fight for control of the Farmers Union. In May, Sartain of Alabama and A. J. Johnson of Iowa joined the earlier petitioners to demand a statement from the board of directors that they had no part in formulating the proposed agricultural adjustment act of 1937. The board ignored them. In July Kennedy got the Minnesota union to demand a national referendum vote on the election of future officers, but the board rejected the plea.[76]

Kennedy was bouncing back from his defeat. He organized a Washington news service to supply his allied state Farm Unions. By fall, however, the Kennedy forces were ready to cut their losses. Morris Erickson, the dynamic young secretary of the North Dakota Farmers Union, demanded that Everson be prohibited from representing the NFU over the radio, be removed as nominal editor of the *National Union Farmer,* and have his expense account cut. Everson bitterly surrendered and announced that he would not seek a new term.[77]

With the Kennedyites admitting their defeat within the National Farmers Union, the rationale for a separate Farm Holiday Association had disappeared. Bosch had already called for unification of the Minnesota Holiday and the two wrangling factions of the state Farmers Union. In November the Holiday and the Cooperative Union—supported by the Northwest Group—merged, while the state Farmers Union, under John Erp and holding the national charter, sullenly stayed out. The South Dakota Holiday had already joined the Farmers Union in October. Finally, on 31 December 1937, the *National Farm Holiday News* ceased publication, calling for continuance of the Holiday spirit within the now fully progressive National Farmers Union.[78]

The Kennedyites fought only a rearguard action at the NFU convention in November 1937. Although the majority for the first time adopted a practical endorsement of the New Deal, they also cheerfully accepted a minority demand for the old Kennedy-Simpson cost-of-production plan. John Vesecky of Kansas unanimously became president, and progressives swept the board of directors.[79]

Kennedy's followers had a new line in view. In December he began publishing the *Union Farmer,* which his allies eagerly adopted. It was, in effect, a declaration of war, and the only question remaining was where the actual hostilities would begin. John Erp, president of the Minnesota Farmers Union and a longtime friend of Kennedy, refused to have anything to do with the unified Farm Holiday–Cooperative Union group in his state—or indeed with the new national leadership. The NFU board of directors met in Saint Paul in mid-December 1937 to try to bring Erp into unity. Erp refused to attend the session and snippily informed them that when he wanted their counsel, he would seek it. The board then authorized George Nelson to begin organizing in Minnesota in the name of the National Farmers Union.[80]

Lem Harris had gotten thirty-five hundred dollars for a Farmers Union drive from the Garland Fund for a committee headed by John Bosch and himself. Nelson held a series of successful meetings under their auspices around the state. Erp and Kennedy countered by calling a meeting of the leaders of the Minnesota, Iowa, Illinois, Michigan, Indiana, and Pennsylvania state unions which protested that the board had violated Minnesota's rights. The board ignored the protest and withdrew Erp's charter. Vesecky followed up by suspending the Michigan charter in April. After the national convention in November 1938 approved these actions, the Illinois, Indiana, and Ohio unions withdrew. In 1939 the seceding and suspended unions formed the National Farmers Guild under Kennedy's leadership, opposed to the New Deal, favoring the cost-of-production plan, and friendly to Father Coughlin.[81]

The purged Farmers Union had bought unity at the cost of losing several of its state organizations. The leaders of the new Farmers Guild angrily charged that the NFU had come under Communist domination. It was an allegation which Farmers Union enemies would repeat for years, but it was not true. For a time Lem Harris was authorized fifty dollars a month to organize for the union, and he received free office space while he wrote for the Communist daily in Chicago, *Midwest Record*. The NFU utilized the services of Farm Research for economic analysis.[82] The Farmers Union, however, was no more dominated by the Communists than was allowed by the real powers: Ricker, Thatcher, Glen Talbott (who succeeded his father in North Dakota), Huff, and that rapidly rising Coloradan, Jim Patton. The Communists, on the other hand, had achieved something of what they were aiming for in this era: the NFU had, to a degree, become a Popular Front organization because those leaders on principal opposed war and fascism.

By 1938, the National Farmers Union had become a firm ally of the Roosevelt administration. The leadership supported the president's policies, and they received favors in return. The Communists were swimming in the same stream, just as they were in several labor unions and other organizations at the time. If, in some states, they achieved a modicum of influence, it was because of hard work and organizing ability. They had found a niche in the Farmers Union at the expense of giving up their own organizations. They could maintain their position only so long as the ideal of the Popular Front prevailed and the policies of the United States and the Soviet Union did not clash.

8

THE SOUTHERN TENANT
FARMERS UNION
AND THE COMMUNISTS

SEVEN BLACK MEN and eleven white men from near Tyronza, Arkansas, formed the pioneer local of the Southern Tenant Farmers Union in July 1934. Their original purpose was to protest the treatment given sharecroppers on the plantation of Hiram Norcross. As the organization grew, however, and began to spread, first throughout the rich delta land of eastern Arkansas and then to neighboring states, it raised its sights to include broad objections against the oftentimes near inhuman treatment of small tenant farmers, sharecroppers, and farm laborers. Members of the STFU were particularly incensed by the effect of the Agricultural Adjustment Act of 1933, which seemed not only to bring them no benefits but to drive large numbers of them from the land.[1]

The STFU soon aroused the enmity of planters and businessmen. Local officials harrassed organizers, and when such tactics failed, a campaign of extralegal violence followed. The organization might well have collapsed except for the moral and financial support of the Socialist party. Norman Thomas served almost as guardian angel from inception, and he helped focus nationwide attention on the crude attempts to crush the STFU.[2]

After a year's existence, the union had grown to include fifteen thousand members. In September 1935 it staged a strike in northeastern Arkansas to demand payment of sixty-five cents a hundredweight for picking cotton—a figure about twice the going rate. The strikers gained little except a lukewarm endorsement from the American Federation of Labor. The STFU followed up with a cotton choppers' strike in May 1936, which caught the nation's fancy when cameras of the popular *March of Time* newsreel captured the drama of the "marching picket lines"—groups of a hundred or more workers, tramping through the fields and pleading with nonstrikers to join them. By early the following year the union had spread to Texas, Mississippi, Tennessee, Oklahoma, and Missouri, and it claimed over thirty thousand members.[3]

Much of the union's fervor came from its executive secretary, H. L. Mitchell, who held it together on a tiny budget. Mitchell, a raw-boned former sharecropper turned dry cleaner, had joined the Socialist party early in the depression. He always emphasized, despite this tie, that the STFU was nonpartisan and nonpolitical.[4] This was probably good policy in the heavily Democratic South. Mitchell, on the other hand, made little secret of his belief that capitalism was dying.[5]

After the union had begun to arouse national attention, it also attracted the interest of the Communist party. If the poor croppers of Arkansas had organized a year or two earlier, the Communists would have condemned the Southern Tenant Farmers Union as social fascist —the term freely applied to Norman Thomas and his ilk. By 1934, however, the new trend was evolving in the party line. The Communists were rapidly abandoning their earlier damnation of all others on the left —characteristic of the Third Period—and were seeking allies against war and fascism. It was in September, two months after the founding of the STFU, that the *Farmers National Weekly* proposed the agrarian Popular Front.[6]

As a result of this change, the STFU found welcome as a potential ally. *Farmers National Weekly* gave Mitchell space to tout his newborn organization, and the Communists invited him to the 1935 drouth conference in Sioux City. The conference of the Sharecroppers Union, late in October 1934, called for class unity between the two groups to fight terroristic planters and the New Deal.[7] The education of the STFU in the tactics of the left wing had begun.

One of the STFU's greatest problems was its abject poverty. Mitchell and the other officers received no salaries, but the search for life's necessities took its toll. One organizer pleaded with Mitchell, "If you know any Commie sources to appeal to for my support, for Gawd's sake do it." Although STFU had no Moscow gold, a few red nuggets had washed ashore elsewhere. Hal Ware had gotten the partial repayment of an earlier loan to the Soviet government from the Garland Fund, and the fund then granted two-hundred dollars to the Sharecroppers Union and twenty-two hundred dollars to the National Committee for the Unity of Agricultural and Rural Workers led by Donald Henderson.[8]

The NCUARW aimed at the unionization of the estimated three million agricultural laborers. Henderson sent organizers to California to study the methods of the party's Cannery and Agricultural Workers Industrial Union, which had led the series of major strikes in that region but was crushed in July 1934.

In the second week of January 1935, Henderson convened a conference in Washington to unite the various organizations of rural workers. He carefully solicited the support of the STFU even though the official proclamation of the Popular Front line was several months in the future. Mitchell and three other delegates took part in the meeting. Henderson picked E. B. McKinney, the eloquent black vice-president of the STFU, as a member of the temporary executive body of the NCUARW.[9]

The STFU was ready to welcome almost any friend it could find. In contrast to the Sharecroppers Union, which feared mixing the races in its membership, the Tenant Farmers Union surprisingly had fairly even numbers of whites and blacks. Its members, however, were the poorest, most depressed, and, regardless of race, usually disfranchised and thus politically powerless. Plantation owners and riding bosses did not take kindly to any challenges to their rule. In mid-January 1935, the authorities at Marked Tree, Arkansas, broke up a STFU meeting and arrested its organizer, Ward Rodgers, a young graduate of Vanderbilt Theological Seminary. The local jury quickly convicted him of criminal anarchy, and the judge sentenced him to six months in jail and a stiff fine.[10]

The Communists immediately began a campaign for Rodgers's defense. The Farmers National Committee for Action circulated a plea for funds to be sent to STFU headquarters. International Labor Defense made Rodgers's case a Popular Front cause. Perhaps more portentous in the long run was the unity pact among students and faculty at Commonwealth College pledging to support Rodgers and the STFU.[11]

Commonwealth, a labor school organized in 1923, had its campus near Mena, Arkansas, across the state from the delta heartland of STFU. It had taken a decided left turn in 1931, and although the party did not dominate the institution, there was a strong Communist fraction among both students and faculty. The school's young director, Lucien Koch, had traveled through the STFU's territory in the late summer of 1934 and had been outspoken in denouncing the oppression he had seen.[12] The Rodgers case brought Koch and several of his students back to eastern Arkansas.

Prominent in the Commonwealth group was Bob Reed, organizer for the Young Communist League. Reed seized the moment for spreading party literature and at one point tried to lead the sharecroppers in singing the "Internationale." It was not very wise tactics, since local officials had already accused Rodgers of being an agent of Moscow, but Mitchell tolerated this until a white STFU leader protested the circulation of maps detailing the party's proposed black soviet republic in the South. After conferring with his close advisor, Howard "Buck" Kester, a classmate of Rodgers at Vanderbilt Seminary, Mitchell gave the Commonwealth delegation its walking papers. He was disturbed also by the glimpse he got of a letter to Reed asking when the party should take over. As he laconically wrote sometime later, "I begun to distrust them."[13]

While Commonwealth was close enough for Mitchell to gauge its importance, the Sharecroppers Union off in Alabama was another story. It was three years senior to the STFU, it already had its martyrs, and it claimed thousands of members. The SCU had fought its strike of cotton choppers, demanding a one-dollar wage for a ten-hour day. It claimed a victory despite a wave of violence by planters. The STFU leaders paid tribute to the fight of their Alabama counterparts and joined them in proclaiming 17 July a memorial day for Ralph Gray, the SCU leader murdered in 1931.[14]

Because of the publicized strength of the Sharecroppers Union, Mitchell was probably somewhat startled when two of its representatives arrived at STFU headquarters in Memphis early in August 1935 to propose merging their supposed twelve thousand members into his younger and slightly smaller organization.[15] A trip to Montgomery to confer with Tom Burke of the SCU raised further doubts. The red hunt was on, and Burke had gone underground with a good deal of justification. Mitchell, however, characteristically showed his disgust by stalking around the city with an unfurled copy of the *Daily Worker.* A hurried visit to a small meeting of blacks in Lowndes County led him to question whether the SCU actually existed as a real organization other than as a part of the Communist party structure. After he returned to Memphis, he continued to give the SCU restrained praise publicly, but privately he advised strongly against any merger.[16]

However much Mitchell had begun to doubt the Communists, he knew that the STFU desperately needed allies. The persecution of the union had aroused sympathy in many liberal and radical circles, but the important truth remained that Chester Davis, head of the Agricultural Adjustment Administration, and Cully Cobb, his chief of the cotton section, favored plantation owners and looked upon sharecroppers as so much human refuse. Mitchell, therefore, followed a policy of cautious friendship well into 1936. Donald Henderson began publication of a monthly paper, the *Rural Worker,* in August 1935, and he solicited articles from the STFU. Lem Harris of the Farmers National Committee for Action pledged solidarity with Mitchell and sent a small contribution for the union.[17]

Henderson continued his courtship. Shortly before the Second Convention of the STFU in January 1936, Mitchell wrote Gardner "Pat" Jackson, a Washington sympathizer, that he hoped both Henderson and Burke would attend. The STFU had no desire to amalgamate with their organizations, he said, but he thought that the two were honest, and he wanted to cooperate with them. The convention itself endorsed both the *Rural Worker* and Henderson's group, finally renamed the National Committee on Agricultural and Rural Workers. Some of Henderson's friends treated the delegates to a movie on cooperative farming in the Soviet Union. When they later suggested that Mitchell circulate it among his locals, he politely declined.[18]

The Communists, for their part, were in a period of redefining their goals in the countryside in accordance with the Popular Front line. They had not clarified their own attitude toward sharecroppers and the STFU. Henderson had delivered a speech, "The Rural Masses and the Work of Our Party," at a meeting in May 1935 of the central committee of the party, in which he quoted Lenin but with important excisions. He omitted the reference to "yellow Socialists" and had apparent problems fitting Lenin's six-tiered structuring of rural classes to the American situation.[19]

The party began to define its position early in 1936. All "toiling farmers" should join the National Farmers Union or the Farm Holiday Association. This class included all owners and tenants who were not exploiters of the labor of others. Agricultural wage-workers, on the other hand, should affiliate with the American Federation of Labor and seek a national charter.[20]

The thought of disbanding the STFU because of some new line appalled Mitchell. Tom Burke wrote him in glowing terms about bringing white Mississippi tenants into the Farmers Union and Tennessee peach pickers into the AF of L, but Mitchell's response dripped acid. He wrote that sharecroppers crossed the line back and forth between tenant and wage-worker so regularly that any attempt to follow Burke's ideas would destroy the STFU. The AF of L was distant and aloof, and the Farmers Union in the past had been a springboard for ambitious politicians in Arkansas. The disclosure that "Tom Burke" was the underground name of Clyde Johnson, a onetime college student activist, irked Mitchell further.[21]

The Communists soon demonstrated their determination to build separate organizations for farmers and agricultural workers, whatever Mitchell thought. A colorful and mercurial character named Odis Sweeden, who was part Cherokee Indian, had formed a branch of the STFU in Oklahoma. A majority of his followers were field workers around Muskogee and not sharecroppers. Henderson decided that these seasonal laborers belonged in the AF of L. He brought Sweeden to his New York headquarters and, from the figurative mountaintop, offered substantial monetary support if the Oklahoman would transfer his allegiance. Although Sweeden resisted the temptation, Mitchell was irate. Henderson self-righteously defended his action, claiming that his genuine desire to help was always unjustly suspected because of his "political character."[22]

The Sweeden affair blew over for the time being, but Mitchell had a more personal complaint. While on his way from Memphis to a meeting in Muskogee, he stopped off at Commonwealth College to confer with J. R. Butler, the president of the STFU. Butler, a mild, Lincolnesque former school teacher, had been instructing at Commonwealth since 1935 over Mitchell's objections. The latter soon learned that several of the faculty had accused him of selling out on a recent cotton chopper's strike, but on the whole he thought he was on safe grounds. He told his bodyguard to relax while he stopped to chat with an STFU organizer who lived on campus. They talked amiably for a few minutes until the organizer stepped in the next room, reappeared with a revolver, and fired several shots at Mitchell. The fusillade missed, and the amazed secretary hightailed for safety.[23]

The assassination attempt shocked Mitchell. He became convinced that Communists at the college had worked on the emotions of the poor sharecropper to make him believe that Mitchell was a traitor to the union. Don Henderson's vehement protestations of his own innocence in the affair only irritated Mitchell further. He decided, with Howard Kester's concurrence, to bar party members from STFU meetings. His resolution was probably bolstered by the complaint from his Texas organizer about two left-wingers in that region: "They always talk bourgesis and Proletariot when people don't even know what that means."[24]

The continuing insistence on the part of the Communists that farmers and laborers should be shunted into separate organizations won few adherents among STFU members who saw in the suggestion only the death of their proud brotherhood. Clyde Johnson tried to modify the party's line slightly when the Sharecroppers Union held its convention in New Orleans late in July 1936. The meeting proposed that the SCU continue to build on its strength in Alabama and that the STFU should do the same in its own area. Elsewhere in the South, however, the delegates resolved that the two groups should enthusiastically support the AF of L and the National Farmers Union. As a token, the SCU would cede its Louisiana locals to the NFU immediately. Johnson was sure that after a few years the various unions could meet to sort their members into the proper categories. The proposal might have pacified the skeptical Mitchell for a time, but in fact it was abortive. Johnson had apparently exceeded his authority, and in an abrupt turnabout, the SCU soon dissolved and split its members between the NFU and a new Alabama Agricultural Workers Union. One of its last activities was to publicize new words for an old spiritual:

> Give me that old Communist spirit,
> Give me that old Communist spirit,
> It was good enough for Ralph Gray,
> And it's good enough for me.[25]

Unlike Johnson, Don Henderson never deviated from the official party position. He used the columns of the *Rural Worker* to continue his calls for "unity." It seemed a strange kind of unity to Mitchell, which he believed would superimpose craft unionism in the cotton fields, break up the alliance of white and black workers, and degenerate into jurisdictional conflicts. When the executive council of the STFU met early in October 1936, it voted to withdraw endorsement from the *Rural Worker* and, on a motion by Odis Sweeden, to rebuff the earlier proposal from the Sharecroppers Union for joint activities.[26]

The STFU council had a more vital complaint against Henderson, which it did not raise publicly. The union had always had money problems. It existed on the tiny dues of its membership, on the pittances contributed by Socialist friends, and on whatever other funds could be raised. Since 1935 the STFU had received the sympathetic attention of Gardner Jackson, who had been appointed as its Washington representative. Pat Jackson—railroad heir, journalist, defender of Sacco and Vanzetti, discharged Agriculture Department radical—was in the mid-period of his true vocation: left-wing ingenue. He organized the Washington Committee to Aid Agricultural Workers in 1936 to raise money among his liberal friends, who were horrified by the unfolding tales of sharecropper oppression and were pleased to help—from a distance.

The Washington Committee was to be the first of a network of similar groups around the nation. The only problem, as far as the STFU was concerned, was that although the union provided a rationale for cocktail parties and other fund-raising festivities, it received only a small portion of the collections. Jackson's committee peeled fifteen dollars a month off the top of its take to support the *Rural Worker*. Only a third of the remainder went to the STFU. The bulk was split between the Sharecroppers Union and the South Jersey Agricultural Workers Union, now headed by Leif Dahl, who had become a devoted lieutenant of Henderson. "Pat's friends are again taking him for a ride so it seems," Mitchell wrote to Norman Thomas. Still, the situation could have been worse. When a similar committee formed in New York, it contributed nothing to STFU.[27]

The executive council of STFU had accumulated enough complaints to have justified breaking relations with Henderson and the Communists. And yet it did not. Mitchell wrote Jackson that he was willing to continue working with them if they kept hands off union policies. Norman Thomas recommended "maximum cooperation"—and unsleeping caution.[28] The key to the situation was probably STFU's yearning for affiliation with a major labor confederation.

The STFU had courted both the AF of L and the fledgling CIO, but with few results.[29] Henderson, on the other hand, seemed able to gain a sympathetic ear despite his denunciations of non-Communist unions a few years earlier. He won a good deal of publicity in sponsoring the National Conference on Rural Social Planning late in March 1936.[30] The

American Federationist published his articles and encouraged him in founding citrus, truck-garden, and sugar-beet unions in Florida, New Jersey, and the West. By November 1936 Henderson was boasting that he represented seventy-two locals affiliated with the AF of L.[31]

Henderson's relationship with the federation was unsatisfactory, however. His committee had no official standing with the AF of L, and each local union was an orphan which had to deal individually with President William Green and his conservative staff. These federal unions, as they were known, tried to win an international charter at the Tampa convention of the AF of L in November 1936, but the greater issues that year sidetracked them.[32]

The pleas of the agricultural unionists were only a poor sideshow at Tampa. The main feature was the final split between the AF of L and the CIO over the issue of industrial unionism. John L. Lewis, leader of the new group, had already undertaken a vast campaign to organize workers in steel, autos, rubber, and other mass industries, which would provide him with powerful legions of dues-paying followers. The sharecroppers, farm hands, and migratory workers looked like a pretty poor harvest in comparison—until his interest was piqued by a grand scheme proposed by Harry Bridges, who was bidding to become Lewis's West Coast satrap.

Bridges, who had won first fame as leader of the massive San Francisco port strike in 1935, was engaged in a struggle to unionize the Pacific slope for the CIO. Late in the spring of 1937 he convinced Lewis that not only could the tens of thousands of agricultural workers be the spearhead of this drive but that they would also pay thirty-six hundred dollars dues every month into the CIO coffers. This was enough inducement, apparently, to swerve Lewis 180 degrees from his previous course of reluctance and to win his blessing for Don Henderson, Bridges's chosen candidate for leader. According to Gardner Jackson, the CIO chieftain previously had never heard of Henderson.[33]

The prospect of an agricultural union, chartered by Lewis, the recent victor over mighty United States Steel and current darling of radicals, brought elation to the hearts of the champions of the cause of thousands of sharecroppers, Okies, Chicanos, and other rural workers. The relationship of the new organization with the older STFU brought a measure of perplexity to both sides, however. Henderson may well have favored excluding the tenant group from his founding convention to be held in

Denver early in July 1937 because of the evidence he already had of its independence, pride, and sometimes cantankerous leadership. On the other hand, Gardner Jackson, now a close advisor of Lewis, insisted on the inclusion of the STFU. Henderson would have been hard put, moreover, to have explained his ignoring a bloc of thirty-five thousand rural workers while favoring only his pet locals, many of which seem to have existed only on paper.[34]

The decision faced by STFU was only less difficult. It had built its strength in numbers during the three years of life, but its strikes and boycotts had not been practical successes. It had won sympathy and support from liberals throughout the nation, but it had failed to halt the transformation of sharecroppers—who, under revised laws, could claim Agricultural Adjustment Administration benefits—into day laborers—who could not. Mitchell concluded that the only solution was entry into John L. Lewis's house of labor, for which Henderson held the latchstring.[35]

Strong circumstances impelled the STFU toward participation in the Denver convention, despite its continuing suspicion of Henderson. Socialist friends, who were vehemently anti-Communist, encouraged Mitchell to play a prominent role at the meeting. The sine qua non for the STFU, however, was a guarantee of autonomy and jurisdiction over cotton workers within its own territory. A press release, which angered Henderson, emphasized these demands.[36]

Henderson and his associates firmly controlled the founding convention of the new union. They cumbersomely christened it the United Cannery, Agricultural, Packing and Allied Workers of America, but it was generally known by the acronym, UCAPAWA (yew-cáp-a-wa or yéw-ca-pá-wa). Gardner Jackson, representing Lewis, later complained that his mail had been opened and read by the Communists at Denver, but if he grumbled at the time, it was not evident. The invited outside speakers included party-liners Harry Bridges; Reid Robinson of the Mine, Mill, and Smelter Workers; and the non-Communist Popular Fronter, John H. Bosch, president of the Farm Holiday Association. The STFU delegates participated in a move by Mary Heaton Vorse, the radical author, to put Leif Dahl at the head of UCAPAWA, but Dahl, according to Gardner Jackson, dissolved in tears at the thought. The convention finally awarded J. R. Butler the honorific—and powerless—title of vice-president, while packing the executive board with Henderson's men. Henderson had privately offered to make Mitchell secretary-treasurer if he secretly joined the Communist party.[37]

The STFU representatives returned to Memphis with the belief that they had won their goal of autonomy as District IV of UCAPAWA. A special convention met, 24–26 September to ratify the affiliation and elect regional officers. Whatever Mitchell's private doubts about Henderson, the CIO seemed the wave of the future, and the delegates hardly debated joining. They chose the old STFU officials as leaders of the new district: Butler as president, E. B. McKinney as vice-president, and Mitchell as secretary-treasurer. Not everything went off smoothly, however. One eloquent white speaker, the Reverend Claude Williams, charged that any doubts about affiliation were purely racial in motivation. He also tried to defeat Mitchell with his own hand-picked black candidate.[38]

Williams, who had hung on the fringes of the STFU since its formation, now began emerging as a storm center as he sought power in the union. The Reverend Claude, a poor hill boy from Tennessee who had become a friend of Howard Kester at Vanderbilt Seminary, had swung away from his early fundamentalism to religious radicalism. His Presbyterian church in Paris, Arkansas, had dismissed him in 1934 for disturbing the orthodoxy of the elders. Two years later he won national attention when a group of white men brutally beat him after an STFU meeting.[39] Somewhere along the line Williams had decided that the Communist party had the answer to the problems of injustice which he saw all around him, and he joined under the name John Gayley or Galey. He dropped formal membership when he became director of the faltering Commonwealth College in August 1937 after giving a pledge of nonpartisanship. He had already won appointment to the executive council of the STFU two months earlier. Ralph Lord Roy, who studied Williams's subsequent career, concluded that he seldom deviated from the party line whatever his formal status.[40]

Mitchell feared that Williams's emotional appeals threatened to split the STFU along racial lines. The problem was doubly dangerous because E. B. McKinney was edging toward black nationalism. Mitchell wrote Jackson that he considered Williams a "serious menace," and he finally appealed to Henderson to have the preacher confine his activities to Commonwealth.[41]

With the ebullient Claude corralled for the time being, the STFU leaders began to try to make sense of their puzzling position within UCAPAWA. They stoutly maintained the right to keep their original name, their constitution, and regional autonomy. Beyond this, much was unclear to them. Their new district status gave them authority over new areas, which they had not organized. What did they know, for instance, of the problems of strawberry pickers in Louisiana or pecan shellers in the Rio Grande Valley? Nor were they quite sure about the relationship with their own state units. Mitchell, honestly but naïvely, told Odis Sweeden to communicate directly with Henderson's office because he simply could not figure out the status of the Oklahoma locals. The STFU secretary, downing his suspicions for the moment, wrote a long conciliatory letter to Henderson, patiently explaining his organization's present position and future prospects.[42]

Henderson's own problems were immense. He was trying to organize a great mass of poor, undereducated, often rootless, generally despised, and economically powerless workers in a field specifically excluded from the provisions of the National Labor Relations Act.[43] He claimed over one-hundred-thousand members for UCAPAWA, but he had, at best, scattered bases of strength. According to the labor grapevine, John L. Lewis had given Henderson fifty-thousand dollars to get his union off the ground. Lewis, however, was no open-handed philanthropist. He wanted dues-paying members, but Henderson's efforts began to flag almost at once. In New Jersey, the Agricultural Workers Union, led by Leif Dahl and with the wholehearted support of the state Federation of Labor, had made large gains in 1935 and 1936, even though they lost their membership at Seabrook Farms. At Denver, Dahl became regional president of District VII of UCAPAWA, encompassing Connecticut, New York, New Jersey, and Pennsylvania. After a few less than successful strikes, he abandoned the attempt to organize field workers to concentrate on packing and cannery employees.[44]

This was a pattern repeated elsewhere across the nation. The Alabama Agricultural Workers Union had received great boosts from the Sharecroppers Union, the Alabama Farmers Union, and the unions of the heavily industrialized Birmingham area. By the time of the Denver convention, it boasted ten thousand members. A year later it was down to seventeen locals and a thousand members, and Henderson rapidly ditched it. District III in the mountain states had another ten thousand members in 1938, especially among beet field workers. In the face of difficult negotiations, Henderson again threw in the towel and abandoned the whole district. He gave up on the citrus fruit pickers of Florida in 1938. Promising organizations in Arizona and the Pacific Northwest shared the same fate.[45]

California, however, was to have been the cornerstone of UCAPAWA under Harry Bridges's tutelege. There had been a promising resurgence of independent and AF of L field union activity in 1935 and 1936, but UCAPAWA's affiliation with the CIO had lost it the support of the powerful Teamsters Union, which now entered into direct competition. There was also a renewal of Associated Farmers activity. Henderson uniformly began losing battles, and his California membership plummeted, although he did not finally give up on the field workers there until 1941.[46]

Declining revenue forced Henderson to economize. In January 1938, he gave the sack to twenty-six of his twenty-eight organizers. J. R. Butler lost his vice-presidential salary of two hundred dollars a month.[47]

Before the foundation of UCAPAWA, Henderson had had the luxury of being a theorist and an ideologue. He had been able to lecture Mitchell and Butler about rural class distinctions until they wearily told him to mind his own business. How different his perspective after becoming president of UCAPAWA! He faced the day-to-day problems of administration and organization—and always the nagging burden of finding adequate funds. Although Mitchell continued to suspect to the end that Henderson wanted to break STFU up on class lines, the issue simmered on a back burner.[48] Henderson no doubt wanted to build UCAPAWA as a pillar of an eventual Communist revolution, but his immediate aims were those of any practical unionist—of a Walter Reuther or a Jim Carey.

Henderson's difficulties elsewhere may well have focused his attention more clearly on the STFU. Here, after all, was a body with 35,000 members. At a per capita of $0.50 a month, this meant a potential $210,000 a year pouring into the union treasury. Despite Mitchell's warning, Henderson never seemed to grasp that to the average sharecropper, $6.00 a year dues was as unrealistic as $60.00 or $600.00. The nominal STFU dues in the past had been $0.10 cents a month, but in 1936 fewer than 10 percent of the membership had been able to pay that.

During the first half year of affiliation, the STFU officially registered only about half its locals, with 21,000 members with UCAPAWA headquarters, and it paid per capita on only 7,389 of these.[49]

From the beginning the issues of autonomy and dues overshadowed all else in the relationship between the two offices in Memphis and Washington. The scattered UCAPAWA locals in the Rio Grande Valley moved almost at once to bypass District IV (STFU) and affiliate with international headquarters. Early in 1938, Henderson's men began work to wean away J. E. Clayton, a black minister and teacher, who was the best STFU organizer in Texas. Across the line in Oklahoma, Odis Sweeden began to see himself surrounded by Communists and threatened to leave not only UCAPAWA but STFU as well.[50]

Mitchell had been lukewarm about the relationship with UCAPAWA from the beginning; he had accepted it as the only way to get CIO affiliation. By April 1938, however, the STFU was close to secession over the issue of autonomy. Sweeden precipitated the matter, demanding the international union communicate with locals and members only through the Memphis office. Howard Kester enthusiastically joined in. A meeting of the executive council seriously debated withdrawal, although Claude Williams posed the classic constitutional argument by saying that the STFU had lost that right when it accepted federation. The council finally withheld action until it presented its case to the execuitve board of UCAPAWA.[51]

Mitchell told the executive board, meeting in Washington, that STFU members were in a state of complete confusion because of the conflicting demands on their loyalties. He asked for either the recognition of his union's complete jurisdiction over all tenants, sharecroppers, and farm laborers throughout the South, or else the peaceful agreement to seek a direct charter from the CIO for the STFU. Henderson countered with a proposal that the STFU become an autonomous district confined to the states of Arkansas, Missouri, and Oklahoma. John Brophy, national director of the CIO and Lewis's troubleshooter, strongly supported the latter motion. For two hours, Henderson's minions poured abuse on the STFU delegation and then voted in favor of their leader's proposal.[52]

Mitchell bitterly concluded that the "cards were stacked" against STFU and moved to secede, but a special session of his executive council decided to make one more appeal to CIO headquarters. A new representation went to Washington to confer with Lewis and his advisors. With John Brophy and Powers Hapgood mediating, the contestants finally hammered out a shaky compromise: the STFU would remain autonomous within the region it already occupied, and its members' dues would be returned for use within the area. Both sides, however, continued to pettishly disagree over the interpretation of the settlement.[53]

In the midst of this atmosphere of general biliousness, Butler released a new element. He discovered a document in Claude Williams's possession purporting to be a plan for the Communist party to seize control of the STFU. The paper chagrined Butler doubly because he had always staunchly defended Williams against Mitchell's distrust. He immediately publicized his find and demanded the minister's resignation from the STFU executive council.[54] Williams declined and denied that the document had any official standing, but after a lengthy trial the council expelled him. He countered by organizing a coalition of malcontents aimed at winning control of the annual convention of the STFU, but eventually dropped the fight on advice of Henderson and Alfred Wagenknecht, district organizer of the Communist party.[55]

Henderson took a reasonable, hands-off attitude toward the Williams affair, and, indeed, told Mitchell to take any action he wanted against Williams because the party didn't trust him anyway; but the long period of mistrust and ill will had taken its toll. The events of the next several months were a chronicle of mutual recrimination between the STFU and UCAPAWA.[56] When nine delegates made the long trip from Memphis to San Francisco for the Second Convention of UCAPAWA, 12–16 December 1938, they met with a cool reception. They received only one vote each despite their claim to represent 146 locals and 35,685 members. When they raised the issue of district autonomy, Henderson's response was to tighten centralized control. Whereas they had previously held four positions on the twenty-four-man executive board, they now retained only one, that of O. H. Whitfield of Missouri, whom Henderson chose as one of his nine vice-presidents.[57]

Whitfield soon proved a weak staff for the STFU to lean on. In January 1939 he led a roadside demonstration of evicted sharecroppers in the bootheel region of Missouri. He ordered Butler and Mitchell to keep out of his territory, and Butler charged that he was being guided by the Communist Al Jackson, a former secretary of the Sharecroppers Union. Late in February Whitfield called a state convention aimed at supporting Henderson in a move to depose the leadership of the STFU.[58]

Henderson had decided to spark a rebellion from below against the Memphis office. He invited executive council member, D. A. Griffith, to lead the Arkansas revolt. Oklahoma, he claimed, had already deserted. On 1 March, he suspended the STFU executive officers and announced that the district would be reorganized on "a democratic and constitutional basis."[59]

Butler and Mitchell responded with a hurried membership referendum which, they claimed, showed overwhelming support for secession. The executive council laid heavy stress on the issue of communism as the reason for their action. They followed up with a special convention, 19 March, which voted unanimously for withdrawal. The delegates purged their feelings with a funeral service led by Howard Kester over a cigar box labeled UCAPAWA. As the members filed past to drop handfuls of dirt on the coffin, a swingtime piano player banged out a union tune, and they joyfully sang:

> She's Ashes to Ashes and Dust to Dust,
> Here lies A Union We Never Could Trust;
> Ashes to Ashes and Dust to Dust,
> This Man Henderson Has Hushed His Fuss.[60]

Henderson did not give up easily. He sent Leif Dahl, whom most STFU leaders respected, to establish an office in Memphis. Mitchell set a guard over his own headquarters and obtained a federal injunction forbidding Henderson and his allies from using the STFU name. The naïve Butler even suggested testifying before the Dies committee.[61]

Henderson's own STFU convention met in Memphis on 2 April. Mitchell and almost a hundred sharecroppers dramatically appeared at the door, but were denied entry. The UCAPAWA leader read a letter from Gardner Jackson, who maundered on at great length about Henderson's sterling qualities. Violence was narrowly averted when Mitchell dissuaded A. B. Brookins, an elderly black, from leading a group which proposed to make a Christian out of Henderson by baptizing him in the Mississippi river.[62]

Henderson had lost the battle despite his claims to the contrary. A number of ambitious leaders like E. B. McKinney, O. H. Whitfield, and

Claude Williams swam in his wake, but only a handful of the STFU locals followed. Henderson could add the Cotton South to his list of failure to organize farm workers in California, Florida, New Jersey, and elsewhere. In 1942 he gave up on the last of his locals in Missouri. He shifted his attention to cannery and packing workers who were regular dues-payers and who were covered by the National Labor Relations Act.[63]

If Henderson failed, the STFU did not win. Its locals were confused and resentful. Mitchell made brave public statements about unanimity and bright prospects, but in private he recognized that only forty of the onetime three hundred locals were active. Funds had almost dried up, and Gardner Jackson was doing his vindictive worst to cut off sources of outside support.[64] Although the STFU lingered on organizationally for another twenty years, in one guise or another—changing names and scrambling for new bases of support—it had been mortally wounded.

Without denigrating the Sharecroppers Union, it can be said that the Southern Tenant Farmers Union represented the most dedicated and sincere effort in the twentieth century to ameliorate the condition of southern farm workers, sharecroppers, and tenant farmers, both black and white. Its amazing strength came from the faith of its humble members, manifested in the face of brutal beatings and persecution. For a brief period of time it touched that sympathetic strain which is best in America.

And yet, the STFU was bound to fail. The provisions of the various New Deal agricultural programs—fostered by Henry Wallace, to whom efficiency and hybrid corn were more important than people—encouraged landowners to wipe out the institution of sharecropping. The increasing mechanization of the next two decades went further in eliminating the need for a vast body of farm workers in the South.

The question remains whether the STFU could have done more to help in this period of transition were it not for Communist interference. The answer lies in large part in the character and actions of the two men, Mitchell and Henderson.

In many ways, Mitchell *was* the STFU. He symbolized the dogged determination of those he led, but he had his own personal quirks. He was hard-working, hard-living, intelligent, and personally honest.[65] His devotion to the STFU held it together where similar organizations had collapsed. He was also intolerant of those with whom he disagreed. He took an early dislike to the Communists he met—the Commonwealth College group, Claude Williams, and Don Henderson. The Communist party line which made strict distinctions between farm workers and sharecroppers or small tenants appalled him because he believed it was impractical in the South. He was lukewarm from the beginning about affiliating with UCAPAWA because it was, without a doubt, dominated by Henderson and other Communists. From the Denver convention on, he saw Henderson's every move as a Communist plot to subvert the STFU.

Henderson was the perfect enemy. He was demanding, dogmatic, and intellectually arrogant. When he decided to take over an independent union in Sugarland, Texas, he could write that he was going to so "regardless of how the sugar refinery workers . . . feel." As early as 1936, Mitchell wrote Norman Thomas, "Two or three centuries ago such people as Henderson were out burning witches." Years later, even Claude Williams reminisced. "You didn't work with Don Henderson, you worked for him."[66] As head of UCAPAWA he surrounded himself with party members. He had little knowledge of sharecroppers' problems, and the STFU was a bastion of those who did not fit his preconceptions.

The relationship, then, was bound to be unhappy and clashes frequent. The wonder was that it lasted as long as it did. From July 1937 onwards, time and energy, sweat and tears, were devoted to an internecine battle rather than the goal of human betterment.

THE DAIRY FARMERS UNION

IN THE LIFE of the American Communist party, New York City has been its most important center of strength and its headquarters since the 1920s. And yet very little heed was paid to one of the most important sectors of American agriculture—the New York dairy industry—throughout the 1920s and much of the 1930s.

Many New Yorkers would have been startled by the dairy statistics for the Empire State. In the 1930s, New York had an estimated 1,400,000 milk cows—about 5.6 percent of the total for the nation. This count ranked the state a close fourth behind Wisconsin, Minnesota, and Iowa. In milk produced, the efficient farmers of the state moved into third place with 7.2 percent of the whole. Moreover, since the major portion of this liquid went to the metropolitan market, upstate producers supplied about a sixth of the nation's "fluid milk"—that is, milk intended for table use rather than for manufacture into cheese, butter, ice cream, or other goods.[1]

A figurative river of fluid milk poured into New York City day after day. Its tributaries and backwaters extended into seven states, but two-thirds of the 4,400,000 quarts used daily came from within the state, with Pennsylvania ranking second and New Jersey third.[2] Farmers themselves thought in that analogy, and when they spoke of the area of supply, they called it the New York milkshed.

The milk industry was indeed big business. Year after year the balance sheets of the great distributing corporations showed respectable profits. But at the other end of the production line, farmers complained bitterly of long hours (milkings twice daily, 365 days a year), low profits, and accumulating debts. The plaint was an old one, and the cause obvious: the farmers were numerous but isolated and individualistic, and they had few chips to cast when bargaining with dealers. On the other hand, two corporations, the Borden Company and Sheffield Farms, handled the overwhelming percentage of milk in the New York market.

During the swirling years of World War I, producers in the milkshed had struck in 1916 by withholding their milk from market until they had won a higher price. An almost dormant organization, the Dairymen's League, Incorporated, had assumed leadership in that strike, and for a time it appeared that farmers could unite their efforts with the league as their bargaining agent. After a much less successful strike in 1919 and a precipitous drop in postwar prices, however, leaders of the old league reorganized as a New York corporation, the Dairymen's League Co-operative Association, Incorporated. The new league quietly dropped the notion of acting as the representative of the individual farmers in bargaining with the dealers. It began buying or building processing plants, with which the producer signed a contract binding him to deliver his entire output for a year at a price to be established by the market.[3] The league had become big business with corporate managers.

Throughout the 1920s the Dairymen's League tried to stabilize conditions in the milkshed. In 1921, it inaugurated the classified plan for members. Henceforth, milk would fall into one of three categories: class 1 for fluid use, class 2 for cream, and class 3 for cheese and butter.[4] Each class brought its own price on the market, but the league member received an average, or blend, price at the end of the month—after the organization had deducted various fees for handling, transportation, a capital levy, and so on. Sometimes the individual farmer had difficulty knowing where the money went.

The league generally signed up nearly half the dairymen of the milkshed. In some areas it retailed its products under the trade name Dairylea, but in 1922 it made a significant arrangement with the Borden Company. The league would abstain from the New York City market, and in return Borden's agreed to buy what it needed for that region from the league. The accord seemed ideal for both parties—a guaranteed supply for one and a guaranteed market for the other. The fly in the ointment was that while Borden's could turn elsewhere for its milk, the financial stability of the league depended on the continuance of the pact. As the result, a onetime president later testified, the league had paid secret rebates to Borden's from the start.[5]

The system, with all its obvious defects, worked not too badly during the 1920s, but the onset of the Great Depression wrought great havoc among dairymen. As urban joblessness increased, the consumption of milk declined. At the same time, farmers desperately increased production in the attempt to compensate for their own falling income. The result was a tremendous surplus. Much passion and effort in the ensuing decade went into attempts to balance price and supply in order to give the producer a decent standard of living.

One hoped-for solution followed another. In 1932, the league tried to win the majority of the producers into one bargaining unit, but failed. The state then stepped in with a price control board, but conditions seemed to go from bad to worse. A strike by independent producers in April 1933 around Rochester brought in the force of state authority. Fred Sexauer, president of the Dairymen's League, charged that a "communistic group" of unemployed and relief workers had wrought violence.[6]

On 1 August, a greater strike broke out, led by Stanley and Felix Piseck, well-to-do independent producers. Within days, ten thousand farmers were holding their milk at home and cruising the highways to convince others to follow their lead. Violence erupted, and Gov. Herbert Lehman dispatched heavy forces of state troopers and encouraged sheriffs to bolster their number of deputies.[7]

Since Communist headquarters were so near, it seemed logical for the party to investigate the strike and to take advantage of its possibilities. Lem Harris and Henry Puro visited the strike area but concluded that the party could do little, and they chose to concentrate their efforts on the Midwest.[8]

The lack of interest of the Communists did not save the strikers from the full force of red-baiting. Congressman Hamilton Fish issued a press release stating that the United Farmers League had rushed organizers to the strike area, seized leadership, and staged a reign of terror. Sexauer claimed that truckloads of "foreigners, . . . pea and bean pickers and city rowdies," hired by a "sinister force" were behind the strike. The Communists, according to Sexauer, were duping the farmers into attacking the Dairymen's League. The Piseck brothers came to believe that the FBI had been brought into the fight against the strike, and they capitulated.[9]

For a time after the strike, the producers had a breathing spell, but state price controls soon failed after the courts declined to allow any regulation of milk from neighboring states. A period of cutthroat price-slashing in the spring of 1937 preceded new legislation which encouraged both producers and dealers to set up bargaining agencies which would deal with questions of quantity and price.[10] The system collapsed in less than a year, and after a new wave of price cutting, the producers of the milkshed sought protection under the umbrella of a federal-state marketing order.

This complicated plan operated under the joint authorization of state law and the Federal Agricultural Marketing Agreement Act of 1937. It incorporated the earlier idea of dealer and producer bargaining agencies, but placed over them as a final authority a federal marketing administrator who would operate across state lines to enforce uniform prices throughout the milkshed.[11]

From September 1938 until 23 February 1939, the federal-state order brought a measure of stability although not of affluence to milk producers. Then United States District Court Judge Frank Cooper declared the federal statute unconstitutional. The Supreme Court rapidly reversed Judge Cooper on 5 June. In the interim, however, and until 1 July, when the secretary of agriculture reinstated the program, dairymen once more found their monthly checks shriveling as dealers joyfully slashed prices.[12]

The system—federal government, state government, the bargaining agencies, the great milk companies, the league—had failed three times in three years to prevent chaos. Little wonder that many farmers began seeking an alternative solution. Moreover, the worst drought within memory struck New York in the summer of 1939. Wells ran dry, and pastures withered; farmers desperately needed cash to buy feed. But even after the reinstatement of the federal-state order, the process of raising the price of milk was slow and seemingly incapable of meeting the emergency situation. After suitable hearings, the market administrator, E. M. Harmon, announced that the class 1 price would be $2.25 per hundredweight of milk. This sounded eminently fair, but since it had to be averaged in with lower-priced classes, the farmer actually received about $1.50 as the blend price. With sinking feelings many producers realized that they would be unable to purchase the fodder necessary to carry their herds through the winter, and on Saturday, 12 August, a special convention of the Dairy Farmers Union called for a strike to begin on the following Tuesday.[13]

It was under those trying circumstances that many farmers in the milkshed heard for the first time of this organization, founded less than three years earlier by eight dissatisfied dairymen meeting at the Oddfellows Hall in Heuvelton.[14] The union had conducted a moderately successful strike in 1937 against Sheffield Farms, which had abruptly canceled the contracts of over two thousand producers in far northern Saint Lawrence, Franklin, and Clinton counties.[15] During the years since, it had built up an enthusiastic following of about thirteen thousand dairymen—out of the sixty to eighty thousand in the milkshed—who demanded an end to the classification system of milk pricing and, to replace it, one rate for all milk, to be arrived at through a system of collective bargaining. Unlike many other farm groups, the Dairy Farmers Union favored close cooperation with consumers and organized labor, and it flirted with the idea of joining the National Farmers Union.[16]

The man who organized the first meeting of the DFU and who remained its leader until 1941 was an Ogdensburg farmer named Archie Wright. A slender, bespectacled man of uncertain health, Wright possessed inner fires which belied his apparent frailty. He had been a pacifist during World War I and had gone to jail after refusing to register for the draft. After the war he had worked as a seaman, joined the IWW in California, and been a reporter for the *Springfield* (Massachusetts) *Union* before going back to the farm in the late 1920s.[17]

Wright had already shown a capacity for leadership; during the strike he underscored it. He recognized that since his own organization had enrolled only a fraction of the dairymen in the milkshed, if he were to win the union's demand for a flat rate of $2.35 for every hundredweight of milk sold, he had not only to maintain unity among his followers but also to gain the support of a majority of nonmembers and the sympathy of the general public. Wright established his headquarters in Utica and began circulation of the printed call for farmers to picket every processing plant in the milkshed. He softened some criticism from the start by guaranteeing a continued supply of milk for children and for hospital patients, and he insisted that picket lines should be absolutely nonviolent. Radio station WFBL agreed to broadcast fifteen minutes of strike news daily. All of these moves meant a drain on the slender treasury of the DFU, but Wright won financial support from various AF of L and CIO unions. The Transport Workers Union, at that time Communist-dominated under Red Mike Quill, sent a representative to advise Wright.[18]

The Dairy Farmers Union convention had allowed a period of two days for the consideration of its demands, but the only answer had been silence from the dealers and a sort of nervous tsk-tsking from the head of the Metropolitan Cooperative Milk Producers Bargaining Agency, Incorporated, which supposedly represented the forty-five thousand members of the Dairymen's League and the Sheffield Producers' Cooperative Association.[19] Thus on 15 August the strike began. It lasted for nine days.

The first day was quiet, and there were conflicting reports of the effectiveness. Wright claimed that the strike was already more successful than that of 1937. City health commissioner John L. Rice estimated that only 7 percent of the normal milk supply had not reached the metropolitan area and termed the result insignificant. Charles Baldwin, executive secretary of the Milk Producers Bargaining Agency said farmers had withheld only four thousand of the usual one-hundred thousand cans shipped daily, and the vice-president of the Dairymen's League insisted that his organization had received more than 98 percent of usual deliveries.[20]

Producers held back more milk on the second day, and this set a pattern which lasted until the end of the strike. The tempo increased in other ways as well. Tempers flared, and both pickets and their opponents disregarded Wright's strictures against violence. Otsego County officials arrested three strikers and charged them with dumping milk from trucks; Dairymen's League officials claimed that they had lost thousands of gallons. As the strike spread outside the state, a milk truck ran over a protesting farmer at Sayre, Pennsylvania.[21]

Governor Lehman, once again, wired the sheriffs of the eleven most affected counties, instructing them to maintain order even if it required hiring a large force of special deputies. Soon thereafter he placed his state troopers on special alert and extended his earlier instructions to other sheriffs. He also suggested that district attorneys might want to summon special grand juries to investigate criminal violence.[22]

The strike had clearly begun to pinch the city by the end of the third day. A jubilant Wright estimated that receipts were down 50 percent; dealers admitted to a shortage of 37 percent, while the city health commissioner suggested a more conservative 28.5 percent. The Milk Producers Bargaining Agency announced suspension of the manufacturing of cheese, butter, and condensed milk; a cutting back on ice cream; and the reduction of deliveries to restaurants, bakeries, and confectioneries. Distributors began demanding that supplies be sought outside the milkshed area. Allan S. Haywood, president of the state CIO, immediately denounced the idea and wired public officials that organized labor would resist it as strikebreaking.[23]

While the vise on the city tightened, violence in the countryside increased. Sheriffs equipped small armies of deputies. Neither the governor nor any of the parties in the dispute seemed willing to take the first step toward settling it peacefully. Into the breach stepped Fiorello H. La Guardia, the ebullient mayor of New York. La Guardia admitted that he knew little about the intricacies of the milk problem, but he did recognize a threat to his city. On Friday, 18 August, the mayor called for all parties to meet him at an informal conference on the following Monday. Never at a loss for any means of publicizing New York's attractions, he insisted that the meeting be held on the grounds of the New York World's Fair.[24]

The Dairy Farmers Union, the Borden Company, and Sheffield Farms accepted almost at once. President Sexauer of the Dairymen's League finally wired La Guardia that he too would attend, although he disclaimed any knowledge of milk shortages except a small amount which he laid to the door of "intimidation by the C.I.O." His intelligence network must have been weak indeed, because by the time the conferees assembled in the shadow of the Trylon and Perisphere, the city's supply was 50 percent below normal, even though constant patrolling had practically eliminated any violence on the highways.[25]

After La Guardia had gotten the representatives of the various interests together, he insisted that they hammer out an agreement. It required ten hours of hard bargaining, but when the weary men adjourned at one in the morning 22 August, they announced a settlement which seemed to meet most of the demands of the DFU. The price paid to producers would rise considerably. The initial statement was vague, but it implied that dairymen would get a flat rate of $2.15 per hundredweight as compared to the $2.35 they had demanded and the $1.50 average they had received for July.[26]

The mayor had hoped that his efforts would bring an immediate end to the strike, but Wright insisted that only a special convention of the union could call a halt to the picketing. A day later, on 23 August, the triumphant group shouted approval of the agreement. In the meantime, while sensing victory, producers had cut the flow of milk into the city to only 46 percent of normal. In the jubilation of the moment, few recognized what a close thing it had been. Archie Wright admitted, years later, that the union had been on the ropes when La Guardia pushed the settlement through.[27]

The DFU claimed to have won the first victory in history for the principle of collective bargaining between farmers and dealers. John L. Lewis wired his congratulations. Mayor La Guardia called the agreement the initial example of successful producer-consumer negotiations. The union received an obvious boost. New members began flocking in at the rate of over one thousand a month until total enrollment surpassed twenty-thousand at the end of the year. As a bitter opponent acknowledged a decade later, ". . . It was only a miracle that the Dairy Farmers Union didn't take over complete control of the New York Milk Shed."[28]

A counterattack against the union began at once. The milk dealers denied that the organization was a party to the settlement which had ended the strike; it was, they claimed, a private arrangement between themselves and Mayor La Guardia. Moreover, when they filed the written agreement with the federal market administrator, there was no mention of the flat price of $2.15 a hundredweight for all milk purchased. There was rather the old system of numerous classes with the price for each modified in a way to bring the theoretical average to the agreed-upon level.[29]

Wright faced a difficult choice. Within days of his great victory, he found two of his principles badly undermined. He could renew the strike to force acceptance of a uniform price for all milk and the recognition of the DFU as a bargaining agent, or he could rest his weary followers and claim the price hike of about sixty-five cents a hundredweight as a great success. Perhaps with inner misgivings he chose the latter course. John J. Dillon, editor of the *Rural New Yorker* and onetime commissioner of marketing, chided him gently for not smashing the milk trust, and almost twenty years later, Wright said ruefully, "Price alone is fatal, yet you are under pressure in that direction all the time."[30]

Very soon even the victory on price turned sour. On 14 October, market administrator Harmon announced that the blended price to be paid for September's milk would be only $2.085. Dealers claimed that they had used less class 1 milk than anticipated and greater amounts in the other classifications and thus brought the average down. An angry Wright assailed the announcement and declared that producers would renew the strike if they were shortchanged.[31]

An even more explosive reaction came from New York City Hall. La Guardia viewed the price cut as a challenge to his own good faith in arranging the settlement, and he pointed out that the dealers had had no hesitation in using it as the reason for raising the price to consumers. When Harmon defended his stand, the mayor's temper flared. "Chiselers," he told reporters, "are always clever in explaining or seeking to hide their misconduct."[32]

The argument over the missing $0.065 dragged on for almost a year. Many smaller dealers settled, but Borden's, Sheffield's, and the Dairymen's League resisted. The Dairy Farmers Union announced a selective boycott, and La Guardia threw his prestige into the balance, but not until 12 August 1940 did the major dealers pay farmers an additional $91,090.25 to rectify the misunderstanding.[33]

These disputes over the terms of the strike settlement were the symptoms of confusion resulting from the challenge to the accepted order of things in the milkshed. For two decades a relatively stable relationship of forces had existed. Two great dealers nearly monopolized sales in New York City, and two large cooperatives provided the milk. The destiny of the Dairymen's League was obviously intertwined with that of the Borden Company, while no one seriously questioned the domination of the Sheffield Producers Cooperative by Sheffield Farms. The advent of the Metropolitan Cooperative Milk Producers Bargaining Agency in 1937 and the federal-state marketing order in 1938 did not alter the situation to any large degree. The Bargaining Agency proved itself largely an extension of the Dairymen's League, acting with the sometimes grudging concurrence of the Sheffield's and smaller cooperatives, while the marketing administrator's office, under E. M. Harmon, accepted the system which had evolved without questioning it. Contributing the middle-level bureaucracy which kept the wheels turning for dealer, cooperative, and government agency alike were the graduates of the Agricultural College of Cornell University.[34]

The Dairy Farmers Union threatened this alignment. Archie Wright not only mocked the knights, rooks, and bishops, so piously occupying their squares, he threatened to sweep them off the board and demand a new game. He damned the dealers, but he knew they would negotiate with him if he had the strength of numbers behind him. He largely ignored the Sheffield Producers Cooperative. Wright knew that the Dairy Farmers Union and the Dairymen's League were mortal enemies. The league had begun as a bargaining unit, but after reorganization in 1919 it had become the processor, manufacturer, distributor, retailer, and wholesaler of milk and milk products—a major business with high-salaried administrators.[35] The union charged that the league had become so property-conscious that it could not represent the interests of its individual members. In contrast, the union insisted that it would remain pure by owning nothing and by encouraging the growth of independent local cooperatives.[36] Although both groups claimed to represent the true interests of milk producers, their opposing philosophies militated against the probability of future coexistence.

The threat posed by the rapid growth of the Dairy Farmers Union brought immediate counterattacks. Opponents took aim at what seemed to be the organization's vulnerable points: its philosophy of collective bargaining, its cooperation with organized labor and especially with the CIO, the vocal support given to it in the *Daily Worker,* and the personal history of Archie Wright. After scattering their shots over all of these targets, the critics soon began grouping them into one accusation—that Wright was using the union as a tool for gaining Communist domination of the milkshed. It was, after all, a technique which had worked well for the Dairymen's League six years earlier. The leaders of the 1933 milk strike had for the most part retired to their farms in silence after Fred Sexauer had called them "misguided puppets" of the Communist party.[37]

The criticisms directed at the DFU during the 1939 strike centered at first largely on the aid given it by the CIO. Strife had followed this new labor group as the result of its organizational drives in autos, steel, and other mass industries. For over a year the editors of the *American Agriculturalist* had been warning farmers against the "C.I.O. radicals."[38] Henry H. Rathbun, vice-president of the Dairymen's League, quickly picked up this theme on the first day of the strike when he charged that some league members had withheld milk because of "threats, intimidation and fear of C.I.O. brutality." On the following day, Charles H. Baldwin, executive secretary of the Milk Producers Bargaining Agency, told of farm families guarding their homes against armed invaders and of the rumored seven hundred automotive workers who were to descend on the state to close dairy plants and "rule the highways." The Dairy Farmers Union, he asserted, was nothing but "an out and out, C.I.O. Communist movement."[39]

After the strike had ended, Baldwin and others redoubled their efforts to depict the DFU as a cat's-paw of the CIO, and Dairymen's League directors held meetings to warn of the dangers. A league advertisement spread the alarm of "A NEW MENACE *over Every Dairy Home!*" with a cartoon showing the shadow of a brutal thug looming over a farmstead and frightening assorted women, children, and cows. "The Most Tragic and Deplorable . . . Coming of the C.I.O.," said the text underneath, had brought poisoned fields, ruined fences, spoiled milk, and much violence. An editorial in the *Dairymen's League News,* lauding the notorious Associated Farmers of California, pondered the necessity for organizing a similar group to restore order to the milkshed.[40]

The alleged radicalism of the CIO gave foes of the DFU a foundation on which to build their charges of communism, as Rathbun had already done. The secretary of the Milk Producers Bargaining Agency soon linked the union, the dealers, and the Communist party together as opponents of higher prices for farmers.[41] League spokesmen persistently hinted at a connection between the DFU and the party.[42] The news sheet of the Sheffield Producers Cooperative Association was more restrained, but within a year it was calling Wright's group a "transmission belt" to Moscow's cause.[43] Heavier attacks came in the pages of the *American Agriculturalist,* controlled by the conservative publisher Frank Gannett.[44]

Within three months after the end of the strike, a flood of anti-DFU material filled rural mailboxes. Mimeographed letters, signed by Robert Eastman, a frequent contributor to *American Agriculturalist,* came from Ithaca bearing the title "The Red Line from Moscow." At the same time, Eastman, using a New York City address, was supplying upstate newspapers with press releases denouncing critics of the established milk system as radicals and Communists. For this latter business he used the letterhead of a public relations firm in which he was associated with Dr. Edward A. Rumely. Dr. Rumely, who had served a federal prison term for concealing his dealings with the German government during World War I, was executive secretary of the anti–New Deal Committee to Uphold Constitutional Government, at the same address, headed by Frank Gannett. Rumely, earlier in the decade, had been secretary of the Committee for the Nation—once again at the same address—of which

Sexauer of the Dairymen's League had been an official. The financial angel for Eastman's numerous mailings remains conjectural. The *Rural New Yorker* repeated the story that the Milk Producers Bargaining Agency "has paid Dr. Rumely a sizeable sum of money for special purposes." A. D. Theobald, at that time publisher of the Bargaining Agency's newspaper, later reported that the Dairymen's League had gotten Baldwin, the administrator of the Bargaining Agency, to organize the Agricultural Industrial Foundation, headed by Frank Gannett, and to give it four thousand dollars. The Bargaining Agency's annual report confirmed that appropriation. The chain of inference is obvious, although the evidence is not absolutely conclusive.[45]

In mid-November a strident new periodical, the *Dairy Farmers Digest,* took up the cudgels against the DFU. The first issue left no doubt of its purpose—it was to combat "Communistic and C.I.O. activities." The proprietor, V. R. Tompkins, had once edited the journal of the Milk Producers Bargaining Agency, where he had attacked the DFU as early as 1937, implying that it had Communist connections.[46] Tompkins seemed to have no financial problems with his new operation. Unsolicited copies of the *Digest* went to almost every farm home in the milkshed. Tompkins often hinted but never specified where his money came from. A. W. Theobald, who had left the service of the Bargaining Agency to publish the *Independent Producers Guide,* left no doubt of his belief that the Bargaining Agency or the league subsidized Tompkins. When Tompkins retired in 1949, the league bought him out through a complicated series of three dummy purchasers.[47]

From birth the *Digest* focused its attention on the Dairy Farmers Union. It approvingly quoted Fred Sexauer's speech to the National Cooperative Milk Producers Federation, in which he linked together the Communist party, the CIO, and the DFU. Tompkins often tried to master the art of innuendo, as when he implied that there were dark secrets surrounding the foundation of the DFU or hidden truths about the strike. But the meat ax and not the rapier was his weapon. He was obviously more comfortable when writing about the "slimy, sneaky, slinking, slobber mouth Communists" in the DFU and when proposing concentration camps for those who disagreed with his conception of American society.[48]

Archie Wright presented Tompkins with a prime target. Because of Wright's opposition to the draft in 1917, the *Digest* referred to him as a "slacker," and his past affiliation with the IWW and his present relations with the CIO brought dark hints that he was controlled by Moscow. Tompkins's mildest complaint was that the DFU leader had made a speech in which he used language similar to that employed by the *Daily Worker;* Wright had mentioned the Bill of Rights—a well-known document "being used in Radical meetings all over the country."[49]

The continuing barrage of accusations against the DFU and its leader inevitably began to get results. Letters to the DFU's *Union Farmer* warned of the dangers of red-baiting. Ernest Wilber, a member of the Union executive committee, sought occasion to deny ever having known of a Communist in the organization.[50]

The specter of radical domination once raised, however, refused to be laid to rest. In late June 1940, Archie Wright resigned as head of the DFU. His executive committee turned down the move but did place him on leave from office. After an absence of two months, Wright returned in triumph at the general convention on 3 September. He led the fight against a resolution which would have denied that the union had Communist membership or was sponsored by the party. It was, he said, a move by the organization's enemies to split it by inviting a witch hunt. When asked about his own affiliation, he freely answered, "I am not a Communist, and I never have been." The convention ended as cheering members gave Wright a standing vote of confidence.[51]

The victory was a personal one and soon clouded. At a time when Hitler's triumph in Europe seemed imminent, foes of the union hinted that its activities were treasonous. An angry crowd of American Legionnaires broke up a DFU meeting at Andover, and in neighboring East Otto, the Legion commander warned both the union and the Communist party to keep out.[52]

The convention had only patched over cracks which soon reappeared. In early November, Wright sued two members of his executive committee, Frank Brill and Sam Schou. He asked one-hundred thousand dollars damages from each for having called him a Communist. Brill answered defiantly that Wright was "using the Dairy Farmers Union as part of the political program of the Communist party." The antagonists worked out a sort of reconciliation two days later. Wright accepted a statement absolving him from "Communist taint," and he withdrew his suit.[53]

The outside sniping of a year's duration had done its job, however. A troubled member of the DFU wrote to the *Rural New Yorker* asking whether there was truth in the many rumors in circulation. The octogenarian editor, John J. Dillon, had spent a lifetime fighting for the welfare of dairymen, and he had stayed largely apart from the strife over the union. He answered that the organization had done a great deal of good in its short period of existence, and he warned that the "paid puppets" of the milk monopoly were out to destroy it. But he went on to caution Wright not to be influenced by the praise or the financial assistance he had received from radical sources. In the next issue of the magazine Wright denied that he was indebted to left-wingers and countercharged the critics with using false issues to destroy the union.[54]

The balloting for officers early in December 1940 clearly indicated the disunity in the DFU. Wright easily won reelection with almost two-thirds of the votes cast, and two of his staunchest foes, Sam Schou and Lyman Rogers, went down to defeat. On the other hand, the five candidates for the governing board on Wright's slate lost, and Frank Brill won a vote second only to that of Wright. Brill and Schou immediately joined in a letter to the membership charging that Wright aspired to "Stalinistic dictatorship" over a "Communist front organization."[55]

The long barrage of criticism had apparently taken its toll on Wright's emotions. The overwhelming personal endorsement given to him by the membership was not enough. He called a showdown convention to meet 27 December. He made the issue plain: he wanted the expulsion of fifty-one members who had signed an open letter urging his defeat. Feeling ran high, and at one point Wright spoke steadily for two hours. Finally, after a day of wrangling, the delegates rejected Wright's demand by a vote of 188–52, and he resigned.[56]

The executive committee of the union announced that all dissension was at an end. They elected as chairman a man relatively uninvolved in the earlier struggles and praised Wright for his past leadership. The wounds inflicted, however, proved impossible to heal. The recruiting of new members had almost ceased. Most of the county leaders earnestly tried to stabilize affairs, but a core of Wright's followers attempted to change the constitution and retain their leader. When the effort failed, they bolted in May 1941 to found a new group called the Farmers Union of the New York Milk Shed.[57]

Wright's new FUNY got off to a slow start with only two or three thousand members out of the thirty thousand claimed by the DFU. The leaders of the old union now wholeheartedly joined in red-baiting

Wright, implying that the Communist party backed him in splitting the organization.[58]

The Dairy Farmers Union, which Wright had nurtured and led for more than four years, continued to exist for little more than a year after his departure. The problems arising from a new drought and rising costs pushed the leaders into calling a strike early in July 1941. Although angry farmers withheld almost as much milk as they had two years earlier, the strike collapsed. Without Wright at the helm, the DFU blundered from one mistake to another. The members of the executive committee soon were bickering among themselves, and rumors abounded that the treasury was running dry. The surprising end came on 7 February 1942 with the announcement that the Dairy Farmers Union would become the United Dairy Farmers, an autonomous section of District 50, United Mine Workers of America, led by John L. Lewis.[59]

The move caused a flurry of speculation. Some observers saw it as the first step by Lewis in a drive to build an industrial union to take in a majority of the nation's farmers. Quite predictably, the *Dairy Farmers Digest* leveled its guns on the new target.[60] Lewis frightened the established powers even more than Wright had done. Whereas in 1939 and 1940, the *Dairymen's League News* and Gannett's *American Agriculturalist* had lauded the Associated Farmers of California and suggested the need for such an organization in the Northeast, they had never followed up on the threat. Now, however, they did.

On 27 March 1942, the Free Farmers, Incorporated, received a charter from the state of New York. Its purpose was to protect members against damage to their property up to ten thousand dollars. The Free Farmers had two offices: one in Ithaca and the other at an advertising agency in New York City. There was no cost for membership, but individuals had no voice in the group. Only organizations with twenty-five or more members had a vote. Dillon of the *Rural New Yorker* asked the obvious question, "Where is the money coming from?"[61]

The answer to both financing and control lay in the records of the establishment organizations. During its first nine months of existence, Free Farmers received contributions of $103,163.40. Of that total, the Dairymen's League gave $48,917.55 and the Grange League Federation —a retail cooperative corporation—gave $49,175.00. Miscellaneous donations made up the remaining $5,070.85. Executive officers of the New York and New Jersey Farm Bureaus, the New York, New Jersey, and

Pennsylvania Granges, the New York Home Bureau, the Eastern States Farmers Exchange, the Dairymen's League, and the GLF made up the board of directors. They assured the members, "You have in the Free Farmers a standing army, the full force of which can move into action at a moment's notice.[62]

For all of the fund raising and general scurrying about, there is no record that the Free Farmers ever paid for damages traced to the minions of John L. Lewis. Friend and foe alike soon realized that Lewis had scant interest in his "milk miners." Within a few years the United Dairy Farmers disintegrated without having exerted much influence in the milkshed.[63]

The Mine Workers excursion into the dairy industry had a side effect, however, which was disquieting to those who thought that they had shunted Archie Wright into obscurity. Throughout 1941, Wright and his Farmers Union of the New York Milkshed had limped along with scant recognition, not even publishing a newsletter. Then in February 1942, shortly after the DFU joined Lewis' camp, FUNY came out with an attractive, professionally prepared sixteen-page monthly, the *Farmers Defender*. Organizational work expanded, and by January 1944 the union had over four thousand members. Where had the money come from? Certainly not from dues—the old Dairy Farmers Union, with many times the membership, had turned out an amateurish, cheaply produced, short monthly. The answer is not obvious, because FUNY issued no financial reports before 1944. The first guess would be the Garland Fund except that, in June 1941, that old standby of radical causes finally expired. Fortunately for the left, however, the millionaire Robert Marshall had died in November 1940, leaving $750,000 to the Marshall Foundation for purposes almost identical to those of the Garland Fund. In 1944, the Marshall Fund gave $4,000 to Wright's organization and continued the gifts for several years thereafter. It had earlier contributed heavily to the National Farmers Union, and the inference perhaps can be drawn that the Marshall Fund began its contributions to FUNY in 1942.[64]

Those on the left—especially Communists and fellow travelers—may have rushed to Wright's assistance in an almost automatic reaction to Lewis's invasion of the milkshed. Lewis had had a complicated relationship with the Communists. In the 1920s he had been a villain when he drove the Communists out of the Mine Workers Union. In the 1930s, however, he had become the labor hero par excellence as he pushed industrial unionism, founded the CIO, utilized Communist organizers, and gave key positions to attorney Lee Pressman and editor Len De Caux. The alliance continued after the Hitler-Stalin Pact of 1939 and the outbreak of the European war. Both Lewis and the Communists favored American neutrality and opposed Roosevelt's rearmament policies. A complete break came on 22 June 1941, when Germany invaded the Soviet Union. The Communists immediately became prowar and favored self-restraint for unions, while Lewis maintained his isolationism and clamored for a bigger share of the expanding economy for his workers. Lewis rapidly regained his status as villain—or even traitor.

Wright had always had the sympathy of the Communists. They had sent representatives to federal and state milk price hearings, whose testimony followed the line of the DFU. Before the milk strike of 1939 the DFU newspaper made the usual vague prolabor statements, characteristic of the National Farmers Union and the National Farmers Alliance before it, but had ignored the Communists. Wright obviously was grateful to the leftist labor unions for their financial assistance during the strike, and he drew closer to them during the year leading up to his resignation as president. Even then the charges against him were obscure, centering mainly on the praise given him by the *Daily Worker.* In the end the strongest accusation came from a disgruntled former employee who claimed that Wright tried to send him to the Communist Jefferson School.[65]

Wright opposed the war, as might be expected of a World War I pacifist. According to his enemies in the Dairy Farmers Union, Wright had echoed the Communist slogan, "The Yanks are not coming," until Hitler's attack on Russia, after which he became interventionist.[66]

Although Wright consistently denied being a Communist—even, at a later date, under oath in federal court—he had become a consummate fellow traveler by February 1942, when the *Farmers Defender* began publication. There was no question of criticism of the Soviet Union. From the time of the very first issues, there was the steady drumbeat of demands for a second front against the Nazis. There was the relegation of the Pacific war to a very secondary status. There was the analogue in farm policy of the Communist labor program of opposition to strikes. For agriculture this took the form of adamant opposition to the Farm Bureau and Grange demands for higher commodity prices, which

Wright characterized as an attempt by the "fascist minded . . . to disrupt the war effort." By 1944, he was charging that the farm bloc in Congress was trying to create price chaos in order to bring a negotiated peace with the enemy.[67] Wright also became one of the staunchest defenders of the efficiency of the small farmer during wartime, but there was no question that he was a firm follower of the Communist party line.

By late 1943, Wright had become convinced that the independent Farmers Union of the New York Milk Shed did not have the funds or the power to have an adequate voice in Washington. He sought affiliation with a larger organization, and there was only one possible direction to move. In a generalized sort of way the National Farmers Union had been following a Popular Front line since 1937. The NFU, unlike the Grange and Farm Bureau, hewed closely to the Roosevelt administration's policies and was moderate in its wartime price demands.

In November 1943, the annual convention of FUNY applied for membership in the larger group. Two months later it became the Northeastern Division of the National Farmers Union.[68] The unified organization looked forward optimistically to a postwar America in which the aims of both the New Deal and the Popular Front would be expanded, domestically and internationally—not foreseeing the wrenching effects of the Cold War and a new red scare.

10
CONCLUSION

THE YEAR 1945 was one of grave crisis for American Communism. In January the French Communist, Jacques Duclos, met with Stalin. In April, the French party's theoretical journal, *Les cahiers du communisme,* published Duclos's article, "À propos de la dissolution du P.C.A.," brutally critical of Earl Browder. In May, the Americans began to discuss it. In July, a special meeting of the national committee unanimously fired the leader to whom they had given unquestioning obedience for fifteen years.[1]

The replacement of Browder by William Z. Foster and Eugene Dennis signaled a clear shift to the left. Unlike the comparable Third Period from 1929 to 1935, during which Communist parties strove to build mass movements among workers and farmers in preparation for imminent revolution, the postwar left turn clearly etched for many observers Stalin's cynical use of those parties for achieving the goals of Soviet foreign policy. As this aim became obvious, the American Communists rapidly lost strength. Most apparent was the near collapse of Communist influence in the labor movement between 1945 and 1950.[2]

For a decade, Browder had guided American Communists in a search for unity with mainstream movements which they hoped to influence or even control. During the initial Popular Front period, from 1935 to August 1939, Communists sought to identify politically with the New Deal; they affiliated briefly with AF of L unions and then wholeheartedly helped to build the CIO; and, as we have seen, they moved first into the Farm Holiday Association and then the Farmers Union. During Stalin's accommodation with Hitler, from August 1939 to June 1941, the Communists attempted to work with those who represented strong strains of pacifism and isolationism in America. And finally, from 1941 until 1945, they went all out in support of the war against Hitler. Browder's greatest error, and the cause of his downfall, was his prediction that the postwar period would witness the continuation of broad political unity at home based on the continuation of the international amity of wartime. He had gone so far, in 1944, as to convert the party into the Communist Political Association.[3]

Browder's downfall saw the immediate reestablishment of the Communist party and a broad reassessment and criticism of the unity policies. During the summer of 1945, meetings, conferences, and conventions frantically sought to define the mistakes of the past and to stake out positions for the future. An internal document from this period analyzed the party's farm work. It raised essential questions about the relationship with farmers and, tangentially, with other groups, especially the labor movement. The anonymous author questioned whether the unity programs had not weakened the party at the same time that they had given the impression of growing influence:

> Since 1935 our farm work has been declining, and although there have been occasions during which some expansion has occurred, the trend has been steadily downward. The early work undertaken at considerable sacrifice by the communists to organize Negro and white sharecroppers and tenants in the South has been almost completely liquidated. In the North this process of liquidation began even earlier, and in fact we can now look back and see that liquidatory tendencies, stemming from a false, undialectical concept of unity, undermined our farm work even before they visibly weakened our work in basic industries. *With each new unity move and each new merger, our farm comrades sooner or later noticed that the Communist Party seemed to be receding from the countryside and they found themselves cut off from their former base of support.* [Italics added][4]

The author was making an immediate case for the condemnation of the official policies of a decade in order to defend a rapid shift of ground, but his argument had a certain logic. The essence of the story of the Communist party and American farmers ended during the rise of the Popular Front. The history of the Dairy Farmers Union was a clear demonstration of this. Fellow travelers and Popular Fronters took the lead, while Communists faded into the background. At the time, however, the path followed by the party had made sense.

In 1938 Communist farm forces had had good reason for an optimistic perception of the future. They and their allies had routed the Coughlin-Kennedy-Everson faction within the National Farmers Union and saw their foes secede to form the ineffectual Farmers Guild. Under the stewardship of John Vesecky, the NFU moved close to the line of the Popular Front. It utilized Robert Handschin of Farm Research as its economist and Washington representative. It made a cooperative pact with Labors Nonpartisan League, the political arm of the CIO, at a time when John L. Lewis was the darling of the Communists. During this period he was depending heavily on the talents of party members and sympathizers from Len De Caux, Lee Pressman, Don Henderson, Harry Bridges, and Gardner Jackson at the top to a host of dedicated organizers at the bottom. The NFU and the CIO united in their support of New Deal policies, and the Farmers Union benefited in return, especially from the programs of the Farm Security Administration and the aid given to various Farmers Union cooperatives. The Communists were satisfied and gave unrestrained praise to the NFU for joining the progressive fight against reaction.[5]

With the backing of Garland Fund money, John Bosch resigned his position as state miller in Elmer Benson's Minnesota Farmer Labor administration to organize for the Farmers Union. During a trip to Louisiana he wrote enthusiastically of the prospects for recruiting strawberry growers into the Louisiana group, the core of which was the old Sharecroppers Union. With the help of Lem Harris he was elected president of a committee to reorganize the Minnesota Farmers Union after Vesecky had suspended the old pro-Kennedy unit.[6]

Bosch worked assiduously to win reelection for Benson after a split between the Popular Front and anti-Communist Farmer Laborites in 1938. The bitter campaign nearly wrecked the party, and Benson went down to a humiliating defeat in the general election at the hands of thirty-one-year-old Harold Stassen. David Saposs, a onetime leftist turned anti-Communist, wrote in 1960 that the Communists had gained control of the Farmer Labor party through manipulation and an influx of "carpet bagger[s]."[7] The claim is probably a Cold War exaggeration, although Walter Harju, Ruth Bert, and Lem and Kay Harris played active roles in the precincts and temporary immigrants included Waldo "Boob" McNutt of Kansas—a leader in both the American League against War and Fascism and the American Youth Congress—and Charles J. Coe of Farm Research.[8]

Benson's two-to-one loss may have caused the Farmers Union to back off from Bosch and incline toward more moderate leadership in Minnesota. Within two years this charismatic leader, who had himself aspired to the governorship, had entered a mid-life career change by becoming a successful insurance man. When interviewed twenty years later, he passionately recalled the glory days of the Farm Holiday movement but remembered only a passing acquaintance with Lem Harris.[9]

Still, the NFU as a whole seemed comfortable in the Popular Front. Important leaders who were sympathetic, if not always uncritical, included Glen Talbott of North Dakota, the Reverend C. M. Mitzell of Pennsylvania, Gordon McIntyre of Louisiana, M. W. Martin of Alabama, George Nelson of Wisconsin, Gladys Talbott Edwards and Chester Graham of educational work, Charles Egley of the livestock service, and old Bill Thatcher, whose financial power within the NFU increased as the New Deal favored his Farmers Union Terminal Association. Most of them undoubtedly approved of the Popular Front line simply because they despised war, feared fascism, and supported the New Deal.

The Farmers Union favored neutrality legislation during the 1930s and opposed American intervention after the outbreak of the European conflict in 1939. Robert Handschin and Gladys Talbott Edwards eloquently fought the peacetime draft bill in 1940. The pronouncements won approbation both from rural pacifists and from Communists who condemned the conflict as imperialist.[10]

In November 1940, the assorted kingmakers in the NFU chose a new president, thirty-eight year old Jim Patton of Colorado. He was tall and movie-star handsome and, when he chose, a dramatic speaker. Patton had fought his way up from a childhood lived in a hardscrabble cooperative agricultural community. He escaped the farm by attending college, then teaching, and, finally, heading the rapidly expanding Farmers Union Life Insurance Company. He would provide a generation of forceful, dramatic, and sometimes Byzantine leadership.[11]

During the first six months of his incumbency Patton displeased both the isolationists and the Communists. He joined William Allen White's Committee to Defend America by Aiding the Allies, and he supported the idea of lend-lease for Britain.[12] He could do little to mollify the isolationists before Pearl Harbor, but the Communists moved in advance of his stand after the German attack on Russia on 22 June 1941.

The global conflict created a wartime Popular Front. The Russian alliance made the American Communists about as respectable as they would ever be to most Americans. They zealously supported administration policies, opposed industrial strikes, advocated an "incentive program" for workers which amounted to old-fashioned piecework, and encouraged government subsidization of small farmers to help them produce at peak efficiency.[13]

Under Patton's strong hand, the Farmers Union became the favored agricultural organization of the Roosevelt administration. It recognized the problems of inflation and supported government programs to curb it—a position criticized by the Farm Bureau and the Grange. Patton served on a variety of Washington's wartime agencies. The NFU strengthened its earlier alliances with labor unions. It fought hard to preserve the Farm Security Administration, the bulwark of small farmers, although in the end an alliance among the Grange, Farm Bureau, and Virginia's reactionary Sen. Harry F. Byrd eviscerated the FSA in the name of wartime patriotism.[14] Patton's vigorous progressivism solidified leftist support for the Farmers Union. In 1941, the Robert Marshall Foundation, under fellow traveling if not Communist aegis, granted thirty thousand dollars, twice renewed, for the NFU to establish a full-time Washington office.[15]

The wartime Popular Front was in full operation during the presidential campaign of 1944 when the Farmers Union joined with the CIO Political Action Committee (CIO-PAC), the National Citizens Political Action Committee (NC-PAC), and the Independent Citizens Committee of the Arts, Sciences, and Professions (ICC-ASP) to support Roosevelt's reelection. Unlike the other groups, the NFU's constitution forbade partisan activities, but its various leaders made the endorsement obvious, and, in addition, Patton became a vice-chairman of the NC-PAC.[16]

Both the ICC-ASP and the NC-PAC decided to keep permanent organizations after the election to provide bases of strength for a broad liberal-left coalition including Communists. They wanted to maintain the wartime Popular Front in the postwar period because many feared that reaction or even fascism would then make a bid for power. In May 1945, Elmer Benson became chairman and C. B. "Beanie" Baldwin executive vice-chairman of NC-PAC, while the sculptor, Jo Davidson, served as head of ICC-PAC. All three firmly believed in the right of Communists to participate in their organizations.[17]

The Roosevelt coalition began to break down soon after his death. Harry Truman seemed to have neither the leadership nor the desire to maintain it. He began replacing Roosevelt's cabinet with his own appointees. Many of them, such as Tom Clark in Justice, John Snyder in Treasury, and Clinton Anderson in Agriculture, seemed hopeless conservatives to many liberals. A wave of strikes swept the nation in 1946, and Truman enraged the labor movement when he threatened to draft workers and used the hated injunction against the mine workers. The lapse of price controls in late summer infuriated consumers as food prices spiraled.

Patton watched these developments with dismay because his own relations with the administration were going sour. In sympathy with his union allies he criticized Truman's proposal for conscription of labor, but he had even more pressing problems. Throughout the war the Farmers Union had loyally held the price line and supported Roosevelt's policies. Patton now feared that Secretary of Agriculture Anderson was throwing him over in favor of the conservative Farm Bureau Federation. The NFU, foreseeing increased foreign markets, favored unrestricted crop acreage; the Farm Bureau, fearing a new depression, was pushing crop restriction. The Farmers Union had good relations with the Bureau of Agricultural Economics and the Farm Security Administration, but Anderson restricted the former and appointed a conservative head for the latter. On 2 May 1946, Patton wrote Truman demanding that he fire Anderson. When Truman refused, the Farmers Union almost broke off relations.[18]

In addition to domestic programs were Truman's foreign policies that led many to fear that he was stumbling toward war with Russia. A flurry of committees and conferences sprang from those concerns. Talk increased about a third party for 1948, particularly after Truman fired his major Democratic rival, Secretary of Commerce Henry A. Wallace, for giving a Madison Square Garden speech mildly critical of American foreign policies.[19]

Patton had become a firm internationalist during the war and placed great faith in the United Nations, which he had helped found. Without being pro-Communist he appeared to believe that a continuation of the domestic Popular Front would best guarantee liberalism at home and peace abroad. The same sentiments prevailed with many other Farmers

Union leaders. Alonzo Hamby, in an astute study of postwar liberalism, writes that Popular Fronters were influential in about half of the fifteen states which contained 90 percent of NFU membership.[20]

NFU leaders in Minnesota, the Dakotas, and Montana supported Patton. Alabama and Louisiana retained strong elements of the old Sharecroppers Union. Archie Wright of the Northeastern Division hewed close to the Communist party line, and the successive presidents of the Eastern Farmers Union—encompassing Pennsylvania, New Jersey, and Delaware—may have been party members.[21] But the strongest, and oftentimes most abrasive, spokesman for the postwar Popular Front was Fred Stover of Iowa.

Stover had had a meteoric rise in the Farmers Union. Born of conservative German Lutheran stock late in the nineteenth century, he had gained prominence as president of the Cerro Gordo County Farm Bureau in the early 1930s. He became one of the first field men for the Agricultural Adjustment Administration, and in 1939 he went to Washington to work in the Commodity Credit Corporation and later the USDA War Board. He resigned his federal position in 1943, returned to Iowa, and joined the Farmers Union with the aim of rejuvenating it. Milo Reno's proud old outfit had fallen on bad days after his death. Successive presidents sourly opposed the New Deal and the Patton leadership. One year the membership fell to fewer than a thousand. The 1944 convention elected Stover vice-president even though he was a known New Dealer and Patton supporter. Within a few months the right-wing president resigned, and Stover became the new leader.[22]

The influence of the Popular Fronters permeated the National Farmers Union for more than two years after the end of the war and survived as an important force for several years longer. Patton cautiously resigned as vice-chairman of the National Citizens Political Action Committee when charges grew that it was Communist-dominated, but he sternly rejected any red hunts in the NFU. Gardner Jackson had drifted from the CIO into the Farmers Union during the war, and somewhere along the line he had converted to fierce anti-Communism. He led a floor fight at the 1946 convention for a resolution critical of Communism. He won, but Patton soon fired him from the staff. In a letter to Patton, Jackson charged that Lem Harris exerted inordinate influence over him by threatening to cut the flow of funds from the Robert Marshall Foundation.

Although Harris was not a member of the foundation's board of directors, such was his power, Jackson claimed, that he had forced Patton to bring a young Communist, Phil Reno, into the NFU headquarters. Both Harris and former representative Jerry O'Connell, a Marshall Foundation director, later denied these allegations before congressional committees.[23]

Patton was unruffled by the criticism. He told a convention of the Iowa Farmers Union that American democracy was not in danger of a Communist takeover but rather of an alliance between "corporatism coupled up with the military."[24] Early in 1947, Truman instituted an FBI check on the loyalty of all federal employees, and he called on Congress for military and economic assistance for Greece and Turkey—soon dubbed the Truman Doctrine—to help them fight Communist subversion. In the late spring, Secretary of State George C. Marshall asked the nation to aid European recovery through massive economic grants. Patton and his board of directors unanimously denounced the loyalty check as a "witchhunt" and implicitly condemned the Truman Doctrine and the Marshall Plan for bypassing the United Nations, propping up undemocratic regimes, and establishing a "new imperialism."[25]

In the 1 September 1947 issue of the *National Union Farmer,* editor James Elmore reprinted a cartoon and an editorial from the *St. Louis Post-Dispatch* mildly critical of the Soviet Union. Patton immediately fired Elmore, saying that he had defied the Farmers Union policy calling for world cooperation. In a surprisingly calm reply, Elmore questioned Patton's own stands. Was Patton himself not dividing the NFU into camps by praising Henry Wallace's criticism of the United States during a European trip, by opposing the American selective service while saying nothing of the Russian, and by condemning aid to Greece and Turkey while remaining quiet over Russian interference in Poland and Hungary? Elmore concluded by warning Pattan not to fall into the trap of thinking that any criticism of the Communists or the Soviet Union was red-baiting: the leadership of the CIO had realized this, and no one called them reactionaries.[26]

The question of Communism had come to divide American liberals sharply by 1947. In December 1946, the Independent Citizens Committee of the Arts, Sciences, and Professions and the National Citizens Political Action Committee had merged to form the Progressive Citizens of America under the leadership of Beanie Baldwin and Elmer Benson.

A week later a number of prominent liberals founded the Americans for Democratic Action. The PCA was frankly Popular Front, believed in the unity of all on the left, and sharply criticized American foreign policies. The ADA rejected Communists and largely supported Truman's diplomatic programs, especially the Marshall Plan.[27] In many ways the Communists themselves had forced this break. When the party reacted to Duclos's criticism in 1945 by removing Browder from leadership, it had also rejected his policy of working within broad organizations for goals of realizable change. It had chosen to promote agressively the programs of international communism. As relations between the United States and the Soviet Union deteriorated, this meant, most often, an unquestioning support of Soviet policies.

Throughout much of 1947 the National Farmers Union leaned toward the PCA. Patton broadcast under its sponsorship a speech critical of the Truman Doctrine.[28] Lem Harris had high praise for the NFU. He singled out Patton, Glen Talbott, and Bill Thatcher for their public recognition of the dangers of fascism and red-baiting. Harris warned that farmers should not be automatically rejected as reactionaries. On the contrary, he wrote, the NFU had been consistently progressive, and this "progressive agrarianism" would be a necessary element in a new political party.[29]

The national convention of the Farmers Union voted down an anti-Communist resolution by a three-to-one margin early in March 1948. Archie Wright led the opposition. In an impassioned address he warned that this had been the very issue, raised by outsiders, which had wrecked the Dairy Farmers Union.[30]

Patton could not completely dampen the issue of Communism in the NFU, however. As early as 1944, the conservative, mass-circulation *Farm Journal* had accused the union of being Communist-infiltrated and warned Patton that he was being duped. The article listed a host of supposed fellow travelers, but it singled out Archie Wright as "a foremost member of the Communist party" who had spoken to its convention in 1936.[31] Wright immediately sued for libel. He swore in federal court that he had never been a Communist and presented evidence that he could not have been at the 1936 convention. The judge narrowed the case to the question of whether calling someone a Communist was libel. The jury decided that it was not. In some ways the Wright suit provided a chilling forecast of the free use of unrestrained innuendo during the McCarthy period and the relative helplessness of the individual.[32]

The *Dairy Farmers Digest* poured a steady stream of accusations at the Farmers Union. *Cooperative Digest* chortled sarcastically over Patton's firing of Elmore. The *Watertown (New York) Times*, for years a friend of the union, turned against it for criticizing American foreign policy. *Counterattack*, a widely circulated anti-Communist newsletter, charged that the party had taken over the NFU and would soon replace Patton with Glen Talbott, whom it characterized as an even more dependable follower of the party line.[33]

The anti-Communist resolutions introduced at the 1946 and 1948 conventions demonstrated that distrust already existed within the NFU itself. In a few states it bubbled to the surface. South Dakota passed its own anti-Communist resolution. Jefferson County New York, one of the largest locals in the Northeastern Division, criticized the NFU's weak stand on Communism and after several months of bickering had its charter lifted. Ken Hones, president of the sizable Wisconsin Farmers Union, fired two members of his staff in 1947 for refusing to say whether or not they were Communists, and Hones, who was no reactionary, began to take the lead in a move to eliminate any Communist influence.[34]

The Farmers Union was only one of a number of liberal organizations kept on the edge of turmoil as speculation increased throughout 1947 that the Progressive Citizens of America would sponsor a third party in the coming presidential campaign. Few Americans were surprised in late December when Henry Wallace announced his candidacy and invited all progressives to join his Gideon's Army.

Patton and the National Farmers Union had good reason to have heeded the call. Wallace, as wartime vice-president, had not only supported the union's domestic policies but had also articulated an idealistic foreign policy admired by Patton and other liberals. Many Americans had look nostalgically toward Wallace as being Roosevelt's true heir when Truman stumbled through one crisis after another during his first year and a half in office. As the Cold War with Russia germinated and grew, the criticism of American policies by Patton, Talbott, and other NFU leaders closely paralleled those of Wallace. In his article for the *New Masses* in 1947, Lem Harris obviously expected Farmers Union support for the new party.[35]

Truman, having lagged about as badly in public opinion as he could in 1946, however, caught a metaphoric second wind. The general public endorsed the Truman Doctrine and Marshall Plan programs for containing the Soviet Union, despite the ill-matched opposition of isolationists, fiscal conservatives, Popular Fronters, and Communists. Organized labor, feeling badly bruised by the Taft-Hartley Act, deeply appreciated Truman's unsuccessful veto. His open support for civil rights brought cautious optimism to blacks. Liberals were heartened by his demands for housing and education programs.

In weaning away potential Wallace supporters, Truman did not neglect the Farmers Union. Patton's longtime friend, Undersecretary of Agriculture Charles F. Brannan, advocated a program of full production, to be consumed by increased exports, and a full-employment economy at home. Truman deftly softened criticism of the Marshall Plan by appointing Patton a member of the advisory board along with the heads of the Grange and Farm Bureau and labor and business leaders. Early in 1948 the liberal Brannan replaced the conservative Anderson as secretary of agriculture.[36]

Wallace had hoped to rally all those, except white southerners, who had formed Roosevelt's coalition: liberals, labor, blacks, urban dwellers, and farmers. Step by step, however, Truman either blocked him, or Wallace thwarted his own aims. When much of his hoped-for support stayed away, he leaned more and more heavily on Communists for their organizational abilities. The result was to alienate others who had initially inclined toward his candidacy.

Wallace almost arrogantly seemed to take farmer support for granted. The top leadership of the new Progressive party was packed with friends of the family farm: Rex Tugwell, Beanie Baldwin, and Elmer Benson all played prominent roles. The small Eastern Farmers Union endorsed Wallace early on. It was the first—and also the last. Archie Wright campaigned vigorously for Wallace, but he did not turn his paper into a propaganda sheet. A group of North Dakota Farmers Union members organized and ran the Progressive campaign in that state. Fred Stover made the powerful nominating address at the Progressive convention, but back home he offered to resign as president of the Iowa Farmers Union if the members wished. They did not.[37]

After a great deal of effort, a small group, including Stover, Wright, Coe of Farm Research, and Ed Yoemans of the Eastern Union, met briefly with Wallace to discuss the agricultural plank. He dismissed them with the admonition that if they needed help, they should seek it from the Department of Agriculture. Stover was furious. In spite of Wallace's lack of interest, the farm plank of the Progressives should have had great appeal to NFU members: strong parity price supports, crop insurance, support for cooperatives, opposition to corporate farming, and so on. During the campaign, however, Wallace continued to ignore farmers. He gave one agricultural speech, arriving two hours late at Moorhead, Minnesota, and getting almost no press coverage.[38]

Lem Harris, like other Communists, worked hard for the Progressive campaign. Almost single-handedly he got the signatures to put Wallace on the ballot in South Dakota. He plaintively asked in a *Daily Worker* column where the Farmers Union was in the campaign. With obvious reference to Glen Talbott, he inquired why courageous leaders did not see that they had the choice of supporting Wallace now or facing a witch-hunt in the future.[39] The obvious answer was that the Farmers Union broke out of the Popular Front mold in 1948. The leadership rejected Wallace and overwhelmingly supported Truman. Wallace, in fact, did more poorly in farm states than did Bill Lemke twelve years earlier. He polled slightly over a million votes nationally—about half from New York City—and ran a lackluster fourth behind Truman, Dewey, and even Strom Thurmond.

Plenty of bruised feelings carried over from the Wallace campaign, but in 1949 an almost magical unity returned to the NFU. Secretary of Agriculture Brannan proposed a bold plan to slow the rapid consolidation in the countryside and to preserve the family farm. The old Popular Front alliance cautiously revived in opposition to the North Atlantic Treaty Organization. Farmers Union leaders feared growing militarism, and Glen Talbott saw a "suicide march" toward war.[40] At the national convention in March 1950, the NFU rejected Ken Hones's anti-Communist resolution and resolved strongly for peace and against the building of hydrogen bombs.[41]

North Korea's invasion of the South in June showed the fragility of the revived Popular Front. Fred Stover immediately opposed American intervention. Archie Wright noted that farmers lost more than they gained from war. Then on 7 September, Sen. Styles Bridges of New Hampshire made a wild swinging attack on the NFU, charging that "Communists, Communist sympathizers, or Communist coddlers," had infiltrated and perhaps taken over.[42] Senators ranging from Hubert Humphrey to Joseph McCarthy rose in rebuttal, and the NFU leadership acted swiftly to certify its patriotism.

At a board of directors meeting, 9 September, the leaders denounced Communism and ratified an official statement supposedly issued by Patton and the executive council 29 July, accusing the North Koreans and their Russian backers of aggression. Stover cast the only negative vote as the rest scurried to rally around the flag.[43]

Patton and his allies now made short shrift of the remaining Popular Fronters. He supported an attempted coup against Stover in October by the outgoing Iowa Farmers Union board of directors, but it failed. In 1951, the national convention revoked the charters of Alabama and the Northeastern Division. The ostensible reason for the latter's expulsion was failure to pay dues. Archie Wright said privately that the NFU wanted him out in order to strengthen ties with Truman and also to bolster a lawsuit against the Utah Farm Bureau, which had publicly charged the NFU with being Communist-controlled.[44]

Patton also fired Clifford Durr, a former member of the Federal Communications Commission, whose wife had been prominent in the Progressive party. An angry Beanie Baldwin wrote Patton to recall all of the help he had given the Farmers Union while head of the Farm Security Administration. Baldwin reminded Patton that not so long ago he had opposed the Marshall Plan and NATO, but now he was persecuting Stover and Durr—men of true integrity—for following the same path of peace. Baldwin claimed that Patton had once told him that since fascism was now fast arriving, it would be necessary to ride with it.[45]

An unruffled Patton moved ahead in his chosen path. The fiftieth anniversary convention held in Dallas, March 1952, turned away from the past activism of the NFU and sealed a bond with the conformism of the decade. There was no mention of the Brannan Plan or of the failure of the administration to support prices at 100 percent of parity. The civil rights resolution was weak, and there was no call for world peace. On the other hand the delegates endorsed the free enterprise system, selective service, and a strong defense program. And, in order to rid themselves of some remaining embarrassment, they gave future conventions the right to revoke the charter of any state with fewer than thirty-five hundred members. Two years later the convention ejected the Eastern and Iowa unions even though some other states had smaller memberships.[46]

The expelled organizations lingered on for some time. Archie Wright's union called a disastrous milk strike in 1957. No one paid the least attention, and by the end of the decade, both the Northeastern and Eastern unions had disappeared. The Iowa union proved the most enduring under the new name, the U.S. Farmers Association. In 1980, the octogenarian Stover still held his little group together with a monthly newspaper and the motto "Peace, Parity, and Power to the People."

In the end, the Communist party failed in its efforts among American farmers, just as it failed among workers, teachers, blacks, and other groups. The little band of visionaries who had founded the party in 1919 eagerly anticipated the imminent proletarian revolution which would end injustice and bring with it an equitable system. Sixty years later the American Communists are a scarred brotherhood of survivors. They cautiously follow Moscow's lead in all things. Even devoted members complain of the dullness of their newspaper. They have not the slightest influence in American life.

'Twas not always so, as we have seen. Even during the prosperity decade of the 1920s, the party attracted dedicated adherents who were willing to lay their very lives on the line to help near hopeless struggles in textile mills and mine fields, or like Al Knutson, to live hand to mouth for years, trying to convince farmers that the system was rotten and needed overthrowing, when oftentimes even the poorest among them believed that all they needed was one good break—maybe next year.

The Great Depression infused new life into the party. As conditions worsened, young idealists flocked to the organization which had the answers, which understood the laws of history, which saw tomorrow clearly. The party seemed to be everywhere: organizing the unemployed, the sharecroppers, the migrants, the blacks, the workers, and the farmers.

But the nation weathered the worst of the depression without a revolution. The idealists, if they stayed in the party, became more sophisticated. They gave up the goal of immediate revolution in order to unite in the Popular Front against the twin evils of war and fascism. Their dedication remained, and they utilized their experience to become some of the best organizers—for example, for the fledgling CIO.

Under Earl Browder's leadership, the Communist party blossomed to its period of greatest influence in the decade between 1935 and 1945. By the simple virtue of hard work, party members had become influential far beyond their numbers in labor unions and Popular Front organizations. Yet this very success brought the downfall of Browder. As the party document on farm work had put it in July 1945, Communists had merged and merged and sought unity so much that the face of the party all too often was no longer evident.

And so, as Eugene Dennis said in 1956, the party made foreign policy issues "the acid test of all united front relationships.[47] For a couple of years after the war the Communist program seemed to be succeeding. Americans dreaded any new conflict, especially with a wartime ally. The new Popular Front based on peaceful accommodation with the Soviet Union held sway in the Progressive Citizens of America, the CIO, and the Farmers Union. But Russian actions in Poland, Hungary, Czechoslovakia, and Berlin turned vast numbers of Americans around. Walter Reuther won leadership away from Popular Fronters in the auto union. Opportunists like Mike Quill and Joe Curran turned on their own Communist supporters and joined the anti-red campaign in the CIO. Between 1948 and 1950, Phil Murray cleaned house in the CIO, revoking numerous charters of party-line unions. The Duclos-inspired insistence on following the Soviet line on foreign policy had deprived the party of its hard-won place in the labor movement.

The Progressive party was an equal disaster. Communists, fellow travelers, and Popular Fronters *had* had considerable influence in that vast coalition, the Democratic party, in 1945. They could have maintained a legitimate slice of power as a peace wing among the Democrats. By deserting, they not only lost that influence, they enhanced the power of their enemies.

Among farmers the story is less clear-cut. In contrast to the labor movement, where a number of union leaders were openly Communist party members, no farm organization leader of significance ever admitted a party link. The two men most often accused, Archie Wright and Fred Stover, consistently and convincingly denied membership under oath in courts and before committees. Joseph Starobin, himself an important party member in the 1940s and later the author of an astute and sensitive study of the party, wrote that one of the great weaknesses of the party was the "inability of thousands of leaders of public, civil, political, and trade union organizations" to make their affiliation publicly known.[48] Did those "thousands" include farm leaders? Those who know will never tell.

The postwar Popular Front was influential within the Farmers Union a considerable time for several reasons. Both pacifism and isolationism can run high among farmers in general. Those farmers who joined the Farmers Union, rather than the Farm Bureau or the Grange, tended to do so because it was politically activist. They reacted adversely to redbaiting. They may also have resisted Truman's increasingly anti-Soviet foreign policies because they were furious over his conservative domestic policies. It finally took the Korean War and Styles Bridges's attack to push Patton firmly into the anti-Communist camp. He used the silken glove more readily than had Murray in the CIO, but he pushed the Popular Fronters out of the NFU just as firmly.

The Communist party's own farm cadres had scattered. Hal Ware had died in 1935. Mother Bloor and Andy Omholt retired to Bucks County, Pennsylvania, and grew old. Al Knutson, after years of unpaid work in the South, returned to North Dakota and a spare existence— always loyal to the party. He lived to be almost ninety, as did Red Flag Charlie Taylor, who left the party in disgust. He became an active Trotskyist and, finally in old age, a democratic socialist. Clyde Johnson and Leif Dahl worked for Don Henderson in UCAPAWA and its successor, the Food, Tobacco, Agricultural, and Allied Workers. After the CIO expelled the latter union in the late 1940s, Henderson left union work and soon died, some said a victim of drink. Dahl turned to cabinetmaking in Philadelphia and Johnson to construction work in California. Gordon McIntyre, a leader in the Sharecroppers Union and the Louisiana Farmers Union, left the country after being investigated by federal authorities in the early 1950s. He became wealthy selling encyclopedias in Europe. Ned Cobb returned home from his long prison term to find his family un-understanding and somewhat ashamed of him. He, however, remained stubbornly proud of his epic days in the SCU. Henry Puro went down hill in the party and left it in the 1940s to start a successful real estate career. Erik Bert remained the perfect party functionary. Charles "Bob" Coe of Farm Research followed the Chinese line when they broke with the Soviets. Rob Hall was a party journalist until the upheavals of the 1950s, when he left to pursue his profession in upstate New York. Lem Harris stayed on as a respected but unobtrusive elder statesman. In late middle age he began a successful industrial insurance business. Later, he started an even more successful travel agency. In his seventies he was still leading tours to the Soviet Union and elsewhere.

Although Eugene Dennis could not say it in so many words, Earl Browder had been right. Browder (or the Comintern) had recognized that the Communist party had very limited potential growth in the foreseeable future. He had observed firsthand that even in the most desperate days of the Great Depression, only a tiny minority of Americans were interested in revolution. The great majority believed that they could be rescued by a little tinkering with the system and by a gallant leader—Roosevelt. Browder accepted this and based his program on the belief that Communists could play a small but important role in a variety of organizations. The anomaly lay, of course, in the question: how long does a revolutionary organization remain revolutionary when it collaborates with reformists? The American Communists were spared this dilemma by Duclos's letter. They followed his strictures, and a decade later Eugene Dennis confessed that the party was in tatters.

The role of the Communist party among American farmers must not be overestimated. Communist revolutions succeeded among farmers and peasants in Russia, China, and Vietnam because there was no social or economic mobility. The future looked darker than the past. Social and economic mobility in the United States, even for sharecroppers, was so much more achievable that the critical mass of despair—and revolution —was never reached. At the best, Communist victories were marginal. Communists had always worked at a disadvantage. They sought, at most, to win farmers as allies in their revolutionary design. They recognized, however, given the individualistic nature of American farmers, that they must mute the goal of collectivization. Farm work was always the party's poor stepchild. On the other hand, their influence should not be dismissed. Because of the dedication of people like Lem Harris, Pat Chambers, Ned Cobb, Charlie Taylor, Leif Dahl, Hal Ware, Caroline Decker, and numerous others, it was probably as successful as in any other area of American life. Their problem was that all of the hard work in the world could not make revolutionaries of a self-satisfied nation.

NOTES

CHAPTER 1

1. Theodore Draper magnificently details the formative period in *The Roots of American Communism* (New York: Viking, 1957). David A. Shannon, *The Socialist Party of America: A History* (New York: Macmillan Co., 1955), is the standard history, but James Weinstein's revisionist *The Decline of Socialism in America, 1912–1925* (New York: Monthly Review Press, 1967) has important insights.

2. Draper, *Roots of American Communism,* pp. 158, 190, 202–25.

3. Ibid., pp. 190, 198.

4. Max Bedacht, "Radicalism in California," *Class Struggle* 3 (August 1919): 270–71; "Communist Party and Socialist Party: The Use of the Ballot," *Communist* 1 (October 1919): 8; *Toiler,* 6 February 1920, p. 3.

5. Ella Reeve Bloor, *We Are Many* (New York: International Publishers: 1940), pp. 266–69. Arthur M. Schlesinger, Jr., with incisive characterization, describes Ware as "a discreet, earnest, quiet man, indistinguishable in a crowd, with rimless glasses on a plain midwestern face" (*The Age of Roosevelt,* vol. 2, *The Coming of the New Deal* [Boston: Houghton Mifflin, 1958], p. 52). Ware and his ancestors, back to the seventeenth century, lived on the Eastern Seaboard. He claimed close kinship with Thaddeus Stevens.

6. V. I. Lenin, "Capitalism and Agriculture in the United States of America," *Selected Works* (New York: International Publishers, 1943), 12:190–282; Bloor, *We Are Many,* pp. 268–70.

7. Theodore Draper, *American Communism and Soviet Russia* (New York: Viking, 1960), pp. 21–27; Bloor, *We Are Many,* p. 270; *Worker,* 2, 11 February 1922.

8. Bloor, *We Are Many,* pp. 270–74; Lenin to Chairman of the Perm Gubernia Executive Committee, 20 October 1922; Lenin to Society of Friends of the Soviet Union, 20 October 1922, reprinted in *Lenin on the United States: Selected Writings by V. I. Lenin* (New York: International Publ., 1970), pp. 588–90; *Worker,* 19 August 1922.

9. Bloor, *We Are Many*, pp. 273–79; Edward Hallett Carr, *Socialism in One Country: 1924–1926* (New York: Macmillan Co., 1964), 3:481–82. Little, unfortunately, has been written on Ware's career in Russia other than his proud mother's encomiums.

10. G. D. H. Cole, *A History of Socialist Thought*, vol. 4, pt. 2; *Communism and Social Democracy: 1914–1931* (London: Macmillan & Co., 1961), pp. 554–72; Edward Hallett Carr, *The Bolshevik Revolution: 1917–1923* (New York: Macmillan Co., 1953), chap. 27, 30; Draper, *Roots of American Communism*, p. 253.

11. Draper, *American Communism and Soviet Russia*, pp. 32–36.

12. Ibid., pp. 57–61.

13. Ibid., pp. 38–43, 57–61.

14. *New York Times*, 13–26 November 1919; 8–16 July 1920 passim; *La Follette's Magazine*, July 1920, p. 93; Belle Case La Follette and Fola La Follette, *Robert M. La Follette* (New York: Macmillan Co., 1953), 2:966–1010.

15. *World Almanac and Encyclopedia, 1921* (New York: New York World Publ., 1920), pp. 685–723. The party name varied in some states.

16. Shannon, *Socialist Party*, pp. 25–40; Edgar Eugene Robinson, *The Presidential Vote, 1896–1932* (Stanford, Calif., Stanford University Press: 1947).

17. Robert M. Morlan, *Political Prairie Fire* (Minneapolis: University of Minnesota Press, 1955), pp. 22–26, 110, 136–37; Alfred Knutson, "The Nonpartisan League," manuscript in author's possession, pp. 7–9.

18. Morlan, *Political Prairie Fire*, 136–37.

19. Ibid., pp. 138–40; Knutson, "The Nonpartisan League," pp. 7–9; Alfred Knutson, interview with author, 5 August 1965.

20. *Minneapolis Journal*, 21 March 1918, quoted in Morlan, *Political Prairie Fire*, p. 190; Morlan, *Political Prairie Fire*, pp. 225–26, 244, 266.

21. Ibid., pp. 190–91, 224–25.

22. Ibid., pp. 207–15.

23. Ibid., pp. 296, 344–45; *New York Times*, 8–16 July 1920 passim.

24. Knutson interview; Solon De Leon, ed., *American Labor Who's Who* (New York: Hanford Press 1925), pp. 127–28.

25. Knutson interview; Charles E. Taylor, interview with author, 2, 3 August 1965.

26. Taylor interview; Homer Ayres, interview with author, 11 November 1969; Harriet Ann Crawford, *The Washington State Grange* (Portland, Oreg.: Binford and Morts, 1940), pp. 269–88, 297–306.

27. *New Majority*, 17 March, 19 May 1923; Draper, *American Communism and Soviet Russia*, pp. 40–43.

28. Draper, *American Communism and Soviet Russia*, pp. 41–42; *New York Times*, 5 July 1923, p. 22.

29. *The Second Year of the Workers Party of America* (Chicago: Workers Library, [1924]), pp. 43–44; *Worker,* 7, 14, 21 July 1923; *New York Times,* 4 July 1923, p. 23; *New Majority,* 14 July 1923; Draper, *American Communism and Soviet Russia,* pp. 43–44.

30. *Producers News* (Plentywood, Mont.), 13 July 1923.

31. Draper, *American Communism and Soviet Russia,* p. 44; John Pepper, "The Workers Party and the Federated Farmer Labor Party," *Liberator* 6 (August 1923): 13–14.

32. *New Majority,* 14 July 1923; Draper, *American Communism and Soviet Russia,* p. 48.

33. Kenneth Campbell MacKay, *The Progressive Movement of 1924* (New York: Columbia University Press, 1947), p. 83; Pepper, *Liberator* 6 (August 1923): 13–14.

34. Edward Hallett Carr, *The Interregnum: 1923–1924* (New York: Macmillan Co., 1954), p. 197; I. Amter, "The Federated Farmer-Labor Party of the United States," *Communist International,* no. 28 (n.d. [ca. August 1923]), p. 63.

35. *Labor,* 14 July 1923; *New York Times,* 7 July 1923, p. 10; *Producers News,* 21 December 1923.

36. Tom Ayres to Henry G. Teigan, 18 July 1923, Henry G. Teigan papers, Minnesota State Historical Society, Saint Paul.

37. *New York Times,* 29 July 1923, pt. 7, p. 11.

38. Draper, *American Communism and Soviet Russia,* p. 80.

39. *The Worker* 4, 11, 25 August, 8 September 1923.

40. Teigan to M. M. Samuelson, 17 September 1923 Teigan Papers.

41. Knutson interview; *Worker,* 27 October 1923.

42. *Producers News,* 5, 23 October, 2 November 1923; Taylor interview; Taylor to Teigan, 8 October 1923, Teigan Papers.

43. Weinstein, *The Decline of Socialism,* pp. 290–92; Teigan to William Bouck, 1 November 1923, Teigan Papers.

44. Taylor to Teigan, 7 November 1923, Teigan Papers; Draper, *American Communism and Soviet Russia,* p. 102.

45. Minutes of unofficial conference, Saint Paul, 15–16 November 1923, National Nonpartisan League Papers, Minnesota State Historical Society, Saint Paul.

46. Ibid.; *New York Times,* 8–16 July 1920 passim; Weinstein, *Decline of Socialism,* p. 293.

47. Draper, *American Communism and Soviet Russia,* p. 91.

48. MacKay, *Progressive Movement,* pp. 54–66.

49. Ibid., pp. 66–72; Weinstein, *Decline of Socialism,* pp. 277–78.

50. Ibid., p. 305; MacKay, *Progressive Movement,* pp. 68, 74–75.

51. Weinstein, *Decline of Socialism,* pp. 304–5. La Follette's family biographers are noticeably silent about these conversations early in 1924 although mentioning Mahoney's trip to Washington to confer with the senator in May (La Follette and La Follette, *Robert M. La Follette* 2:1098–99).

52. J. A. H. Hopkins to Teigan, 22 January 1924, Teigan Papers; *Daily Worker,* 29 January 1924.

53. *North Dakota Nonpartisan* (Bismarck), 13 February 1924; *Daily Worker,* 9 February 1924; Thorwald Mostad to Teigan, 10 February 1924, Teigan Papers.

54. *Daily Worker,* 19, 27 February 1924.

55. Weinstein, *Decline of Socialism,* pp. 304–7.

56. *Daily Worker,* 19 January 1924.

57. Draper, *American Communism and Soviet Russia,* p. 98.

58. Ibid., p. 103; Weinstein, *Decline of Socialism,* pp. 306–7; *Daily Worker* 10–13 March 1924.

59. La Follette and La Follette, *Robert M. La Follette,* 2:1098; *Labor,* 5 April 1924; Hall to Lemke, 26 April 1924, William Lemke Papers, University of North Dakota Library, Grand Forks.

60. Weinstein, *Decline of Socialism,* pp. 310–12; La Follette and La Follette, *Robert M. La Follette,* 2:1098–99; *Labor,* 5 April 1924; *New Majority,* 24 May 1924.

61. La Follette and La Follette, *Robert M. La Follette,* 2:1099–1103.

62. Teigan to C. A. Hathaway, 5 June 1925, Teigan Papers; *New York Times,* 24 April 1924, p. 2; 29 May 1924, p. 1.

63. Walker to Lemke, 30 May 1924, Lemke Papers.

64. Taylor to Teigan, 8 June 1924, Teigan Papers.

65. *Producers News,* 6 June 1924, *New York Times,* 29 May 1924, p. 1.

66. Carr, *Socialism in One Country,* 3:243–44; Draper, *American Communism and Soviet Russia,* p. 109.

67. Carr, *Socialism in One Country,* 3:244. Years later, Earl Browder hypothesized that La Follette had learned of the Comintern order prior to his letter and wrote it as a result. Even if he had—which seems unlikely—the pressures from the labor leaders would still have been the most important motivation (Draper, *American Communism and Soviet Russia,* pp. 113–14, 461).

68. Draper, *American Communism and Soviet Russia,* pp. 461–62; *New York Times,* 18 June 1924, p. 1; *New York Herald Tribune,* 18 June 1924; p. 1. Both Weinstein, *Decline of Socialism,* p. 317, and Draper, *American Communism and Soviet Russia,* p. 115, accept a somewhat larger figure, between five and six hundred delegates.

69. *New York Times,* 18 June 1924, p. 1; *New York Herald Tribune,* 18 June 1924, p. 1.

70. Jaspar Haaland, letter, *Worker*, 13 April 1965.

71. *New York Times*, 18 June 1924, p. 1; *Producers News*, 20 June 1924.

72. *New York Times*, 16 June 1924, p. 2; 17 June 1924, p. 2, 19 June 1924, p. 1; Weinstein, *Decline of Socialism*, pp. 317–18; Draper, *American Communism and Soviet Russia*, pp. 115–16.

73. Ibid., pp. 116; Irving Howe and Lewis Coser, *The American Communist Party* (New York: Praeger, 1962), p. 138; Benjamin Gitlow, *I Confess* (New York: E. P. Dutton, 1940), p. 208; *New York Times*, 20 June 1924, p. 1.

74. *Labor*, 28 June 1924; *New York Times*, 20 June 1924, p. 1.

75. Weinstein, *Decline of Socialism*, p. 318; Draper, *American Communism and Soviet Russia*, p. 116.

76. MacKay, *Progressive Movement*, pp. 110–22.

77. Draper, *American Communism and Soviet Russia*, pp. 117–18.

78. *New York Times*, 15 July 1924, p. 2; Lemke to Covington Hall, 2 July 1924, Lemke Papers; "North Dakota's Communist Legislator," *Workers Monthly*, 4 (April 1925): 272–73.

79. In 1922, the Farmer Labor candidate got 24.7 percent of the vote; in 1924, the Progressive candidate got 10.0 percent and the Farmer Laborite 13.5 percent (*World Almanac 1925* [New York, 1925], p. 849). *Western Progressive Farmer*, 15 August 1926.

80. Weinstein, *Decline of Socialism*, p. 319; George H. Mayer, *The Political Career of Floyd B. Olson* (Minneapolis: University of Minnesota Press, 1951), pp. 30–36.

81. *Producers News*, 11, 18 July, 8 August, 12, 19 September 1924. The independent electors got 61,105 votes and the FLP slate only 4,771 (Robinson, *The Presidential Vote*, p. 388.)

CHAPTER 2

1. Theodore Draper, *American Communism and Soviet Russia* (New York: Viking, 1960), pp. 127–29; Edward Hallett Carr, *Socialism in One Country: 1924–1926* (New York: Macmillan Co.), 3:247.

2. Draper, *American Communism and Soviet Russia*, p. 131; Carr, *Socialism in One Country*, 3:283–88.

3. Draper, *American Communism and Soviet Russia*, p. 130; Carr, *Socialism in One Country*, 3:283–90.

4. George D. Jackson, Jr., *Comintern and Peasant in Eastern Europe: 1919–1930* (New York: Columbia University Press, 1966), pp. 81–82.

5. Ibid., pp. 83, 92–94; Draper, *American Communism and Soviet Russia*, p. 135; Carr, *Socialism in One Country*, 3:309–10.

6. Draper, *American Communism and Soviet Russia*, pp. 133–41.

7. Jackson, *Comintern and Peasant,* especially pp. 60–76; U. Krasni, "The International Peasants' Council," *Communist International,* no. 4 (July–August 1924), p. 155; International Peasant Council, *First International Peasant Conference* (Paris: Bibliotheque Paysonne, 1924), trans. from French in *The Red Peasant International: A Minor Item in the Forgotten Byways of Recent History,* International Peasant Union Documents, no. 19 (New York, n.d.), p. 2. See also Lowell K. Dyson, "The Red Peasant International in America," *Journal of American History* 58 (March 1972): 958–73.

8. Alfred Knutson, interview with author, 5 August 1965.

9. Draper, *American Communism and Soviet Russia,* pp. 141–48, 467th n. 35.

10. *The Fourth National Convention of the Workers (Communist) Party of America* (Chicago: Daily Worker Publishing Co., [1925]), pp. 113–14.

11. *Daily Worker,* 3 September 1925; Draper, *American Communism and Soviet Russia,* pp. 179, 205. The other commission members were Ruthenberg, Lovestone, Earl Browder, Bob Minor, and Alex Bittelman.

12. I summarize the typical problems of western farmers in the study of one state: Lowell K. Dyson, "Was Agricultural Distress in the 1930s a Result of Land Speculation during World War I? The Case of Iowa," *Annals of Iowa,* 3d ser. 40 (Spring 1971): 577–84.

13. Charles E. Taylor to author, 28 April 1964; *United Farmer* (Bismarck, N.D.), August, September, October, 1926. Party friends, if not exactly fellow travelers, in this period included South Dakota Farm Laborites Tom Ayres and Alice Lorraine Daly; North Dakotans R. H. "Dad" Walker, William Lemke, State Senator Ralph Ingerson, and Fargo Labor Council secretary, H. R. Martinson. There were also friendly newspapers in Bowbells, North Dakota, and Sisseton and Wentworth, South Dakota.

14. Charles E. Taylor, interview with author, 2, 3 August 1965; Charles Vindex, "Radical Rule in Montana," *Montana: The Magazine of Western History* 18 (January 1968): 2–18.

15. Lemke to Frazier, 8 November 1925; Frazier to Lemke, 16 November, 14 December 1925; Lemke to Richard McCarter, 23 November 1925, William Lemke Papers University of North Dakota, Grand Forks.

16. *North Dakota State Record* (Bismarck), 17, 24, 31 December 1925, 7 January 1926; *North Dakota Nonpartisan* (Bismarck), 30 December 1925.

17. Lemke to Covington Hall, 13 January 1926; Lemke to R. H. Walker, 25 July 1924, Lemke Papers.

18. *North Dakota State Record,* 11 February 1926; *North Dakota Nonpartisan,* 17 February 1926; *United Farmer,* 1 March 1926.

19. Knutson interview; Alfred Knutson, "The Agricultural Situation," *Workers Monthly* 5 (March 1926): 218–23.

20. *United Farmer,* 1 March, April 1926. There was no chairman, and there is no evidence that the committee ever met. Its membership consisted of R. H. Walker, A. C. Miller, James E. Wenstrum, and H. R. Martinson of North Dakota; O. F. Carlson, South Dakota; E. R. Meitzen, Texas; Charles E. Taylor, Montana; J. B. Della Vedova, Iowa; William Bouck, Washington; Yalmer Karnoven, Minnesota. Martinson and Bouck were not Communists; Walker and Meitzen almost certainly were not.

21. *United Farmer,* 1 March, April 1926.

22. Robert Lee Hunt, *A History of Farmer Movements in the Southwest: 1873–1925* [College Station, Tex., 1935], pp. 156–60; Harold Ware, "Introducing John Farmer," *Liberator* 6 (July 1923): 27.

23. Hunt, *A History of Farmer Movements,* pp. 184–90.

24. William Bouck, "Autobiographical Sketch," University of Washington Library, Seattle; Harriet Ann Crawford, *The Washington State Grange: 1889–1924* (Portland, Ore., 1940), pp. 189–245.

25. Crawford, *The Washington State Grange,* pp. 278–304; Draper, *American Communism and Soviet Russia,* pp. 116–18; *Western Progressive Farmer* (Prosser, Wash.), 20 July 1923, 20 July 1924.

26. *Producers News* (Plentywood, Mont.), 16 October–13 November 1925 passim. The paper was temporarily under the command of P. J. "Paddy" Wallace, a flamboyant Irishman. Taylor lived in Saint Paul between June 1925 and May 1926, having caught the get-rich-quick spirit of the decade. He headed the quack medicine outfit called Radium Remedies Company, which went out of business only after the death of one of the promoters lost for the rest the location of the essential pool of radioactive mud (Lem Harris, interview with author, 15 December 1976).

27. *Western Progressive Farmer, Producers News,* and *United Farmer* carry extensive coverage on organizing, especially in 1926.

28. *United Farmer,* April 1926.

29. *Western Progressive Farmer* 20 February, 15 April 1926.

30. Ibid., 15 April 1926; Shoemaker to H. G. Teigan, 4 May 1926, Henry G. Teigan Papers, Minnesota State Historical Society; [Helmuth] Ihlenfeldt to A. G. Kringlock, 7 February 1927, Kringlock Papers, in the author's possession.

31. *Western Progressive Farmer,* 20 February 1926; *United Farmer,* September 1926; Teigan to Shoemaker, 18 May 1926, Teigan Papers.

32. *United Farmer,* November 1926. The estimate is mine.

33. *United Farmer,* December 1926; *Producers News,* 17 December 1926; *Western Progressive Farmer,* 12 January 1927; A. G. Kringlock, "History of the Progressive Farmers Movement in Iowa," p. 47, Kringlock Papers.

34. *United Farmer,* December 1926; *Western Progressive Farmer,* 12 January 1927.

35. *United Farmer,* December 1926; *Western Progressive Farmer,* 12 January 1927. Neither Taylor nor Knutson would answer as to Wallace in separate interviews with the author some forty years later; each called him an opportunist. Mother Jones, of course, was the aged heroine of organized labor.

36. *Producers News,* 17 December 1926.

37. *Western Progressive Farmer,* 22 December 1926; *United Farmer,* November 1926; Larry Remele to author, 2 August 1977. The Lemke candidacy is puzzling. His papers at the University of North Dakota are voluminous. Generally, there is one file folder or more of correspondence per month. The period April to December 1926, however, is contained in one folder, which has the official notification of his nomination and no other references to his senatorial candidacy.

38. *Western Progressive Farmer,* 12 January 1927; Draper, *American Communism and Soviet Russia,* p. 118.

39. *United Farmer,* September, December 1926.

40. Kringlock, "History of the Progressive Farmers Movement in Iowa," pp. 47–50.

41. See, for example, French to National Director, 5 April 1927; Bouck to National Directory, 9 April 1927; Shoemaker to National Council of Action, P.F.A., 11 May 1927; Wallace to Shoemaker, 27 May 1927; Kringlock to Bouck, 7 July 1927; Kringlock Papers.

42. Minutes, National Directory, P.F.A., 6, 7, 8 September 1927, Kringlock Papers.

43. Teigan to Wallace, 1 November 1927; Teigan to Gale Plagman, 19 May 1928, Teigan Papers; Wallace and Green to P.F.A. officers, 20 April 1928, Kringlock Papers.

44. Charles Anthony Mast, "Farm Factionalism over Federal Agricultural Policy: The National Farmers Union, 1926–1937" (Master's thesis, University of Maryland, 1967), pp. 18–25; *Farmers Union Herald,* March–December 1927 passim.

45. Much of my analysis is based on Mast, "Farm Factionalism," pp. 18–25.

46. *United Farmer,* 1927 passim; Draper, *American Communism and Soviet Russia,* p. 184, 474th n. 81.

47. Draper, *American Communism and Soviet Russia,* pp. 243–67, 492th n. 33.

48. Franz Borkenau, *World Communism* (New York: W. W. Norton, 1939), pp. 274–331; Gunther Nollau, *International Communism and World Revolution,* Trans. Victor Andersen (London: Hollis and Carter, 1961), pp. 97–105.

49. Jackson, *Comintern and Peasant,* p. 117, Draper, *American Communism and Soviet Russia,* p. 305; Isaac Deutscher, *The Prophet Unarmed: Trotsky, 1921–1929* (London: Oxford University Press, 1959), pp. 403–5.

50. Draper, *American Communism and Soviet Russia,* pp. 278–81.

51. Ibid.

52. *United Farmer,* 7 December 1927–15 February 1928 passim.

53. Ibid., 7 March 1928.

54. Ibid., 14, 21 March, 4 April, 16 May 1928.

55. Ibid., June 1928.

56. Draper, *American Communism and Soviet Russia,* pp. 301–9; Jackson, *Comintern and Peasant,* p. 122.

57. Knutson interview; *United Farmer,* September 1928.

58. Draper, *American Communism and Soviet Russia,* pp. 284–99, 380; *United Farmer,* June, October, December 1928, January 1929.

59. Ibid., January–April, 1929 passim.

60. Ibid., January 1929.

61. Draper, *American Communism and Soviet Russia,* pp. 405–41, 523th n. 68; William Z. Foster, *History of the Communist Party of the United States* (New York: International Publ., 1952), pp. 270–74, 292.

62. Untitled report on ["Frank Brown"], obtained from the Federal Bureau of Investigation under the Freedom of Information Act, containing an excerpt of the letter written by Knutson ("Brown").

63. *United Farmer,* April, November 1929.

64. *Producers News,* 26 July, 9 August, 20 September, 25 October 1929.

65. Ibid., 27 December 1929.

66. "U.S. Agriculture and the Tasks of the Communist Party, U.S.A.," *Communist* 9 (February 1930): 105.

67. Ibid., pp. 107–17.

68. Ibid., (March 1930), pp. 280–85.

69. Ibid., (April 1930), pp. 359–75.

70. *Producers News,* 30 May 1930.

71. *Daily Worker,* 10 January, 16, 17, 27 June 1930. George cited former Communist legislator A. C. Miller of North Dakota as an extreme example of Trotskyism for again running on the Republican ticket. Erik Bert criticized the draft program in the *Daily Worker,* 23, 24 May 1930.

72. *United Farmer,* May 1930.

73. Ibid., July 1930.

74. The equivocality of my statement comes from the nature of the evidence. The FBI files which I received on the United Farmers League under the Freedom of Information Act have almost all names deleted. Copies of three letters, dated September [day obliterated] 1930, 1 October 1930, and 2 October 1930, from Bismarck, North Dakota, appear to me to have been written by Knutson. The addressee of the first is "Polburo Distr. #11"; the addressees of the second two have been deleted, although they would seem to be to party officials in New York.

75. Earl Browder, "The Bolshevization of the Communist Party," *Communist* 9 (August 1930): 690–92.

76. U.S., Congress, House, Special Committee to Investigate Communist Activities in the United States, *Hearings,* pt. 4, vol. 3, 71st Cong., 2d sess., 1930, p. 85. The latter statement rests on letter, [deleted], Bismarck, N.D., to [deleted], 2 October 1930, FBI files.

77. [Deleted], Bismarck, N.D., to Polburo Distr. #11, September [day obliterated], 1930, FBI files. Years later Taylor said that Knutson had been accused of using party funds for his family's support.

78. [Deleted], Communist Party of the United States, New York City to [deleted], 27 September 1930, FBI files. Almost certainly to Knutson.

79. [Deleted] to [deleted], 1 October, 2 October 1930, almost certainly from Knutson to Communist party officials in New York; Vern Smith to [deleted], 10 November 1930, almost certainly to Knutson: untitled report on ["Frank Brown"], FBI files; Knutson interview.

CHAPTER 3

1. H. Haines Turner, *Case Studies of Consumer's Cooperatives: Successful Cooperatives Started by Finnish Groups in the United States Studied in Relation to Their Social and Economic Environment* (New York: Columbia University Press, 1941), pp. 179–80; *Cooperative Pyramid Builder,* January 1931, p. 7.

2. Turner, *Case Studies,* p. 149.

3. Ibid., pp. 156–57; Leonard C. Kercher, Vant W. Kebker, and Wilfred C. Leland, Jr., *Consumers' Cooperatives in the North Central States,* ed. Roland S. Vaile (Minneapolis: University of Minnesota Press, 1941), p. 18.

4. Kercher, Kebker, and Leland, *Consumers' Cooperatives,* pp. 18–20.

5. Ibid., pp. 21–22; Turner, *Case Studies,* p. 159.

6. Kercher, Kebker, and Leland, *Consumers' Cooperatives,* p. 23; John I. Kolehmainen and George W. Hill, *Haven in the Woods: The Story of the Finns in Wisconsin* (Madison: State Historical Society of Wisconsin, 1951), pp. 12–24; A. William Hoglund, *Finnish Immigrants in America: 1880–1920* (Madison: University of Wisconsin Press, 1960), pp. 4–9, 13–16.

7. Kercher, Kebker, and Leland, *Consumers' Cooperatives,* p. 23.

8. David J. Saposs, *Left Wing Unionism* (New York: International Publ., 1926), p. 139; Philip S. Foner, *History of the Labor Movement in the United States,* vol. 4, *The Industrial Workers of the World, 1905–1917* (New York: International Publishers, 1965), pp. 491–517; Hoglund, *Finnish Immigrants,* 74–75; Michael Gary Karni, "Yhteishyva—or, For the Common Good: Finnish Radicalism in the Western Great Lakes Region, 1900–1940" (Ph.D. diss., University of Minnesota, 1975), p. 268.

9. John I. Kolehmainen, *The Finns in America: A Bibliographical Guide to Their History,* Finnish American Historical Library, (Hancock, Mich.: Suomi College, 1947), pp. 56–57; Kolehmainen and Hill, *Haven in the Woods,* pp. 127–28.

10. Turner, *Case Studies,* pp. 166–69.

11. Ibid., pp. 159, 161; Kercher, Kebker, and Leland, *Consumers' Cooperatives,* p. 24.

12. Turner, *Case Studies,* pp. 160–61, 167–68; Kolehmainen and Hill, *Haven in the Woods,* pp. 136–37.

13. Turner, *Case Studies,* pp. 171–72.

14. Ibid., pp. 174–75; Kercher, Kebker, and Leland, *Consumers' Cooperatives,* p. 81.

15. Turner, *Case Studies,* pp. 174–75; Karni, "Yhteishyva," pp. 275–76.

16. Turner, *Case Studies,* pp. 175–76; Kercher, Kebker, and Leland, *Consumers' Cooperatives,* p. 81.

17. Kercher, Kebker, and Leland, *Consumers' Cooperatives,* p. 81; Turner, *Case Studies,* pp. 176–77.

18. Turner, *Case Studies,* pp. 183–84; 199–201.

19. *Communist 1* (18 October 1919): 7; Kohlehmainen and Hill, *Haven in the Woods,* p. 129.

20. Theodore Draper, *Roots of American Communism,* (New York: Viking, 1947), pp. 332, 341; Hoglund, *Finnish Immigrants,* p. 76; Theodore Draper, *American Communism and Soviet Russia* (New York: Viking, 1960), p. 190.

21. This was the phrase used by Fahle Burman, secretary of the Finnish Workers Federation, in his report to the party. *The Fourth National Convention of the Workers (Communist) Party of America* (Chicago: Daily Worker Publ. Co., [1925]), p. 46.

22. Solon De Leon, ed., *American Labor Who's Who* (New York: Hanford Press, 1925), pp. 2, 174, 199, 227. That the board were Communists was certainly true by 1929, according to the *Cooperative Pyramid Builder,* January 1931, p. 7. The president of the Cooperative League of the U.S.A. made the latter claim (J. B. Warbasse to L. S. Herron, 21 February 1927, Herron Papers, Nebraska State Historical Society, Lincoln).

23. *The Second Year of the Workers Party of America* (Chicago, [1924]), p. 113; Draper, *American Communism and Soviet Russia,* p. 95.

24. Irving Howe and Lewis Coser, *The American Communist Party: A Critical History* (New York: Praeger, 1962), pp. 157–58; Karni, "Yhteishyva," p. 234. The party Bolshevized in 1924–25 by forming cell units under central discipline and disbanding language federations.

25. Edward Hallett Carr, *Socialism in One Country: 1924–1926* (New York: Macmillan Co., 1964), 3:970.

26. Ibid., pp. 970–76; *International Press Correspondence,* 16 February 1928, pp. 182–83; *Cooperation,* April 1924, pp. 62–64; September 1924, pp. 153–54.

27. Turner, *Case Studies,* p. 202; *Cooperation,* December 1924, pp. 199–201; *Cooperative Pyramid Builder,* December 1926, p. 163; April 1927, p. 107.

28. *Cooperative Pyramid Builder,* December 1926, pp. 163–64; Turner, *Case Studies,* pp. 202–3.

29. De Leon, ed., *American Labor Who's Who,* pp. 199, 241. An example of Ronn's attitude can be seen in his article, "Pink Pills for Pale People," *First Yearbook, Northern States Cooperative League* (Minneapolis, Minn.: Northern States Cooperative League, 1925), pp. 78–80.

30. *Cooperative Pyramid Builder,* January 1927, pp. 3–5; *Cooperation,* December 1926, p. 229.

31. Warbasse and Cedric Long to Board of Directors, 21 February 1927, enclosing four-page mimeographed report; Warbasse to L. S. Herron, 23 February 1926, Herron Papers.

32. J. T. Murphy in *International Press Correspondence,* 14 July 1927, pp. 912–13.

33. *International Press Correspondence,* 15 September 1927, p. 1192. The others were sixty-five Soviets, ten Czechs, two Finns, and one Norwegian.

34. *Cooperative Pyramid Builder,* September–October 1927, pp. 263–66; December 1927, p. 358; *International Press Correspondence,* 15 September 1927, pp. 1192–93; *Cooperation,* October 1927, p. 184.

35. Warbasse to Herron, 21 January 1928, Herron Papers.

36. Herron to Warbasse, 26 January 1928, Herron Papers.

37. Kolehmainen and Hill, *Haven in the Woods,* p. 143.

38. Draper, *American Communism and Soviet Russia,* p. 422; *Cooperative Pyramid Builder,* August 1929, p. 241; May 1930, p. 104.

39. Ronn to Herron, 17 December 1929, Herron Papers; Kolehmainen and Hill, *Haven in the Woods,* pp. 143–44; Karni, "Yhteishyva," pp. 290–94.

40. Karni, "Yhteishyva," pp. 297–301; *Cooperative Pyramid Builder,* May 1930, pp. 104–5; January 1931, p. 7.

41. *Cooperative Pyramid Builder,* January 1931, p. 7; Karni, "Yhteishyva," pp. 303–4.

42. Kolehmainen and Hill, *Haven in the Woods,* p. 145; De Leon, ed., *American Labor Who's Who,* p. 2; Turner, *Case Studies,* p. 205.

43. For example, *Cooperative Pyramid Builder,* January 1927, p. 5.

44. Herron was surely the most dogmatic cooperator in the nation; he opposed federal food and drug acts, feeling that cooperatives should hire their own chemists to test products (Herron to Prof. George Virtue, 16 May 1924, Herron Papers).

45. Herron to Warbasse, 26 January 1928, Herron Papers. There are numerous letters between Ronn and Herron in the Herron Files for 1928 and 1929.

46. *Cooperative Pyramid Builder,* January 1931, p. 7.

47. Karni, "Yhteishyva," p. 305.

48. Ibid., pp. 305–8; Turner, *Case Studies,* pp. 205–6; Draper, *American Communism and Soviet Russia,* p. 493; *Cooperative Pyramid Builder,* December 1929, p. 363; April 1930, pp. 77–78; May 1930, pp. 104–7; January 1931, pp. 7–8.

49. *Cooperative Pyramid Builder,* April 1930, p. 77; Kolehmainen and Hill quote the key sentence from *Tyomies* in *Haven in the Woods,* pp. 143–44.

50. *Cooperative Pyramid Builder,* April 1930, p. 79; January 1931, p. 10.

51. Ibid., November 1929, pp. 323–25.

52. Karni, "Yhteishyva," pp. 311–12; Carl Reeve, interview with author, 17 December 1977.

53. Ronn to Herron, 17 December 1929, Herron Papers.

54. Karni, "Yhteishyva," pp. 313–15; Walter Harju, "Halonen and the Comintern Line," Immigration History Research Center Papers, University of Minnesota, Minneapolis, Xerox copy in author's possession.

55. Reeve interview.

56. *Cooperative Pyramid Builder,* November 1929, p. 324; April 1930, pp. 77–79; May 1930, pp. 98–99; Karni, "Yhteishyva," pp. 319–21.

57. Karni, "Yhteishyva," pp. 321–23.

58. Ibid., pp. 325, 379; *Cooperative Pyramid Builder,* April 1930, p. 79.

59. *Cooperative Pyramid Builder,* May 1930, pp. 97–99; Karni, "Yhteishyva," p. 335.

60. Karni, "Yhteishyva," p. 335; *Cooperative Pyramid Builder,* July 1930, p. 164; January 1931, p. 4; April 1931, p. 111.

61. *Cooperative Pyramid Builder,* November 1930, pp. 304–5; Reeve interview; Kercher, Kebker, and Leland, *Consumers' Cooperatives,* p. 378.

62. Karni, "Yhteishyva," p. 340; *Cooperative Pyramid Builder,* January 1931, p. 4; April 1931, pp. 105–6; Turner, *Case Studies,* p. 212.

63. *Cooperative Pyramid Builder,* April 1931, pp. 98–111; *Cooperative Builder,* April (postconvention issues) 1932–1937 passim; *Central Cooperative Wholesale Yearbook: 1934* (Superior, Wisc.: Central Cooperative Wholesale, [1934]).

64. *Cooperative Pyramid Builder,* April 1931, p. 99.

65. *Cooperative Builder,* 2 July 1938, p. 3; Karni, "Yhteishyva," pp. 363–70. *Farmers National Weekly* always had a once a year spread on the CUA, 1933–36.

66. *Cooperative Builder,* 18 April 1936, p. 4; 17 April 1937, p. 2; 2 July 1938, p. 3; Turner, *Case Studies,* p. 150.

67. Ronn to Herron, 17 December 1929, Herron Papers.

CHAPTER 4

1. Harrison George, "Report on the Agrarian Question," Seventh National Convention, Communist Party, U.S.A., New York, 25 June 1930, mimeographed, Lem Harris Papers, private possession, Norwalk, Conn.

2. "U.S. Agriculture and Tasks of the Communist Party, U.S.A.," *Communist* 9 (February, March, April 1930): 104–20, 280–85, 359–475.

3. Ibid., pp. 283–85, 369–70, 372.

4. George, "Report on thé Agrarian Question."

5. Earl Browder, "The Bolshevization of the Communist Party," *Communist* 9 (August 1930): 690–92.

6. George, "Report on the Agrarian Question."

7. U.S., Department of Agriculture, *Yearbook 1935,* (Washington, D.C.: Government Printing Office, 1935) pp. 3–11; *Yearbook 1931* (Washington, D.C.: Government Printing Office, 1931), p. 31.

8. *Producers News,* 22 November, 13 December 1929; 19 September 1930.

9. H. Puro to Communist Party District Committees, 27 May 1931, Harris Papers; *United Farmer,* January 1931.

10. *Producers News,* 24 July 1931; H. Puro to All District Committees, 27 May 1931, Harris Papers.

11. Allan James Mathews, "The History of the United Farmers League in South Dakota, 1923–1936," (Master's thesis, University of South Dakota, 1972), pp. 2–6; *Producers News,* 27 November 1931.

12. "Directives for Agrarian Work: Endorsed by the Central Committee Plenum," 21–23 August 1931, Harris Papers.

13. Mathews, "The United Farmers League in South Dakota," p. 8.

14. *Producers News,* 11 December 1931; Agrarian Departmental Central Committee to All Districts of the C.P.U.S.A., 19 January 1932, Harris Papers.

15. "Directives for Agrarian Work," 21–23 August 1931; Agrarian Department Central Committee to All Districts, 19 January 1932; "The United Farmers League and How to Organize It," 4 February 1932, Harris Papers.

16. *Producers News,* 22 January 1932.

17. Ibid., 29 January, 11 March, 29 April, 1932.

18. There is no adequate biography of Reno. Roland A. White, *Milo Reno: Farmers Union Pioneer* (Iowa City: Athens Press, 1941), is a cut-and-paste job which, however, draws on material no longer available.

19. White, *Milo Reno,* pp. 35–36, 86–87.

20. Theodore Saloutos and John D. Hicks, *Agricultural Discontent in the Middle West, 1900–1939* (Madison: University of Wisconsin Press, 1951), p. 238.

21. Ibid., pp. 429–32.

22. *Iowa Union Farmer,* 27 July 1932. Lauren K. Soth, *Agricultural Economic Facts Basebook of Iowa,* Iowa Agricultural Experiment Station and Iowa Agricultural Extension Service Special Report no. 1 (Ames, Iowa, 1936), p. 26.

23. The cost-of-production plan was discussed in almost every issue of the *Iowa Union Farmer* after 1930 and later in the *Farm Holiday News.* Richard Bosch gave an intelligent exposition in the *Willmar* (Minn.) *Daily Tribune,* 30 August 1932. John A. Simpson explained it several times in hearings, for example, U.S., Congress, House, Committee on Agriculture, *Hearing, Program of National Farm Organizations,* 72d Cong., 1st sess., 1932, pp. 23–31.

24. *Iowa Union Farmer,* 2 December 1930; Victor Kenneth Heyman, "The National Farmers Union in Its Political World: A Case Study in Influence and the Factors of Influence Potential" (Ph.D. diss. Washington University, 1957), p. 67.

25. U.S., Congress, Senate, Committee on Agriculture and Forestry, *Hearing on H.R. 13991, Agricultural Adjustment Relief Plan,* 72d Cong., 2 sess., 1933, p. 28; *Iowa Union Farmer,* 7 May 1930.

26. *Iowa Union Farmer,* 23 September, 2 December 1931.

27. Ibid., 10 February, 9 March 1932.

28. *Madrid* (Iowa) *Register-News,* 25 February 1932; *Farmers Union Herald,* March 1932; *Des Moines Register,* 4 May 1932, p. 1. There are two extensive accounts of the Farm Holiday Association, with differing interpretations: John L. Shover, *Cornbelt Rebellion (Urbana: University of Illinois Press, 1965); and Lowell K. Dyson, "The Farm Holiday Movement" (Ph.D. diss., Columbia University, 1968).

29. *Producers News,* 13 May 1932.

30. Ibid., 29 April, 6 May 1932.

31. Ibid., 29 April–22 July 1932.

32. *Farm News Letter,* 29 July 1932.

33. *Farmers Union Herald,* September 1932; *Sioux City Journal,* 6 August 1932, p. 2.

34. *Sioux City Journal,* 9 August 1932, p. 2; 10 August 1932, pp. 3, 7.

35. Ibid., 10 August 1932, p. 7.

36. Ibid., 12 August 1932, pp. 4, 7; 21 August, p. A-9.

37. *Producers News,* 12 August 1932; Harrison George, "Causes and Meaning of the Farmers' Strike and Our Task as Communists," *Communist* 11 (October 1932): 930; *Producers News,* 19 August 1932; H. Puro, "The American Farmers Are Beginning to Fight," *Communist* 11 (September 1932): 809–10.

38. Dyson, "The Farm Holiday Movement," p. 83; *Sioux City Journal,* 19 August 1932, p. 1.

39. *Sioux City Journal,* 27 August 1932, p. 1.

40. Ibid., 22 August 1932, p. 2; *Omaha World-Herald,* 26 August 1932, p. 1; *Des Moines Register,* 26–31 August 1932 passim.

41. *Sioux City Journal,* 22 August 1932, p. 2; 23 August 1932, p. 2; 27, 28 August 1932 passim; *Des Moines Register,* 23, 25 August 1932 passim.

42. *Sioux City Journal,* 27 August 1932, p. 1; 1 September 1932, p. 1.

43. Ibid., 15 August 1932, p. 8; *Producers News,* 26 August–9 September 1932 passim.

44. *Farm News Letter,* 8 September 1932.

45. "Farmers! On with the Strike!"; "Toiling Farmers! Unite for Struggle!"; "Striking Farmers: Do Not Betray the Hungry Masses by Signing a Profitteers' Agreement"; flyers in Harris Papers. Ella Reeve Bloor, *We Are Many* (New York: International Publ., 1940), pp. 234–35.

46. Bloor, *We Are Many,* pp. 234–35.

47. *Farm News Letter,* 16 September 1932; a wordier version is in *Sioux City Journal,* 10 September 1932, p. 1.

48. *Sioux City Journal,* 12 September 1932, p. 4.

49. *Farm News Letter,* 16 September 1932; John L. Shover, "The Communist Party and the Midwest Farm Crisis of 1933," *Journal of American History* 51 (September 1964): 254.

50. *Sioux City Journal,* 11 September 1932, p. 1.

51. Ibid., 12 September 1932, p. 1.

52. *Willmar* (Minn.) *Daily Tribune,* 12–22 October 1932 passim.

53. *Sioux City Journal,* 16 September 1932, p. 1.

54. Ibid.; Shover, "The Communist Party and the Midwest Farm Crisis of 1933," p. 253.

55. *Farm News Letter,* 27 October, 30 November 1932.

56. Ibid., 14 November 1932.

57. *The Farmers Make Their Own Program* (Washington, D.C.: National Committee For Action, [1933]), pp. 7, 8. Charles E. Taylor, interview with author, 2, 3 August 1965, made the estimate of party members.

58. Lowell K. Dyson, ed., "Manuscript of Notes of the Farmers National Relief Conference," Group L, *Agrarian Publications* (Westport, Conn., microform, 1976); Malcolm Cowley, "A Remembrance of the Red Romance," *Esquire,* March 1964, p. 128. Matthew Josephson, who supported the Communist ticket in 1932 along with Cowley, took a similar romanticized view in *Infidel in the Temple* (New York: Knopf, 1967), p. 96.

59. Dyson, ed., "Manuscript of Notes of the Farmers National Relief Conference."

60. Ibid.; also summarized in *The Farmers Make Their Own Program,* pp. 13, 14.

61. *The Farmers Make Their Own Program,* p. 18.

62. Ibid., pp. 19, 20.

CHAPTER 5

1. Stuart Jamieson, *Labor Unionism in American Agriculture,* U.S. Department of Labor, Bureau of Labor Statistics Bulletin no. 836 (Washington, D.C.:

Government Printing Office, 1945), pp. 59–70, 261–64; Philip S. Foner, *History of the Labor Movement in the United States*, vol. 4, *The Industrial Workers of the World, 1905–1917* (New York: International Publishers, 1965), pp. 473–85.

2. "Concerning the Convocation of the Second World Congress of the Communist International," *Communist International* 1 (June–July 1920): 2164–75.

3. William Z. Foster, *History of the Communist Party of the United States* (New York: International Publ., 1952), pp. 257–59.

4. Jim Dann, "In the Great Depression—1930–1940: Communists Try to Organize 'Factories in the Fields,'" *PL: Progressive Labor* 6 (February 1969): 73–75; Jamieson, *Labor Unionism in American Agriculture*, pp. 43–46.

5. Ellen Lois Holcomb, "Efforts to Organize the Migrant Workers by the Cannery and Agricultural Workers Industrial Union in the 1930s" (Master's thesis, Chico State College, 1963), p. 1.

6. Dann, "In the Great Depression," pp. 73–74.

7. Jamieson, *Labor Unionism in American Agriculture*, p. 73.

8. Ibid., pp. 81–82.

9. Ibid., pp. 82–83.

10. Ibid., p. 80; Irving Bernstein, *Turbulent Years: A History of the American Worker, 1933–1941* (Boston: Houghton Mifflin, 1970), p. 148.

11. Jamieson, *Labor Unionism in American Agriculture*, p. 84.

12. Ibid., pp. 83–84, 86; Bernstein, *Turbulent Years*, pp. 148–150; Al Richmond, *A Long View From the Left: Memoirs of an American Revolutionary*, (Boston: Houghton Mifflin, 1973), p. 215.

13. *Southern Worker*, 11 October, 1 November 1930; 31 January 1931; Tom Johnson to H. Puro, 19 January 1931; Johnson to Earl Browder, 25 January 1931; [H. Puro] to Johnson, 2 February 1931, Lem Harris Papers, in private possession, Norwalk, Conn.

14. Theodore Draper, *American Communism and Soviet Russia* (New York: Viking, 1960), pp. 342–53; *Southern Worker*, 27 June 1931.

15. Jamieson, *Labor Unionism in American Agriculture*, pp. 284–89; Dale Rosen, "The Alabama Share Croppers Union" (honors' essay, Radcliffe College, 1969), p. 31.

16. Rosen, "Share Croppers Union," pp. 31–32; *Southern Worker*, 25 July 1931.

17. Rosen, "Share Croppers Union," pp. 33–34; John Beecher, "The Share Croppers Union in Alabama," *Social Forces* 13 (October 1934): 126–27.

18. Beecher, "The Share Croppers Union in Alabama," pp. 125–27; Rosen, "Share Croppers Union," pp. 38–40.

19. Rosen, "Share Croppers Union," pp. 43–56, 133–35; Beecher, "The Share Croppers Union in Alabama," pp. 131–32. Ned Cobb's oral history, edited

by Theodore Rosengarten, was published as *All God's Dangers: The Life of Nate Shaw* (New York: Knopf, 1974).

20. Dann, "In the Great Depression," p. 80; Jamieson, *Labor Unionism in American Agriculture,* pp. 87–88.

21. Jamieson, *Labor Unionism in American Agriculture,* p. 20.

22. Ibid., pp. 89–90; Dann, "In the Great Depression," pp. 80–81.

23. Ibid., p. 81.

24. Ibid., pp. 83–85; Bernstein, *Turbulent Years,* p. 156; Jamieson, *Labor Unionism in American Agriculture,* pp. 93–100.

25. Jamieson, *Labor Unionism in American Agriculture,* p. 103.

26. Dann, "In the Great Depression," pp. 85–86; Bernstein, *Turbulent Years,* pp. 156–57.

27. Bernstein, *Turbulent Years,* p. 157; Jamieson, *Labor Unionism in American Agriculture,* p. 100.

28. Bernstein, *Turbulent Years,* pp. 157–58; Dann, "In the Great Depression," p. 86.

29. Dann, "In the Great Depression," p. 86; Bernstein, *Turbulent Years,* p. 158.

30. Bernstein, *Turbulent Years,* pp. 158–59; Dann, "In the Great Depression," pp. 86–87.

31. Dann, "In the Great Depression," p. 88; Jamieson, *Labor Unionism in American Agriculture,* p. 104; Bernstein, *Turbulent Years,* p. 159.

32. Bernstein, *Turbulent Years,* p. 159; Jamieson, *Labor Unionism in American Agriculture,* p. 104.

33. Dann, "In the Great Depression," p. 88; Jamieson, *Labor Unionism in American Agriculture,* pp. 104–5.

34. John Monfross, "The Associated Farmers of California," (Paper read before the Southwest Labor Studies Conference, April 1976), p. 45.

35. Monfross, "Associated Farmers," p. 47; Dann, "In the Great Depression," pp. 90–91; Table "Prepared by the [La Follette] Staff from Data Submitted under Subpoena by the Associated Farmers of California, Inc.," Simon J. Lubin Society Papers, Bancroft Library, University of California, Berkeley; Monfross, "Associated Farmers," p. 50.

36. *Agricultural Worker* (Sacramento), 20 February, 10 April 1934; Bernstein, *Turbulent Years,* p. 153.

37. Bernstein, *Turbulent Years,* p. 160.

38. Ibid., pp. 160–65.

39. Ibid., pp. 165–68; Jamieson, *Labor Unionism in American Agriculture,* p. 109.

40. Monfross, "Associated Farmers," p. 53; Bernstein, *Turbulent Years,* p. 169.

41. Bernstein, *Turbulent Years*, pp. 263–71.

42. Ibid., pp. 169–70; Dann, "In the Great Depression," p. 91.

43. Bernstein, *Turbulent Years*, p. 170.

44. Jamieson, *Labor Unionism in American Agriculture*, pp. 343–45.

45. Ibid., p. 345; Leif Dahl, "Some Aspects of the Work in South Jersey," printed as Appendix O in ibid., pp. 448–51.

46. James A. Wechsler, *The Age of Suspicion* (New York: Random House, 1953), pp. 48–53.

47. Jamieson, *Labor Unionism in American Agriculture*, pp. 345–452; Dahl, in ibid., pp. 449–50.

48. Jamieson, *Labor Unionism in American Agriculture*, p. 345–46; Dahl, in ibid., p. 449.

49. Jamieson, *Labor Unionism in American Agriculture*, p. 346.

50. Ibid., pp. 346–47.

51. Richard Hofstadter, "The Southeastern Cotton Tenants Under the AAA, 1933–1935" (Master's essay, Columbia University, 1938), p. 95.

52. *Southern Worker*, 12 July, 15 November 1933.

53. Ibid., December 1934.

54. Rosen, "Share Croppers Union," p. 62.

55. Ibid., p. 88; Jamieson, *Labor Unionism in American Agriculture*, p. 298.

56. Jamieson, *Labor Unionism in American Agriculture*, p. 298; Rosen, "Share Croppers Union," p. 66.

57. Rosen, "Share Croppers Union," p. 66; Jamieson, *Labor Unionism in American Agriculture*, pp. 299–300.

58. Jamieson, *Labor Unionism in American Agriculture*, pp. 299–300.

59. Lem Harris to Roger Baldwin, 22 February 1934, enclosing "Budget and Plan of Work for Organization of First National Convention of Wage Workers in Agricultural Industry"; undated memorandum of 28 June appropriation, American Fund for Public Service Papers, New York Public Library.

60. "National Conference Agricultural, Lumber, Rural Workers: Program and Resolutions," National Committee for Unity of Agricultural and Rural Workers, Washington, D.C., 1935, mimeographed, American Fund for Public Service Papers; Jamieson, *Labor Unionism in American Agriculture*, p. 22.

61. Jamieson, *Labor Unionism in American Agriculture*, p. 23.

62. Ibid., pp. 23–24.

63. Ibid., pp. 300–301; Rosen, "Share Croppers Union," pp. 105–13.

64. Jamieson, *Labor Unionism in American Agriculture*, pp. 25–26.

CHAPTER 6

1. *Des Moines Register*, 2 October 1932, p. L-4; 2–4 January 1933 passim; 21 January 1933, p. 4.

2. "Memorandum of the Polburo on the Work among Farmers," 15 March 1933, Lem Harris Papers, private possession, Norwalk, Conn., *Farmers National Weekly,* 17 April 1933, 24 August 1934.

3. Alan James Mathews, "The History of the United Farmers League of South Dakota, 1923–1926: A Study of Farm Radicalism" (Master's thesis, University of South Dakota, 1970), pp. 19–30.

4. *Iowa Union Farmer,* 21 September, 19 October 1932; Lowell K. Dyson, "The Farm Holiday Movement" (Ph.D. diss. Columbia University, 1968), p. 131.

5. Dyson, "Farm Holiday Movement," pp. 131–33.

6. Reno to Thomas Horsford, 6 January 1933; Reno to Dr. R. W. Hewes, 15 January 1933, Milo Reno Papers, Special Collections, University of Iowa Library.

7. Dyson, "Farm Holiday Movement," p. 134.

8. *Producers News,* 4 December 1931; John Bosch, interview with author, 4 November 1961.

9. *Sioux City Journal,* 5 January 1933, p. 1; 17 August 1933, p. 3.

10. Ibid., 20 August 1932, p. 5; 9 October 1932, p. B-1.

11. U.S., Congress, Senate, Committee on Agriculture and Forestry, *Hearings on S. 3133, To Abolish the Federal Farm Board and Secure to the Farmer Cost of Production,* 72d Cong., 1st sess., 1932 p. 26.

12. *Sioux City Journal,* 6 December 1932, p. 10; *Des Moines Register,* 6 December 1932, p. 1.

13. *Farmers National Weekly,* 10 February 1933; notes, 14 April [1933] meeting, Harris Papers.

14. *Farmers National Weekly,* January–November 1933 passim; Charles E. Taylor, interview with author, 2–3 August 1965.

15. *Sioux City Journal,* 8 January 1933, p. 1; 9 January 1933, p. 1.

16. Lem Harris, "An American Workman in Russia," *Outlook* 157 (25 February 1931): 295–97; U.S., Congress, House, Committee on Un-American Activities, *Hearings,* 82d Cong., 1st sess., 1951, pp. 1833–1923; Lem Harris, interview with author, 15 December 1976.

17. Leif Dahl, "Nebraska Farmers in Action," *New Republic* 73 (18 January 1933): 265–66.

18. Dahlsten to Harold Ware, 20 January 1933; notes, 14 April [1933] meeting, Harris Papers.

19. *Sioux City Journal,* 24 January 1933, p. 1; 5 February 1933, p. B-1; 12 February 1933, p. B1; 14 February 1933, p. 2; 15 February 1933, p. 3.

20. Ibid., 17 February 1933, p. 8.

21. "Know the Truth About Communism"; notes, 14 April [1933] meeting, Harris Papers; Lem Harris to Harold Ware, 22 February 1933, Harris Papers; *Sioux City Journal,* 17 February 1933, p. 8.

22. Notes, 15 April [1933] meeting, Harris Papers.

23. Charles E. Taylor to Harold Ware, 20 February 1933, Harris Papers.

24. *Des Moines Register,* 14 January 1933, p. 1; 20 January 1933, p. 1.

25. *Sioux City Journal,* 9 February 1933, p. 1; *Des Moines Register,* 12 February 1933, p. L-2.

26. Henry Puro, "Report on Situation and the Tasks of the Party among Farmers," Polburo, 15 May 1933, Harris Papers.

27. See, for example, *Sioux City Journal,* 1 April 1933, p. 3, 2 April 1933, p. B-1; 23 April 1933, p. B-1.

28. *Farmers National Weekly,* 17 April 1933, 2 March 1934.

29. *Sioux City Journal,* 28 April 1933, pp. 1–2; ex-sheriff Ed Leemkuill, interview with author, 6 September 1962.

30. *Sioux City Journal,* 28 April 1933, p. 1; *Le Mars Globe Post,* 3 May 1933.

31. *Sioux City Journal,* 2 April 1933, p. 1; 30 April 1933, p. 1; *Des Moines Register,* 29 April 1933, p. 1; 30 April 1933, p. 1.

32. Ella Reeve Bloor, *We Are Many* (New York: International Publ., 1940), p. 238; Otto Anstrom, interview with author, 17 March 1962.

33. Lem Harris, "Special Bulletin," Harris Papers.

34. "Why National Guard in Le Mars?," Harris Papers.

35. *Sioux City Journal,* 2 May 1933, p. 1; 5 May 1933, p. 12.

36. Harris, "Special Bulletin," Harris Papers; former member of Plymouth County council of defense, O. N. Kelley, interview with author, 16 November 1961.

37. *Des Moines Register,* 4 May 1933, p. 1; *Farmers National Weekly,* 19 May 1933; Rob Hall to Washington [Headquarters], 6 May 1933, Harris Papers.

38. Hall to Washington, Harris Papers; *Des Moines Register,* 4 May 1933, p. 1.

39. *Des Moines Register,* 4 May 1933, p. 1; 5 May 1933, p. 1.

40. M. L. Wilson, interview with author, 9 May 1962.

41. *Des Moines Register,* 5 May 1933, p. 1.

42. Hall to Washington, Harris Papers. Lux evaded the dilemma by resigning from Townley's committee (*Farmers National Weekly,* 19 May 1933).

43. Hall to Washington, Harris Papers.

44. *Sioux City Journal,* 11 May 1933, p. 1.

45. Floyd B. Olson to Milo Reno, 12 May 1933, Reno Papers; *Sioux City Journal,* 13 May 1933, p. 1.

46. On Reno: Thomas Horsford to Reno, 15 May 1933; John C. Scott to Reno, 18 May 1933, Reno Papers. On Communists: *Farmers National Weekly,* 19 May 1933; Henry Puro, "Report on Situation and the Tasks of the Party among Farmers," Polburo, 15 May 1933, Harris Papers.

47. *Sioux City Journal,* 17 May 1933, p. 1; 23 June 1933, p. 1; 28 July 1933, p. 1; *Des Moines Register,* 20 July 1933, p. 1.

48. Loren K. Soth, *Agricultural Facts Basebook of Iowa,* Agricultural Experiment Station and Iowa Agricultural Extension Service Special Report no. 1 (Ames, 1936), p. 26.

49. *Farmers National Weekly,* 10 July 1933; Dyson, "Farm Holiday Movement," pp. 203–5.

50. Charles E. Taylor to Harold Ware, 20 February 1933, Harris Papers; *Agricultural Worker* (Sacramento), 10 April 1934; *Organized Farmer* (Dublin, Pa.), September 1932–July 1933 passim; Taylor interview.

51. Leif Dahl to Harold Ware, 4 March 1933; notes, 14 April [1933] meeting; Henry Puro, "Report on Situation and the Tasks of the Party among Farmers," Polburo, 15 May 1933, Harris Papers.

52. H. Puro, "The Tasks of Our Party in the Work among Farmers," *Communist* 12 (September 1933): 482; *Farmers National Weekly,* 5 June 1933.

53. *Farmers National Weekly,* 5 June 1933; William D. Rowley, " 'Grass roots' and Imported Radicalism in Nebraska, 1932–1934" (Master's thesis, University of Nebraska, 1963), p. 5.

54. *Farmers National Weekly,* 30 January, 3 March 1933.

55. Ibid., 25 July 1933; John Wiita [Henry Puro], "My Experience in Work among American Farmers during the 1930s Agrarian Crisis," Immigration History Center, University of Minnesota, pp. 5–6.

56. H. Puro, "The Class Struggle in the American Countryside," *Communist* 12 (June 1933): 547–58.

57. H. Puro, "The Tasks of Our Party in the Work among Farmers," pp. 475–87.

58. *Farmers National Weekly,* 1 September, 2 October 1933.

59. *Sioux City Journal,* 14 August 1933, p. 5; 30 September 1933, p. 2; 19 September 1933, p. 2.

60. *Farmers National Weekly,* 28 October 1933.

61. *Sioux City Journal,* 23 September 1933, p. 1; *Des Moines Register,* 23 September 1933, p. 1.

62. Wallace to Roosevelt, 11 September 1933, Official Files, Franklin Delano Roosevelt Library, Hyde Park, N.Y.

63. *New York Times,* 8 October 1933, p. 13; Reno to F. C. Crocker, 8 October 1933, Reno Papers.

64. Telegram, Langer to Floyd B. Olson, 17 October 1933, Vincent A. Day Papers, Minnesota State Historical Society, Saint Paul; *Des Moines Register,* 20 October 1933, p. 1.

65. Telegram, Murphy to Roosevelt, 20 October 1933, Farm Relief File, USDA, National Archives, Washington, D.C.; Henry J. Morgenthau, Jr., "Farm Credit Diary," 24 October 1933, Morgenthau Papers, Franklin Delano Roose-

velt Library; *Des Moines Register,* 21 October 1933, p. 1; *Sioux City Journal,* 23 October 1933, p. 2.

66. *Sioux City Journal,* 31 October 1933, p. 1; 1 November 1933, p. 8; *Des Moines Register,* 2–4 November passim; Lorena Hickock to Harry Hopkins, 10 November 1933, FERA-WPA Narrative Field Reports, Franklin D. Roosevelt Library.

67. *Farmers National Weekly,* 28 October 1933.

68. *Des Moines Register,* 26 October 1933, p. 1; *Sioux City Journal,* 5 November 1933, pp. A-1, B-4; 6 November 1933, p. 1; 7 November 1933, p. 1.

69. *Le Mars Globe Post,* 26 October 1933; *Des Moines Register,* 26 October 1933, p. 1; *Sioux City Journal,* 6 November 1933, p. 1; 7 November 1933, p. 14.

70. *Des Moines Register,* 10 November 1933, p. A-1; 12 November 1933, p. L-1; 21 November 1933, p. 1; 23 November 1933, p. 2; 24 December 1933, p. L-1; *Le Mars Sentinal,* 10 November 1933; *Le Mars Globe Post,* 16 November 1933; telegram, Paul Appleby to Donald R. Murphy, 8 November 1933; Murphy to Wallace, 18 November 1933, Murphy File, USDA, National Archives.

71. *Farmers Unite Their Fight* (Chicago: Farmers National Committee for Action, 1934), pp. 4–8, 51–53.

72. Ibid., pp. 53–54.

73. Ibid., pp. 56–58.

74. Ibid., pp. 59–61.

75. Taylor interview.

76. Ibid.; *Farmers National Weekly,* 2 October 1933.

77. Ibid., 9 March 1934; *Farmers Unite Their Fight,* pp. 77–79; Wiita [Puro], "My Experiences," pp. 6–8.

78. Taylor interview.

79. *Farmers National Weekly,* 2 March 1934.

80. Mathews, "United Farmers League of South Dakota," pp. 56–70.

81. J. Barnett, "On the Draft Program of the United Farmers League," *Communist* 12 (November 1933): 1140–51.

82. J. Barnett, "Leninism and Practical Work among the Farmers," *Communist* 12 (January 1934): 40–46; H. Puro, "Lenin's Teachings on the Farmer as an Ally of the Proletariat," *Communist* 12 (January 1934): 32–39.

83. Taylor interview; *Farmers National Weekly,* 6 April 1934.

84. Taylor interview; H. Puro, "The Farmers Are Getting Ready for Revolutionary Struggles," *Communist* 13 (June 1934): 574.

85. Taylor interview; Rowley, " 'Grass roots' and Imported Radicalism in Nebraska," p. 109; *Farmers National Weekly,* 18 May 1934.

86. J. Barnett, "The United Farmers League Convention," *Communist* 13 (August 1934): 810.

87. *Farmers National Weekly,* 29 June, 18 May 1934.

88. Ibid., 29 June 1934.

89. Ibid., 6 July 1934.

CHAPTER 7

1. William Z. Foster, *History of the Communist Party of the United States* (New York: International Publ., 1952), pp. 265–66; Theodore Draper, *American Communism and Soviet Russia* (New York: Viking, 1960), pp. 302–6; Franz Borkenau, *European Communism* (New York: Harper & Bros., 1953), p. 71; Julius Braunthal, *History of the International,* vol. 2, *1914–1943* (New York: Praeger, 1967), pp. 345–46; Gunther Nollau, *International Communism and World Revolution: History and Methods,* Trans. Victor Andersen (London: Hollis and Carter, 1961), pp. 106–7.

2. In the context of the 1930s, the *fellow traveler* accepted Communist dogma and revelation but for one or another reason (sometimes a feeling of unworthiness) failed to join the party. *Popular Fronters,* in this book, are those non-Communists who believed in the necessity of a broad liberal-left alliance to combat the depression, fascism, and militarism. Many Popular Fronters were skeptical of the Communists and accepted them only in the spirit of nonexclusivity. Archie Wright of New York (Chapter 9) exemplifies the fellow traveler, John Bosch the Popular Fronter.

3. Braunthal, *History of the International,* 2:415–23; Franz Borkenau, *World Communism: A History of the Communist International* (New York: W. W. Norton, 1939), pp. 382–83.

4. Braunthal, *History of the International,* 2:425–28; Borkenau, *European Communism,* pp. 120–26; Celie and Albert Vassart, "The Moscow Origins of the French 'Popular Front,' " in *The Comintern: Historical Highlights, Essays, Recollections, Documents,* ed. Milorad M. Drachkovitch and Branko Lazitch (New York: Praeger, 1961,) pp. 234–52.

5. *Farmers National Weekly,* 29 June, 6 July 1934. Irving Bernstein believes that Jack Stachel revealed the new line in the sentence, "Our basic task is to win these millions within the A.F. of L.," in June. I find it doubtful that the American party was so well informed; rather, it would appear to me that this is one more in the long list of pledges to win rank-and-file workers to the party despite their leaders—in other words, the "united front from below" (Irving Bernstein, *Turbulent Years: A History of the American Worker, 1933–1941* [(Boston: Houghton Mifflin, 1970], p. 170). Jack Stachel, "Some Problems in Our Trade-Union Work," *Communist* 13 (June 1934): 527.

6. *Farmers National Weekly,* 10, 17 August 1934.

7. Ibid., 31 August 1934.

8. Ibid., 14 September 1934.

9. Ibid., 21 September 1934.

10. *Des Moines Register,* 21 September 1934, p. 1.

11. *Farmers National Weekly,* 14 December 1934; Reno to William Moxness, 26 November 1934, Lem Harris Papers, in private possession, Norwalk, Conn.

12. *Farmers National Weekly,* 28 September, 12 October 1934.

13. Ibid., 29 October, 14 December 1934; 11 January–8 February, 1, 15 March 1935.

14. Charles E. Taylor, interview with author, 2–3 August 1965. Taylor spent much the rest of his working life as a proofreader on the West Coast and as an active Trotskyist. In his eighties he retired to the Minnesota of his youth and returned to his old democratic socialist faith.

15. *Farmers National Weekly,* 19 October–16 November 1934 passim, "Report of the Annual Convention, Minnesota Farmers: Holiday Association, Oct. 9–10, 1934," mimeographed, Harris Papers.

16. *Farmers National Weekly,* 7 December 1934.

17. Ibid., 2 November, 14 December 1934.

18. John Barnett, "Unity of the Farming Masses—A Paramount Issue," *Communist* 14 (February 1935): 180.

19. *Farmers National Weekly,* 25 January 1935.

20. Lem Harris, *Farmers Plan United Action* (Philadelphia: Farmers United Committee for Action, 1935), p. 52.

21. Ibid., pp. 3, 5, 23–25, 32–33; Taylor interview.

22. *Farmers Plan United Action,* pp. 18–19, 32–36, 41–45, 54–56.

23. *Farmers National Weekly,* 5 April 1935; John Wiita [Henry Puro], "My Experiences in Work among American Farmers during the 1930s Agrarian Crisis," Immigration History Center, University of Minnesota, p. 11.

24. *Farmers National Weekly,* 12 April 1935.

25. Ibid., 19 April 1935.

26. Ibid.

27. Telegram, John Dewey, Alfred Bingham, Thomas R. Amlie to Olson, 1 April 1935, Vincent A. Day Papers, Minnesota State Historical Society, Saint Paul; Howard Y. Williams to Bingham, 23 April 1935; Amlie to Williams, 24 April 1935, Howard Y. Williams Papers, Minnesota State Historical Society.

28. *Farmers National Weekly,* 26 April 1935; *Des Moines Register,* 24 April 1935, p. 1.

29. *Des Moines Register,* 28 April 1935, p. 1; *Farmers National Weekly,* 10 May 1935.

30. *Farmers National Weekly,* 3, 10 May 1935.

31. Ibid., 5 October 1934, 10 May 1935.

32. Ibid., 31 May 1935.

33. Ibid., 3 May, 7 June 1935.

34. Clarence A. Hathaway, "Let Us Penetrate Deeper into Rural Areas," *Communist* 14 (July 1935): 641–60.

35. Lem Harris, interview with author, 15 December 1976.

36. *Farmers National Weekly,* 5 July 1935.

37. Ibid., 2 August 1935.

38. "Barley" [Charles Garland] to Roger Baldwin, 14 August 1935, American Fund for Public Service (AFPS) Papers, New York Public Library.

39. *Farmers National Weekly,* 23 August 1935; Taylor interview; Wiita [Puro], "My Experiences," pp. 2, 11–12; Baldwin to Garland, 19 August 1935, AFPS Papers. I do not discuss the so-called Ware Cell of Agriculture Department employees in Washington because they seem to have had no connection with the Communist farm movement.

40. Lem Harris to Roger Baldwin, 22 February 1934, AFPS Papers.

41. Ibid.

42. Thomas to Baldwin, 3 March 1934; extract of minutes of Board Meeting, 7 March 1934; marked ballots, undated; Baldwin to Board of Directors, 23 April 1934; Harris, Ware, and Garland to AFPS, 19 March 1935; Harris to AFPS, 8 February 1936, AFPS Papers; Harris interview.

43. *Farmers National Weekly,* 13 March 1936, was the last issue carrying Bert on the masthead. Wiita [Puro], "My Experiences," p. 13.

44. *Farmers National Weekly,* 20 September–6 December 1935 passim.

45. Ibid., 13 December 1935.

46. Ibid., 20 December 1935; Reno to Harris, 23 December 1935; Reno to Bert, 11 February 1936, Harris Papers.

47. Dale Kramer, interview with author, 1 December 1961.

48. This analysis of the Farmers Union is based on the author's extensive reading of Farmers Union newspapers and minutes for the period. An excellent summary is in Charles Anthony Mast, "Farm Factionalism over Federal Agricultural Policy: The National Farmers Union, 1926–1937 (Master's thesis, University of Maryland, 1967).

49. Ibid., pp. 129–30.

50. Ibid., pp. 118–20; *Farmers National Weekly,* 10 January 1936.

51. *Farmers National Weekly,* 7 February 1936. I am unable to categorize J. W. Hanson of Wisconsin with the information available.

52. Ibid.

53. Mast, "Farm Factionalism," pp. 120–21; *Farmers National Weekly,* 12, 28 February 1936; *National Union Farmer,* 2, 16 March 1936.

54. Mast, "Farm Factionalism," pp. 121–23; *Farmers National Weekly,* 8 May 1936; *New York Times,* 17 February 1936, p. 1; 13 May 1936, p. 1; 14 May 1936, p. 1.

55. *Farmers National Weekly,* 22 May 1936; Mast, "Farm Factionalism," p. 122; *National Union Farmer,* 13 May, 15 June 1936.

56. Lowell K. Dyson, "Father Coughlin and the Election of 1936" (Master's essay, Columbia University, 1959), pp. 15–39.

57. *New York Times,* 20 June 1936, p. 1; 28 June 1936, p. 23.

58. Dyson, "Father Coughlin," pp. 47–50; Mast, "Farm Factionalism," pp. 111–15, 124–26; *Farmers National Weekly,* 26 June, 10 July 1936.

59. *Farmers National Weekly,* 3 January, 8 May 1936.

60. Ibid., 10 July 1936; "Minutes of the 1936 Annual Convention of the National Farmers Holiday Association," mimeographed, Harris Papers.

61. *Farmers National Weekly,* 10 July 1936; *Des Moines Register,* 3 July 1936, p. 13; 8 July 1936; p. 12; *National Farm Holiday News,* 13 November 1936.

62. *Farmers National Weekly,* 14 August 1936; *Farm Holiday News,* 14 August 1936; *National Farm Holiday News,* 20 August 1936.

63. *National Union Farmer,* 1 July, 15 August, 1 October, 2 November 1936.

64. *National Union Farmer,* 15 October, 2 November 1936; Mast, "Farm Factionalism," pp. 125–26.

65. *National Farm Holiday News,* 9 October 1936.

66. National Farmers' Holiday Association: Minnesota Division, "Report of Annual Convention," mimeographed, Harris Papers; Irving Howe and Lewis Coser, *The American Communist Party: A Critical History* (New York: Praeger, 1962), pp. 329–30.

67. Edward A. Stinson to George A. Nelson, 3 November 1936; Stinson to Charles Talbott, 2 November 1936, George A. Nelson Papers Special Collections, University of Wisconsin Library, Madison. *National Union Farmer,* 1 October, 2 November 1936.

68. Dyson, "Father Coughlin," pp. 60–64, 94–96.

69. "Official Minutes of the 32nd Annual Convention of the Farmers Educational and Cooperative Union of America, Des Moines, November 17, 18, 1936," mimeographed, Nelson Papers; Mast, "Farm Factionalism," pp. 127–28.

70. C. C. Talbott to Jesse W. Scott, 26 January 1937, mimeographed copy; E. E. Kennedy to C. C. Talbott, 25 March 1937, mimeographed copy, Nelson Papers. The Indiana state secretary charged also that the state president had padded membership rolls, giving Kennedy more votes (Edward A. Stinson to George A. Nelson, 3 November 1936, Nelson Papers).

71. *National Farm Holiday News,* 27 November 1936; Dale Kramer, "Farewell to Bryanism," *Common Sense* 7 (January 1937): 15–17; "Official Minutes, 1936 Farmers Union Convention," Nelson Papers.

72. E. E. Kennedy to William Lemke, 24 November 1936; Lemke to Kennedy, 3 December 1936; Kennedy to Lemke, 16 February 1937, William Lemke Papers, University of North Dakota, Grand Forks. *Kansas Union Farmer,* 28 January 1937; *National Union Farmer,* 15 January 1937; Mast, "Farm Factionalism," pp. 136–37.

73. John Bosch and Dale Kramer to American Fund for Public Service, 1 September 1936; Roger Baldwin to George A. Nelson, 15 September 1936, Nelson Papers; Anna Marnitz to Lem Harris, 30 November 1936, AFPS Papers; John Bosch to Oliver Rosenberg, 27 October 1936, Oliver Rosenberg Papers North Dakota State University, Fargo; *National Farm Holiday News,* 16 October, 13, 27 November, 11 December 1936, 22 January 1937. Years later, Lem Harris told the author that Bosch had spend so much on the Holiday that he lived on "fried snowballs."

74. *National Farm Holiday News,* 11, 18 December 1936; 8, 15 January, 5 February 1937.

75. Ibid., 12, 19, 26 February, 12 March, 2, 30 July 1937.

76. Mast, "Farm Factionalism," pp. 136–37.

77. Kennedy to Lemke, 16 February 1937; Kennedy to "My Dear Congressman," 11 May 1937, Lemke Papers; Erickson to Nelson, 20 July 1937, Nelson Papers; *National Union Farmer,* 1 October 1937.

78. *National Farm Holiday News,* 10, 24 September, 22 October, 8 November, 31 December 1937.

79. Mast, "Farm Factionalism," p. 138.

80. Gladys Talbott Edwards to John Vesecky, 5 January 1938; "Minutes of the Board of Directors," Nelson Papers.

81. Appropriation, 2 February 1938, AFPS Papers; Roger Baldwin to Committee of Five: John Bosch, John Cox, Lem Harris, Harry Haugland, George Nelson, 3 February 1938; "Minutes, Farmers Unity Council Meeting," 18 March 1938; untitled resolutions adopted at a conference of six eastern and midwestern Farmers Union states, 28, 29 January 1938; Nelson to National Board, 31 January 1938; John Vesecky to Ira Wilmoth, 5, 18 April 1938; "Official Minutes of the 34th Annual Convention of the Farmers Educational and Cooperative Union of America, Madison, Wis., November 15–17, 1938," George A. Nelson Papers. John A. Crampton, *The National Farmers Union: Ideology of a Pressure Group* (Lincoln: University of Nebraska Press, 1965), pp. 144, 229; *Dairy Farmers Digest,* 20 October 1940, p. 2.

82. "Minutes, Farmers Unity Council Meeting," 18 March 1938, Nelson Papers; *National Union Farmer,* 25 May 1938. Vesecky therein also stated Farm Research "will act as the National Farmers Union Research Bureau in Washington, and also as our contact with the different departments of Government."

CHAPTER 8

1. David Eugene Conrad, *The Forgotten Farmers: The Story of Sharecroppers in the New Deal* (Urbana: University of Illinois Press, 1965), pp. 84–86; Stuart Jamieson, *Labor Unionism in American Agriculture,* U.S. Dept. of Labor, Bureau of Labor Statistics Bulletin no. 836 (Washington, D.C.: Government

Printing Office, 1945), pp. 307–8; H. L. Mitchell, *Mean Things Happening in This Land* (Montclair, N.J.: Allanheld, Osmun, 1979), pp. 41–43, 47–49.

2. Jerold S. Auerbach, "Southern Tenant Farmers: Socialist Critics of the New Deal," *Labor History* 8 (Winter 1966): 5–13; Mitchell, *Mean Things*, pp. 60–74.

3. Jamieson, *Labor Unionism in American Agriculture*, pp. 307–14; Donald H. Grubbs, *Cry from the Cotton: The Southern Tenant Farmers' Union and the New Deal* (Chapel Hill University of North Carolina Press, 1971), pp. 86–87.

4. See, for example, H. L. Mitchell to Chester Hunt, 24 March 1936; Mitchell to A. S. Bayne, 7 April 1936, Southern Tenant Farmers Union (STFU) Papers, Southern Historical Collection, University of North Carolina Library, Chapel Hill. Auerbach, "Southern Tenant Farmers," on the other hand, strongly emphasizes a Socialist orientation.

5. H. L. Mitchell to A. S. Bayne, 7 April 1936; Mitchell to Clyde Johnson, 20 April 1936, STFU Papers.

6. *Farmers National Weekly*, 21 September 1934.

7. Ibid., 7 September, 16 November, 14 December 1934, 25 January 1935; *Southern Worker*, December 1934.

8. "Bob" to H. L. Mitchell, 4 April 1935, STFU Papers; Lem Harris to Roger Baldwin, 22 February 1934; Lem Harris and Harold M. Ware to Roger Baldwin, 20 July 1934, American Fund for Public Service (AFPS) Papers, New York Public Library.

9. National Conference Agricultural, Lumber, Rural Workers, *Program and Resolutions* (Washington, 1935), pp. 1–5.

10. Grubbs, *Cry from the Cotton*, pp. 70–71.

11. Lem Harris, circular letter, mimeographed, 28 January 1935, STFU Papers; *Labor Defender*, March 1935, p. 7; Commonwealth College press release, 24 January 1935, Socialist Party Papers, Manuscripts Division, Duke University Library, Durham, N.C..

12. William H. Cobb and Donald H. Grubbs, "Arkansas' Commonwealth College and the Southern Tenant Farmers' Union," *Arkansas Historical Quarterly* 25 (Winter 1966), 294–95.

13. H. L. Mitchell Memoir, Columbia Oral History Collection (COHC), Butler Library, Columbia University, New York, pp. 42–43, 71; Mitchell to Gardner Jackson, 3 September 1936, STFU Papers.

14. *Southern Worker*, March / April, June 1935; *Sharecroppers' Voice*, July 1935; *Labor Defender*, August 1935, p. 21.

15. *Sharecroppers' Voice*, August 1935.

16. Mitchell to Gardner Jackson, 3 September 1936, STFU Papers; *Sharecroppers' Voice*, strike issue, n.d. [ca. September 1935].

17. Cully Cobb Memoir, Oral History Collection, Bancroft Library, University of California, Berkeley, pp. 50–55; Donald Henderson to J. H. Butler, 12 July 1935; Lem Harris to *Sharecroppers' Voice,* 26 December 1935, STFU Papers.

18. Mitchell to Gardner Jackson, 26 December 1935, STFU Papers; STFU; *Convention Proceedings: 2nd Annual Convention* (Memphis, 1936); Herbert Goldfrank to Mitchell, 17 January 1936; Mitchell to Goldfrank, 20 January 1936, STFU Papers.

19. Donald Henderson, "The Rural Masses and the Work of Our Party," *Communist* 14 (September 1935): 866–80. Compare Henderson's quotation, p. 868, with the full translation in Lenin, *Selected Works* (New York: International Publ., 1938), 10:219–25.

20. *Southern Farm Leader,* May 1936.

21. *Sharecroppers' Voice,* July 1936; Tom Burke to Mitchell, 2 March 1936; Mitchell to Burke, 9 March 1936; Clyde Johnson to Mitchell, n.d. [ca. 15 April 1936]; Mitchell to Johnson, 20 April 1936, STFU Papers.

22. Jamieson, *Labor Unionism in American Agriculture,* pp. 268–69; Mitchell to Norman Thomas, 27 April 1936; Thomas to Mitchell, 4, 14 May 1936; Henderson to Thomas, 7 May 1936; Henderson to Mitchell, 10 June 1936, STFU Papers.

23. Mitchell to Butler, 31 January 1936; Edwin "Little Boy" Mitchell to H. L. Mitchell, 6 May and n.d. 1936, STFU Papers; Mitchell Memoir, COHC, pp. 59–62; Mitchell, *Mean Things,* pp. 94–96.

24. Mitchell Memoir, COHC, pp. 61–62; unsigned [Fred Mathews?] to Mitchell, n.d. [ca. February 1936], STFU Papers [original spelling].

25. *Southern Farm Leader,* July, August, November, December 1936; *Southern Worker,* July, December 1936.

26. Mitchell to Henderson, 12 August, 8 October 1936; minutes, STFU executive council, 4 October 1936, STFU Papers.

27. Mitchell to Sidney Hertzberg and A. S. Gilmartin, 30 August 1936; James Myers to Howard Kester, 4 November 1936; Walter White to Kester, 3 December 1936; Mitchell to Thomas, 3 September 1936, STFU Papers. Years later Jackson called himself "a guileless instrument of a Commie operation" (Jackson Memoir, COHC, p. 657). After the Sharecroppers Union ceased operations, the Washington committee sent its forty-five dollars a month to the Agricultural Workers Union of Alabama with 150 members to start and the same amount to STFU with 35,000 members (M. W. Martin to Roger Baldwin, 7 January 1937, AFPS Papers).

28. Mitchell to Jackson, 14 September 1936; Thomas to Kester and Mitchell, 7 December 1936, STFU Papers.

29. Grubbs, *Cry from the Cotton,* pp. 86–87; John Brophy to Mitchell, 24 March 1936, STFU Papers.

30. A decade and a half later, Gardner Jackson, by then an anti-Communist warrior, described the dramatic unmasking of some party fakery. A transcript indicates—to put it in the kindest light—that his memory had failed (Jackson Memoir, COHC, p. 702). Compare with "Typescript of National Conference on Rural Social Planning, Washington, D.C., March 27–28, 1936," Farm Research, Inc., Papers, New York City.

31. Donald Henderson, "Agricultural Workers," *American Federationist* 43 (May 1936): 488–93; "Unions of Agricultural Workers," ibid. (June 1936) pp. 632–33; Leif Dahl, "Agricultural Labor and Social Legislation," ibid. 44 (February 1937): 137–45; *Rural Worker*, November 1936.

32. Jamieson, *Labor Unionism in American Agriculture*, p. 25. American unions are generally known as "internationals" because they have Canadian branches.

33. Jackson to Mitchell, 5 June 1937, STFU Papers; *[Farm] Worker* (Berkeley, Calif.), 25 February 1938.

34. Mitchell Memoir, COHC, p. 85; *[Farm] Worker*, 25 February 1938. Henderson to Butler, 27 June 1937, STFU Papers, indicates Henderson's less than overwhelming joy at the STFU participation.

35. Mitchell to Gordon McIntyre, 8 September 1937, STFU Papers.

36. Frank N. Traeger to Butler, 17 June 1937, STFU Papers; STFU press release, 23 June 1937; Henderson to Butler, 27 June 1937, STFU Papers.

37. Jackson Memoir, COHC, pp. 710, 712–13; *Daily Worker*, 10, 13 July 1937; Grubbs, *Cry from the Cotton*, p. 167; Mitchell, *Mean Things*, pp. 164–66.

38. Mitchell to Henderson, 30 September 1937; memorandum, Gardner Jackson to John L. Lewis, John Brophy, Ralph Hetzel, and Donald Henderson, 1 October 1937; STFU press release, 30 September 1937, STFU Papers.

39. Ralph Lord Roy, *Communism and the Churches* (New York: Harcourt Bruce and Co., 1960), pp. 271–73; Grubbs, *Cry from the Cotton*, pp. 111–13. There are at least two editions of a sympathetic biography of Williams by Cedric Belfrage, *South of God* (New York: Modern Age Books, 1941), and *A Faith to Free the People* (New York: Dryden Press, 1944).

40. Mitchell Memoir, COHC, pp. 87–88; Grubbs, *Cry from the Cotton*, p. 173; Cobb and Grubbs, *"Arkansas' Commonwealth College,"* p. 304; Roy, *Communism and the Churches*, pp. 273–80.

41. Mitchell to Jackson, 9 July [9 October?] 1937; Mitchell to Henderson, 30 September 1937, STFU Papers.

42. Mitchell to Henderson, 6 October 1937, STFU Papers.

43. B. Patricia Dyson, "The Farm Workers and the N.L.R.B.: From Wagner to Taft-Hartley," *Federal Bar Journal* 36 (Summer-Fall 1977): 121–44.

44. Benjamin Stolberg, "Communist Wreckers in American Labor," *Saturday Evening Post* (2 September 1939), p. 169; Jamieson, *Labor Unionism in American Agriculture*, pp. 347–54.

45. Jamieson, *Labor Unionism in American Agriculture,* pp. 199–202, 214–16, 249–55, 301–2, 336–40.

46. Ibid., pp. 116–88.

47. Mitchell to Butler, 4 January 1938, STFU Papers; Mitchell Memoir, COHC, p. 88; Grubbs, *Cry from the Cotton,* p. 169.

48. See, for example, statement of H. L. Mitchell to UCAPAWA executive board, 28 April 1938, STFU Papers.

49. Mitchell to Jackson, 9 July [9 October?] 1937, STFU Papers; *Sharecroppers' Voice,* September 1936; Jamieson, *Labor Unionism in American Agriculture,* p. 317; Grubbs, *Cry from the Cotton,* p. 169.

50. Mitchell to Clayton, 4 May 1938; Clayton to Mitchell, 10 May, 4 June 1938; Henderson to Sweeden, 21 December 1937; Sweeden to Mitchell, 24 December 1937; summary, Oklahoma STFU meeting, 13 January 1938, STFU Papers.

51. Resolution passed at the Oklahoma State Convention of the STFU, 23 April 1938; Kester to STFU executive council, telegram, 25 April 1938; minutes, special meeting of STFU executive council, 25 April 1938, STFU Papers.

52. Statement of H. L. Mitchell to UCAPAWA executive board, 28 April 1938; minutes, UCAPAWA executive board meeting, 28 April 1928; Mitchell to Powers Hapgood, 16 May 1938; STFU Papers.

53. STFU press release, 29 April 1938 (marked "not released"); Mitchell to Kester, 5 May 1938; Butler to Mitchell to John L. Lewis 23 May 1938; Henderson to Mitchell, 4 June 1938; Mitchell and Butler to Henderson, 6 June 1938; Henderson to Butler, 29 July 1938, STFU Papers.

54. Butler to Williams, 22 August 1938; untitled plan to take over STFU, n.d. [August 1938], STFU Papers. Williams later told Donald Grubbs that Cedric Belfrage had written most of the document Cobb and Grubbs, "Arkansas' Commonwealth College," p. 310.

55. Butler to Williams, 22 August 1938; proceedings, trial of Claude C. Williams, 6–17 September 1938, STFU Papers; Grubbs, *Cry from the Cotton,* pp. 175–79.

56. See, for example, Henderson to Butler, 5 October 1938; Butler to H. A. Davie, 17 October 1938; Butler to UCAPAWA executive board, 27 October 1938; minutes, STFU executive council, 21 January 1939; Henderson to Mitchell, 28 January 1939; Butler to executive board, CIO, 14 February 1939, among many other STFU papers. Mitchell, *Mean Things,* p. 161.

57. Mitchell to Evelyn Smith, 13 December 1938; Evelyn Smith to David L. Clendenin, 20 December 1938; report of San Francisco delegation to Fifth STFU Convention, 29 December 1938 to 1 January 1939, STFU Papers.

58. STFU executive council to John L. Lewis, n.d. [? February 1939]; Whitfield to locals and members, 24 February 1939, STFU Papers; Grubbs, *Cry from*

the Cotton, pp. 180–83. Louis Cantor, *A Prologue to the Protest Movement: The Missouri Sharecropper Roadside Demonstration of 1939* (Durham, N.C.: Duke University Press, 1969), is a monographic study.

59. Henderson to Griffin, 23 February 1939; Henderson to Mitchell, Butler, and executive board, District IV, UCAPAWA, 1 March 1939, STFU Papers.

60. STFU press release, 12 March 1939, STFU Papers; *S.T.F.U. News,* 21 March 1939.

61. Mitchell to Butler, 3 March 1939; Mitchell to Harriet Young, 13 March 1939; Henderson to STFU locals, 22 March 1939; UCAPAWA press release, 24 March 1939, STFU Papers.

62. STFU press release, 2 April 1939, STFU Papers; *Agricultural Unionist,* March 1953. Jackson had already viciously attacked Mitchell and had tried to sabotage the fund-raising activities of National Sharecroppers Week. Jackson to Mitchell, 13 March 1939; Mitchell to Harriet Young, 17 March 1939; Mitchell to Jackson, 3 April 1939, STFU Papers.

63. Jamieson, *Labor Unionism in American Agriculture,* pp. 164–92, 336–40, 351–55; *Tenant Farmer,* 15 November 1941; *Farm Labor News,* August 1946.

64. Mitchell to Kester, 1 May 1939; Butler to Kester, 5 May 1939; Mitchell to Blaine Treadway, 9 May 1939; Jackson to Frank R. Crosswaite, 24 February 1940; Walter White to Jackson, 27 February 1940; Mitchell to Jackson, 27 February 1940, STFU Papers.

65. Mitchell's recent autobiography, *Mean Things Happening in This Land,* is remarkably frank about his private as well as his professional life.

66. Henderson quoted in F. Ray Marshall, *Labor in the South* (Cambridge, Mass.: Harvard University Press, 1967), p. 238; Mitchell to Thomas, 17 November 1936, STFU Papers; Williams quoted in Grubbs, *Cry from the Cotton,* p. 82.

CHAPTER 9

1. U.S., Department of Agriculture, *Yearbook: 1935* (Washington, D.C.: Government Printing Office, 1935), pp. 598–602.

2. Ibid., p. 606; *New York Times,* 16 August 1939, p. 25.

3. John J. Dillon, *Seven Decades of Milk: A History of New York's Dairy Industry* (New York Orange Judd Publ. Co., 1941), pp. 84–102, 150–60, 201.

4. Ibid., p. 178.

5. Ibid., pp. 186, 277. A state audit for the fiscal year ending 31 March 1937 disclosed over six million dollars for "price adjustments" to customers (pp. 292–93).

6. Dairymen's League Cooperative Association, Inc., *Story of the Year: 1932–1933* (New York, 1933), pp. 16–17; Dillon, *Seven Decades of Milk,* pp. 196–97; Dairymen's League, *Story of the Year: 1933–1934* (New York, 1934), p. 26.

7. Paul Abrahams, "Agricultural Adjustment during the New Deal Period: The New York Milk Industry: A Case Study," *Agricultural History* 39 (April 1965): 95; *Farmers National Weekly,* 12 August 1933. The paper charged that Lehman's family firm had heavy investments in Borden and Sheffield.

8. John Wiita [Henry Puro], "My Experience in Work among American Farmers during the 1930s Agrarian Crisis," Immigration History Center, University of Minnesota, Minneapolis, p. 5.

9. Press release, mimeographed, 8 August 1933, John D. Miller Papers, Special Collections, Cornell University Library, Ithaca, N.Y.; Dairymen's League, *Story of the Year: 1933–1934,* pp. 28–30; Abrahams, "The New York Milk Industry," p. 95.

10. Dillon, *Seven Decades of Milk,* pp. 225–34, 307–8.

11. Ibid., pp. 240–49.

12. Ibid., pp. 250–51; *New York Times,* 25 February 1939, p. 1; 6 June 1939, p. 1; Dillon, *Seven Decades of Milk,* pp. 269–70.

13. *New York Times,* 13 August 1939, p. 1; 20 August 1939, p. 21.

14. *Union Farmer* (Ithaca), 25 September 1940.

15. *New York Times,* August–December 1937 passim; *Dairymen's League News,* 10 August–14 December 1937 passim; Dillon, *Seven Decades of Milk,* p. 235.

16. *Dairy Farmer* (Ogdensburg), 25 March 1939.

17. *New York Times,* 21 August 1939, p. 2; *Union Farmer,* March 1941; *Dairy Farmers Digest,* 20 September 1941, pp. 76–77.

18. *New York Times,* 13 August 1939, p. 1; 14 August 1939, p. 2; *Farmers Defender,* February 1942, p. 3; U.S., Congress, Senate, Subcommittee of the Committee on the Judiciary, *Hearings, Investigation of the Administration of the Internal Security Act and Other Internal Security Laws,* 83d Cong., 2d sess., 1954, pp. 1628–36.

19. *New York Times,* 14 August 1939, p. 2.

20. Ibid., 16 August 1939, p. 25.

21. Ibid., 17 August 1939, p. 42.

22. Ibid., 18 August 1939, p. 1.

23. Ibid., 18 August 1939, p. 1.

24. Ibid., 19 August 1939, p. 1.

25. Ibid., 20 August 1939, p. 21.

26. Ibid., 22 August 1939, p. 1; *Union Farmer,* 25 August 1939.

27. *Union Farmer,* 25 August 1939; *New York Times,* 22 August 1939, p. 1; 24 August 1939, p. 21; Raymond Knack, Acting President, Farmers Union of the New York Milkshed, circular letter, mimeographed, 24 June 1957, Leo Ars Papers, in author's possession.

28. *New York Times,* 23 August 1939, p. 1; 24 August 1939, p. 21; *Union Farmer,* 25 September 1939; 25 January 1940; *Dairy Farmers Digest,* September 1948, p. 6.

29. *New York Times,* 23 August 1939, p. 1; *Rural New Yorker,* 9 September 1939, p. 485.

30. *Rural New Yorker,* 9 September 1939, p. 485; Archie Wright to Leo Ars, 22 January 1957, Ars Papers.

31. *New York Times,* 15 October 1939, p. 7.

32. Ibid., 17 October 1939, p. 1; 18 October 1939, p. 15; 22 October 1939, p. 9.

33. Ibid., 25 October 1939, p. 34; 26 October 1939, p. 25; 27 October 1939, p. 25; 14 August 1940, p. 21.

34. In 1933, Governor Lehman sponsored an independent investigation of the milk situation. The investigator was Professor Leland Spencer—of the Agricultural College of Cornell University (Dillon, *Seven Decades of Milk,* p. 208).

35. Dairymen's League, *Story of the Year: 1933–1934,* pp. 23–24.

36. See, for example, *Dairy Farmer,* 25 March 1939.

37. Diarymen's League, *Story of the Year: 1933–1934,* p. 36; *Dairymen's League News,* 15 August 1933, p. 1; *Sheffield Producer,* September 1933, p. 1; *American Agriculturist,* 19 August 1933; "Re: Situation in Milk Strike New York State," George N. Peek Papers, Western Historical Manuscripts Collection, University of Missouri, Columbia.

38. *American Agriculturist,* 8 October 1938, p. 5. See also 30 July 1938, p. 5; 22 October 1938, p. 3; 19 November 1938, p. 5; 7 January 1939, p. 5.

39. *New York Times,* 16 August 1939, p. 25; 17 August 1939, p. 42. For the similar views of Fred Sexauer, see 19 August 1939, p. 7; 23 August 1939, p. 10.

40. Director L. M. Hardin to members, circular letter, mimeographed, 9 September 1939, Ars Papers; *American Agriculturist,* 16 September 1939, p. 9; *Dairymen's League News,* 5 September 1939, p. 4.

41. J. C. Treat to producers, circular letter, mimeographed, 9 September 1939, Ars Papers.

42. See, for example, *Dairymen's League News,* 24 October 1939, p. 1; 28 November 1939, p. 1; 5 December 1939, p. 1; 19 December 1939, p. 2.

43. *Eastern Milk Producer,* October 1939, June 1940.

44. See, for example, *American Agriculturalist,* 2 September 1939, pp. 5, 8; 16 September 1939, p. 11; 3 February 1940, p. 4; 2 March 1940, p. 4.

45. *Rural New Yorker,* 10 February 1940, p. 86; 27 December 1941, p. 661. Arthur Derounian [John Roy Carlson], *Undercover* (New York: E. P. Dutton, 1943), pp. 473–74; E. A. Piller, *Time Bomb* (New York: Arco, 1945), pp. 17–24; Rumely to Sexauer, 12 August 1937, Dairymen's League Cooperative Associa-

tion, Inc., (DLCA) Papers, Special Collections, Cornell University Library, Ithaca, N. Y.; Theobald to Archie Wright, 26 August 1946, Farmers Union of the New York Milkshed (FUNY) Papers, Special Collections, Cornell University Library, Ithaca, N.Y.

46. *Dairy Farmers Digest,* 15 November 1939, pp. 4–5; *Milk Producers Market News,* n.d. [ca. October 1937], p. 57.

47. *Dairy Farmers Digest,* 15 November 1939, p. 23; Theobald to Wright, 3, 9 August 1942, FUNY Papers; *Independent Producers Guide,* November 1944, p. 2; Dillon, *Seven Decades of Milk,* p. 271. Legal document of sale, V. R. Tompkins to Foster Strader, 21 January 1949; unsigned document of assignment, [Strader] to Edward Shoeneck, 21 January 1949; Seward A. Miller, General Counsel of Dairymens' League, to Schoeneck, 21 January 1949, enclosing $15,000, S. A. Miller Legal Files, DLCA Papers.

48. *Dairy Farmers Digest,* 15 December 1939, p. 21; 20 January 1940, p. 27; 20 March 1940, pp. 84–85; 20 June 1940, p. 20; 20 December 1940, p. 50.

49. Ibid., 20 June 1940, p. 22; 20 April 1940, pp. 108–9.

50. *Union Farmer,* 25 January, 25 March, 25 April 1940.

51. Ibid., 25 September 1940.

52. *Metropolitan Milk Producers News,* 16 September, 1 October 1940; *Dairy Farmers Digest,* 20 October 1940, p. 7.

53. *New York Times,* 10 November 1940, p. 6; 13 November 1940, p. 18; *Union Farmer,* 25 November 1940; *Dairy Farmers Digest,* 20 November 1940, pp. 12, 17.

54. *Rural New Yorker,* 30 November 1940, p. 611; 28 December 1940, p. 648.

55. *Union Farmer,* December 1940; Brill and Schou to Member (copy), 11 December 1940, FUNY Papers.

56. *Union Farmer,* December 1940; *New York Times,* 28 December 1940, p. 17.

57. *New York Times,* 29 December 1940, p. 27; 2 January 1941, p. 10; 12 May 1941; *Union Farmer,* January–June 1941 passim; Carl Peters to Chairman, 6 May 1941, FUNY Papers.

58. *Union Farmer,* March–December 1941 passim.

59. *New York Times,* 1–10 July 1941 passim; *Union Farmer,* July 1941, January 1942; *Dairy Farmers Digest,* March 1942, p. 74; *United Dairy Farmer,* 2 May 1942.

60. See, for example, Dale Kramer, "John L. Lewis: Last Bid?" *Harpers* 185 (August 1942): 275–83; *Dairy Farmers Digest,* 20 March 1942, pp. 69, 74–76.

61. *Rural New Yorker,* 25 July 1942, p. 410.

62. George Monroe, Secretary, Free Farmers, Inc., to L. A. Chapin, 25 January 1944, DLCA Papers; form letter, Free Farmers, Inc., [ca. May 1943], DLCA Papers.

63. *United Dairy Farmer,* 2 May 1942–20 August 1945 passim.
64. Benjamin Stolberg, "Muddled Millions," *Saturday Evening Post,* 15 February 1941, p. 9; "Mr. Garland's Million," *Time,* 30 June 1941, p. 17; *Dairy Farmers Digest,* 20 December 1941, p. 26; *Farmers Defender,* May-June 1945, p. 12.
65. *Union Farmer,* 1939–1940 passim; *Dairy Farmers Digest,* 20 January 1941, p. 61.
66. *Union Farmer,* December 1941.
67. *Farmers Defender,* May 1942–January 1944 passim.
68. Ibid., November 1943, p. 6; January 1944, pp. 1–2.

CHAPTER 10

1. Irving Howe and Lewis Coser, *The American Communist Party: A Critical History* (New York: Praeger, 1962), pp. 442–448; Joseph R. Starobin, *American Communism in Crisis, 1943–1957* (Cambridge, Mass.: Harvard University Press, 1972), pp. 77–106.
2. Cold War products are Max M. Kampelman, *The Communist Party vs. the C.I.O.: A Study in Power Politics* (New York: Praeger, 1957), and David J. Saposs, *Communism in American Unions* (New York: McGraw-Hill, 1959). More balanced in interpretation but not a full chronological history is Bert Cochran, *Labor and Communism: The Conflict That Shaped American Unions* (Princeton, N.J.: Princeton University Press, 1977). The supposedly definitive study, financed by the Fund for the Republic, has never appeared.
3. Starobin, *American Communism in Crisis,* pp. 55–65.
4. "Farm Work and the Draft Resolution," typescript, undated [ca. July 1945], Lem Harris papers private possession, Norwalk, Conn.
5. Jerry Coleman, "Farmers Advance in the Movement for the People's Front," *Communist* 17 (February 1938): 169–176.
6. John Bosch to John Vesecky, 18 February 1938, copy, George A. Nelson Papers, Special Collections, University of Wisconsin Library, Madison; *Midwest Daily Record* (Chicago), 4, 18 May 1938.
7. David J. Saposs, *Communism in American Politics* (Washington, D.C.: Public Affairs Press, 1960), p. 59.
8. List of Delegates to the 1938 Farmer Labor Convention; Charles J. Coe to Elmer Benson, n.d. [ca. July 1941], Elmer Benson Papers, Minnesota State Historical Society, Saint Paul.
9. Bosch to Benson, 5 February 1941, Benson Papers; John H. Bosch, interview with author, 4 November 1961.
10. John A. Crampton, *The National Farmers Union: Ideology of a Pressure Group* (Lincoln: University of Nebraska Press, 1965), p. 27; *National Union Farmer,* 23 July 1940.

11. C. E. Huff and Perry Eberhart, *The Voice of the Family Farmer* (n.p., n.d.), pp. 62–64, 72.

12. Crampton, *National Farmers Union,* p. 28; Wesley McCune, *The Farm Bloc* (Garden City, N.Y.: Doubleday, Doran, 1943), p. 200.

13. Howe and Coser, *American Communist Party,* pp. 405–36.

14. Grant McConnell, *The Decline of Agrarian Democracy* (New York: Atheneum, 1969), pp. 97–111.

15. U.S., Congress, House, Committee on Un-American Activities, *Hearings,* 82d Cong., 1st sess., 1951, p. 1901.

16. Alonzo L. Hamby, *Beyond the New Deal: Harry S. Truman and American Liberalism* (New York and London: Columbia University Press, 1973), pp. 33–34.

17. Ibid., pp. 35–36.

18. Ibid., pp. 75–77.

19. Ibid., pp. 102–3, 138–140.

20. Ibid., p. 150.

21. Gardner Jackson to James Patton, 3 August 1946, reprinted in U.S., Congress, Senate, *Congressional Record,* 81st Cong., 2d sess., 1950, 96, pt. 11:14289.

22. Steven A. Chambers, "Relations between Leaders of the Iowa and the National Farmers Union Organizations, 1941 to 1950" (Honors' essay, University of Iowa, 1961), pp. 25–40.

23. Jackson to Patton, 3 August 1946, pp. 14287–90; U.S., Congress, House, Committee on Un-American Activities, *Hearings,* 82d Cong., 1st sess., 1951, p. 1918; *Investigation of Communist Activities in the Seattle, Wash., Area,* 84th Cong., 1st sess., 1955, pp. 530–31.

24. Quoted in Chambers, "Relations between Leaders," p. 54.

25. Resolution of NFU board of directors, [March 1947], Farmers Union of the New York Milk Shed (FUNY) Papers, Special Collections, Cornell University Library, Ithaca, N.Y.

26. James Elmore to James Patton, 9 September 1947, reprinted in U.S., Congress, Senate *Congressional Record,* 81st Cong., 2d sess., 1950, 96, pt. 11:14290–91.

27. Hamby, *Beyond the New Deal,* pp. 159–61.

28. Ibid., pp. 165, 177, 192; Curtis D. MacDougall, *Gideon's Army* (New York: Marzani and Munsell, 1965), 1:134.

29. Lem Harris, "You're Wrong about the Farmers," *New Masses,* 16 September 1947, pp. 3–6.

30. Archie Wright to All Officers and Delegates, 20 March 1948, mimeographed, FUNY Papers.

31. Robert Cruise McManus, "Communist Beachhead in Agriculture," *Farm Journal* 68 (October 1944): 23, 84–85.

32. *Farmers Defender,* November 1944, pp. 2, 9; February 1945, p. 14; February 1946, p. 5.

33. See various issues of *Dairy Farmers Digest* of this period; "Keeping Up with Co-ops," *Cooperative Digest* 8 (October 1947): 17–18; *Northeastern Union Farmer,* May-June 1948, p. 1; *Counterattack: Facts to Combat Communism,* 19 March 1948.

34. U.S., Congress, Senate, *Congressional Record,* 81st Cong., 2d sess., 1950, 96, pt. II:14283, 14291; *Northeastern Union Farmer,* May-June 1948, p. 2; December 1948, p. 2.

35. Harris, "You're Wrong About the Farmers," pp. 3–6.

36. Hamby, *Beyond the New Deal,* pp. 223–24; Huff and Eberhart, *Voice of the Family Farmer,* pp. 80–81.

37. MacDougall, *Gideon's Army,* pp. 604, 608, 795; Chambers, "Relations Between Leaders," pp. 58–59.

38. MacDougall, *Gideon's Army,* pp. 604–7.

39. *Daily Worker,* 25 July 1948.

40. Chambers, "Relations between Leaders," p. 60; Hamby, *Beyond the New Deal,* p. 358; Talbott quoted, p. 365.

41. Chambers "Relations between Leaders," pp. 60–61; Charles J. Coe to Jimmy Youngdale, 15 March 1950; Fred Stover to Elmer Benson, 24 March 1950, Benson Papers; *Facts for Farmers,* April 1950.

42. Chambers, "Relations between Leaders," p. 61; *Northeastern Union Farmer,* August 1950, pp. 2, 11; U.S., Congress, Senate, *Congressional Record,* 81st Cong., 2d sess., 1950, 96, pt. 11:14276–91.

43. Chambers, "Relations between Leaders," p. 63.

44. *The Inside Story of the Outside Interference in the Iowa Farmers Union,* printed flyer [ca. April 1951], in author's possession; Wright to Ulster local, 3 April 1951, FUNY Papers.

45. Baldwin to Patton, 22 March 1951, copy, Benson Papers.

46. *Whither the National Farmers Union?,* printed flyer [ca. April 1952], in author's possession; Crampton, *National Farmers Union,* pp. 226–27.

47. Quoted by Starobin, *American Communism in Crisis,* p. 17.

48. Ibid., p. 38.

BIBLIOGRAPHICAL ESSAY

THE READER WILL FIND a variety of sources listed in the footnotes. I want to use this essay to comment on some of the more significant ones and in certain cases to indicate their location.

Any student of the history of the Communist party in the United States must begin with the two volumes by Theodore Draper, *The Roots of American Communism* (New York: Viking, 1957) and *American Communism and Soviet Russia* (New York: Viking, 1960), which take the party to the end of the decade of the 1920s. Although Draper and his work have often been criticized by party leaders, I find his books carefully researched and well thought out. An old standard, *American Labor Who's Who* (New York: Hanford Press, 1925), edited by Solon De Leon, is an indispensable source which some enterprising publisher should reprint.

There is no adequate history of the most important period, 1930–45. A number of scholarly and many nonscholarly works tackle various facets, but until Harvey Klehr publishes his work in progress, the best bridge is Irving Howe and Lewis Coser, *The American Communist Party: A Critical History* (New York: Praeger, 1962). Joseph R. Starobin's *American Communism in Crisis, 1943–1957* (Cambridge, Mass.: Harvard University Press, 1972) is sensitive, thoughtful, and provocative. David A. Shannon has covered similar ground in *The Decline of American Communism* (New York: Macmillan Co., 1959), one of the volumes sponsored by the Fund for the Republic. Some of the other volumes in this series are quite useful although sometimes not untouched by the Cold War attitudes of the 1950s. Several promised works have never appeared. A splendid guide to the postwar break between Popular Fronters and liberal anti-Communists is Alonzo L. Hamby, *Beyond the New Deal: Harry S Truman and American Liberalism* (New York: Columbia

University Press, 1973). No student can ignore William Z. Foster, *History of the Communist Party of the United States* (New York: International Publ., 1952), for the party's authorized view of itself.

Edward Hallett Carr's multivolume History of Soviet Russia is a necessity for understanding not only the Russian background but also the interplay of forces in the world movement in its first decade and a half (*The Bolshevik Revolution, 1917–1923,* 3 vols.; *The Interregnum, 1923–24; Socialism in One Country, 1924–1926,* 3 vols.; *Foundations of a Planned Economy, 1926–1929,* 2 vols. [London and New York: Macmillan Co., 1950–71]).

Frank Borkenau, *World Communism* (New York: W. W. Norton, 1939), and Gunther Nollau, *International Communism and World Revolution,* Trans. Victor Andersen (London: Hollis and Carter, 1961), are somewhat dated but still useful histories of the Third International. Scholarly but frankly Socialist interpretations are contained in G. D. H. Cole, *A History of Socialist Thought,* vol. 4, pt. 2, *Communism and Social Democracy: 1914–1931* (London: Macmillan & Co., 1961), and Julius Braunthal, *History of the International,* vol. 2, *1914–1943,* Trans. Henry Collins and Kenneth Mitchell (New York: Praeger, 1967). Most useful in dealing with the Krestintern, or Farmers' International, is George D. Jackson, Jr., *Comintern and Peasant in Eastern Europe: 1919–1930* (New York: Columbia University Press, 1966).

I am surprised that there are no adequate histories of the general farm organizations of the twentieth century. In Robert M. Morlan's history of the Nonpartisan League, *Political Prairie Fire* (Minneapolis: University of Minnesota Press, 1955), the author loses focus after the movement spread beyond North Dakota. Kenneth Campbell MacKay, *The Progressive Movement of 1924* (New York: Columbia University Press, 1947), is solid but has an anti-Communist bias. Neither Morlan nor MacKay recognizes the significance of the Farmer Labor parties of the early 1920s. John L. Shover, *Cornbelt Rebellion: The Farmers' Holiday Association* (Urbana: University of Illinois Press, 1965), retells the story in fine fashion but misses the importance of the revolutionary antidispossession movement in the winter of 1932 and the impact which the May (threatened) and October (actual) 1933 strikes had on New Deal farm programs. Stuart Jamieson, *Labor Unionism in American Agriculture,* U.S. Department of Labor, Bureau of Labor Statistics Bulletin no. 836 (Washington, D.C.: Government Printing Office, 1945), has no index and presents other frustrations, but it is still irreplaceable. No one can understand the STFU without reading both Donald H. Grubbs, *Cry from the Cotton: The Southern Tenant Farmers Union and the New Deal* (Chapel Hill: University of North Carolina Press, 1971), and H. L. Mitchell, *Mean Things Happening in This Land* (Montclair, N.J.: Allanheld, Osmun 1979).

All too often, much well-researched work in unpublished essays, theses, and dissertations goes unsung. I must note a few, although I have probably missed many more: Charles Anthony Mast, "Farm Factionalism over Agricultural Policy: The National Farmers Union, 1926–1937" (Master's Thesis, University of Maryland, 1967); Allan James Mathews, "The History of the United Farmers League in South Dakota, 1923–1936: A Study in Farm Radicalism" (Master's Thesis, University of South Dakota, 1972); Ellen Lois Holcomb, "Efforts to Organize the Migrant Workers by the Cannery and Agricultural Workers Industrial Union in the 1930's" (Master's Thesis, Chico State, 1963); Dale Rosen, "The Alabama Share Croppers Union" (Honors' essay, Radcliffe College, 1969); William D. Rowley, " 'Grass roots' and Imported Radicalism in Nebraska, 1932–1934" (Master's Thesis, University of Nebraska, 1963); and Steven A. Chambers, "Relations between Leaders of the Iowa and the National Farmers Union Organizations, 1941 to 1950" (Honors' essay, University of Iowa, 1961). Unfortunately, the late Gordon Smith does not seem to have left a manuscript of his extensive research into 1930s farm radicalism.

Tracing sometimes ephemeral radical publications in the first half of the twentieth century is a labyrinthine task. There is an excellent key to the path, however. Walter Goldwater, *Radical Periodicals in America, 1890–1950* (New Haven, Conn.: Yale University Library, 1966) is a guide not only to the journals themselves but also to the groups which published them. Goldwater, for example, sorts out the various journals entitled *Communist* (eight). In smaller fashion I have tried to do the same in "Radical Farm Organizations and Periodicals in American, 1920–1960," *Agricultural History* 45 (April 1971): 111–20. Greenwood Press has reprinted a large number of those listed by Goldwater. The same publisher has microfilmed many of the journals listed in my article, along with pamphlet material and the manuscript record of the Farmers Relief Conference of 1932, under the general title *Agrarian Periodicals in the United States* (1976). This is the prime source for runs of the various sharecropper papers, the *United Farmer, Cooperative Pyramid Builder, Farmers National Weekly,* Charlie Taylor's *Producers News,* and many others.

As most researchers are acutely aware, manuscripts dealing either with Communism or with farming organizing tend to be scarce. I consider myself lucky in the access to as much material as I have had. Of primary importance are the papers of Lem Harris, in his possession. They are an uneven feast, the collection of a man keenly aware of history but also with an active life including numerous changes of residence. I know that John Shover, Dale Rosen, and myself have benefited greatly from their use. The Federal Bureau of Investigation may or may not have extensive files on the subject of this book. My request for material on the United Farmers League brought a thin sheaf of letters, with names heavily censored, apparently provided to the bureau by an informer. Subsequent to the completion of this book I have seen a much larger file, considerably less censored, provided to another researcher. My request for material on the Farmers National Committee for Action brought the answer that the bureau did not have a file on the FNCA, but if I had reason to believe otherwise, I should let them know!

Gould Colman of the Cornell University Library is to be commended for acquiring the papers of both the Farmers Union of the New York Milk Shed and its arch-foe, the Dairymen's League Cooperative Association, Incorporated (Dairylea). The officers of the latter organization should be thanked by historians for not culling their files of material which could be interpreted as less than complimentary to earlier leaders.

The Milo Reno Papers at the University of Iowa are highly useful. Unfortunately, one of his associates apparently destroyed all correspondence except that for 1933. The William Lemke Papers at the University of North Dakota and several collections at the University of Wisconsin and the Minnesota State Historical Society have proven most useful. The Southern Tenant Farmers Union Papers at the University of North Carolina are marvelous.

I could never have unraveled the story of the Progressive Farmers of America without Alex Kringlock's generous donation of his papers to me. Leo Ars also gave me his collection, which proved helpful in writing Chapter 9. The Kringlock, Ars, Taylor, Knutson papers and other material including duplicates of the Harris material in my possession will eventually go to a proper repository.

Lorena Hickock's letters to Harry Hopkins, written as she toured disaster areas in 1933, are a graphic depiction of the Great Depression by a first-rate journalist. Henry Morgenthau's unpublished diary helps disclose the serious view that the Roosevelt administration took of the October 1933 farm strike. These materials are at the Franklin D. Roosevelt Library at Hyde Park. A running account of the importance of the farm problem is contained in the thousands of letters in the Department of Agriculture files in the National Archives. Pointed and sometimes amusing exchanges are in the folders of Donald R. Murphy, editor of *Wallaces Farmer*.

Finally, this work has benefited from my sometimes imperfect use of oral history techniques. The late Louis Starr generously had several of my interviews transcribed, and they now rest in the Columbia University Oral History Collection.

INDEX